breakthrough
ON the
new skis

Say goodbye to the intermediate blues

Lito Tejada-Flores

MOUNTAIN SPORTS PRESS

Boulder, Colorado   USA

Printed in the United States of America

International Standard Book Number: 0-9676747-2-7

Library of Congress Cataloging-in-Publication Data applied for.

Disclaimer: Skiing is an adventurous outdoor sport, and as such has always entailed a certain risk of injury; this risk can be minimized, but never entirely eliminated, by good physical conditioning, good judgment, well-maintained and adjusted equipment, and skillful technique. Neither the publisher, editors, nor the author shall be held liable for the use or misuse of information contained in this book. Like all skiers, readers of this book assume the risks and responsibilities inherent in skiing.

Mountain Sports Press
929 Pearl Street, Suite 200
Boulder, Colorado 80302 USA
Phone (303) 448-7610

Contents

Acknowledgments

Special thanks to:

My many students who, on many mountains, have always taught me more than I've taught them.

The dedicated Aspen-area ski pros who have worked with me to make our annual "total-saturation" ski weeks such an innovative success.

The Aspen Skiing Company, one of the most creative and environmentally responsible ski companies in North America, for welcoming and supporting my ski-filming and ski-teaching projects.

A handful of exceptionally gifted skiers—including Jerry Berg, Kim McDonald, Paul Ruid, and Harald Harb—who not only inspired me with their dazzling technique, but volunteered to ski for my cameraman, Edgar Boyles, so that their skiing not only enriched my Breakthrough on Skis *videos, but, eventually, the illustrations for this book.*

Bill Grout, my friend, long-time editor at SKIING Magazine, *and today the publisher of this book, who has always helped me to focus and clarify the way I write about skiing.*

Linde Waidhofer, partner, true love, and ideal ski companion, for sharing my ski-teaching life with such enthusiasm and the rest of my life with such grace.

Introduction

Why Become an Expert Skier?

Nothing equals a perfect morning on skis: diamond sparkles in fresh powder, endless slow-motion turns, champagne air in your lungs. Nothing, except perhaps sharing such experiences with other skiers. That's the real motivation of the ski-teaching life, my life. Not a big pay check but a big payoff: the impossibly happy grin of students who have just done the impossible—skied an expert run like real experts. For years, my life as a ski teacher has been based on a bold premise—that there really is an expert, hidden, waiting to emerge, inside every skier. This is not exactly an idea shared by most ski instructors or most ski schools. But it's true. And I've been proving it true for years—on the slopes with my students, in my articles and books, with my skiing videos. Still, this notion that every skier is potentially an expert is hardly the first image one gets when visiting ski resorts in the United States, in the Alps, anywhere.

Most skiers, alas, are simply survivors: They cope with the mountain instead of collaborating with it. They "get down" runs more often than they fly down them. In a word, most skiers at most ski areas are dyed-in-the-wool, rough-at-the-edges intermediates. Cynics might go so far as to say "terminal intermediates." I disagree with that verdict, but I have to admit that most skiers exhibit neither grace nor efficiency, neither poise nor poetry as they slide down the mountain. Is this merely the bell-shaped curve at work?

Are most skiers destined to be mere participants rather than performers? Are only a handful, a small percentage, capable of breathtaking, almost effortless expert performance? I don't believe it for a minute, and you shouldn't either. I didn't believe it when I wrote my classic ski book *Breakthrough on Skis: How to Get Out of the Intermediate Rut.* I didn't believe it when I made my series of *Breakthrough on Skis* videos. I don't believe it today. And for good reason.

My experience has been the exact opposite. I believe average skiers can become true experts because I've seen it happen again and again, because I've been helping average skiers to do just that for years, because the proof is in the skiing. And there's even more good news. It's much easier to ski like an expert today than it was even a few years ago because of revolutionary changes in ski design. Even long-time experts are now skiing better than ever before on their new skis. I certainly am—after all these years. Why shouldn't you?

I know that's a rhetorical question, but I'll answer it anyway. Of course you should! If you've ever been tempted, fascinated, intrigued by skiing, I want to tell you that life is too short not to live it as an expert skier. We'll talk in more detail about just what it means to be an expert skier, but let's start with this simple notion: Expert skiing, expert ski technique, is freedom—freedom to move, to slide, to turn or not to turn, to ski as fast, or as slowly, as you want to, to be yourself and to express yourself on a snowy mountainside, the most aesthetic winter playground imaginable.

Here's the first technical insight I want to share with you—the foundation of this book and the key insight that continues to keep me as passionate about ski instruction as about skiing itself: Expert skiing is no harder than intermediate-level skiing; it's merely different.

I hope you'll remember this all-important notion as you read and reference this book and as you view and review the companion videotapes. Again: *Expert skiing is not harder than intermediate-level skiing; it's merely different.*

Certainly, some expert skiers are also amazing athletes; top-level ski racers, in particular, are wonderfully fit and superbly trained athletes. But in general, expert skiing does not depend on athletic gifts or prowess or on sheer muscular strength. The forces that propel us down the mountain are borrowed forces, free for the asking. The pull of gravity and the friction of skis against snow give us more power to move over a snow-covered planet than Olympic sprinters have at the peak of their form. Expert skiing is a sport of balance and coordination—and I'm convinced you can develop both. I've spent a great deal of time in the world of ski instruction, teaching all kinds of lessons and all kinds of students (students who taught me as much as I ever taught them) and training instructors, at major resorts including Squaw Valley, Telluride, Vail, and Aspen, and at a few smaller resorts like Leysin and Villars-sur-Ollon in western Switzerland that most American skiers have never even heard of. And I can tell you that most ski instructors are not great athletes, although most ski instructors are indeed expert skiers.

When I said that expert skiing isn't any harder than intermediate skiing, merely different, I was really making several points: First, that expert skiers use a fundamentally different set of movements to guide and control their skis than you do (if you are an intermediate skier, that is). And second, that these expert movement patterns are no harder—and generally, in fact, are physically easier and much less fatiguing—than the movements used by average skiers. Why? Because experts let their equipment, particularly their skis, do most of the work for them. In contrast, average intermediate skiers tend to do most of the work of skiing—that is to say, turning—with their muscles. This is a critical difference, which we'll explore in detail later.

But there is an interesting corollary to my assertion that although expert skiing is no harder than intermediate skiing, its basic movement patterns are really different. The sad fact is that most ski lessons at most ski schools are not designed to transform you into an expert skier. Instead, most ski lessons, even lessons that seem to produce results, simply create more skilled intermediates. Is this what you're after? I don't think so. My goal is not to take the way you already ski and polish it up a bit. That strategy will only turn you into a more polished average skier. But it will never get you out of the intermediate rut. It will never cure the intermediate blues.

Instead, I want to ask you to join me in an experiment, a bold plan, designed to turn you into a brand new skier. Together we are going to build your expert technique almost from scratch. Together we are going to master a very few critically important movement patterns, the key moves of modern expert skiing. And then I'll help you fine-tune those patterns to coax the best performance from your revolutionary new skis. This book is not a compilation of little tips to make you ski just a wee bit better. Together we're going after the big prize. I'm going to sketch out the whole program and launch you on a campaign that will change the way you ski, dramatically—and for good.

For now, I'd like to welcome you to a new vision of winter: You are about to become the star, the main player, the leading lady or leading man in a new adventure—the adventure of expert skiing.

How to Use This Book

And Its Companion Videotapes

This is a book of ski lessons. But it's not a random sampler of random ski lessons. There's method in my madness—method and methodology. The sequence of steps I'm going to lay out to get you from average to expert skiing is just as important as the steps themselves. If you get excited and rush ahead to follow my advice about skiing bumps, for example, without first working on linking short turns, I don't think you'll have much success. And linking short turns depends on mastering a certain form of weight shift, and so on.

Even though I can promise you that expert skiing is pretty simple, it will soon become obvious that this ski-course-in-a-book contains far more—more explanations, more moves, more techniques, and more practice patterns— than you can possibly absorb in one sitting or in one reading. So I want to encourage you to look at this book as something between a narrative and a reference work. Ultimately, I think you will find the book most helpful when you take it in small chunks, focusing on one chapter at a time, reading about and visualizing a certain aspect of ski technique, and then going out to practice and integrate that aspect into your skiing. You are going to become an expert skier one step, one skill at a time.

Nonetheless, human nature is human nature. It's natural and inevitable that many of you will want to read straight through to the end—rather than bite off small lesson-sized chunks. So be it. That's not all bad. If you do read this book from cover to cover, it will certainly give you a good overview of modern expert skiing.

But reading this book from cover to cover won't make you an expert skier. What will make you an expert skier is patiently practicing a handful of key moves, acquiring step-by-step the building blocks of expert ski technique. So I'm hoping that once you've taken an overall look, you will slow down, thumb back through the pages, and tackle each chapter separately, a little more patiently, a little more thoroughly.

Chapter 1 is devoted to the *why* of expert skiing: *why* our skis turn, and especially *why* our new "shaped," or "super-sidecut," skis turn so much better than the ones we used only a few years ago. The rest of the book is about doing it, mastering and integrating expert patterns into your skiing at a deep level. The organization of this book reflects my conviction that there is a natural progression that virtually all skiers have to pass through on their way to top performance. Skiers ignore this natural progression at their own risk.

It's a question of putting A before B, B before C, and keeping the few key elements of expert skiing in their proper order. So please don't be too flighty a student; don't pick and choose at random what to practice. Follow the overall sequence of this book and your journey into expert skiing will be faster than you can imagine. Make a point of breaking your progress into small, manageable, achievable chunks: Read, visualize, practice; then relax and enjoy. And on your next ski weekend, do it again.

How Much Should You Practice?

You wouldn't think that an aspiring expert skier could practice too much, too hard, too long. Yet it happens all the time. When skiers, or any athletes, practice too long, too seriously, too hard, they often regress rather than continue to progress. Muscles tighten; movements lose their spontaneity and fluidity; everything goes wrong. You will learn more, faster, and better if you alternate intense, focused runs, serious single-minded practice runs, with totally relaxed, playful, to-hell-with-ski-technique runs.

How much practice is enough? I recommend one carefully focused practice run for every two or three playful fun runs. And do try to get in your serious practice time in the morning when you are fresh, when you can easily concentrate on the subtle nuances of balance and movement.

The Companion Videos

The exact same principles apply to the use of my *Breakthrough on Skis* videotapes. As a ski writer, I've always challenged myself to paint pictures of good ski technique with words, not to rely on illustrations to clarify something that I was unable to express in writing. But both skiing itself and learning to ski have a powerful visual component. Out on the hill, your eyes provide the most important input to your balance. And watching, then imitating, remains the oldest and often the most effective way of learning any sport, any physical activity, any motor skill.

So a few years ago, I decided to use my background in documentary filmmaking to produce a videotape to accompany my earlier *Breakthrough on Skis* book. One of the main reasons this video succeeded was the amazingly skillful camera work of my friend Edgar Boyles, who skis just as well with a heavy professional 16-mm camera on his shoulders as most instructors can with a ski pole in each hand. After the success of my first ski-teaching video, I went on to make several more. The second is a sort of graduate course, focusing on moguls and deep powder, perhaps the two biggest challenges in expert skiing. My third video is an exploration of the new shaped, or super-sidecut, ski designs and ways of obtaining the best performance from these amazing skis. All three videos can be combined with the instruction I offer in this book in a thoroughly complementary way.

My goal in producing these videos was to use rhythmic, often repetitive, slow-motion footage to distill the most important skiing images into an easy-

skiing and teaching and start searching for something, anything, new that would work with these new skis. This kind of grasping after novelty goes on more than you can imagine in the ski-teaching world—and more than is really necessary. But even when I explain basic expert patterns—like early weight shift, like riding the outside ski—patterns I've been teaching and writing about for years, I try to do so in a fresh way with fresh images.

To be sure, there are more than a few new moves and new feelings I want to pass on. Yes, some things do change. And have changed. And are still changing. Most of the new techniques and subtleties I share in this book, like the mysteriously named "phantom edging," involve carving—slicing beautiful narrow-track arcs instead of skidding our turns. On our new skis, carving— once reserved for a minority of experts, at racing speeds only—has now become a sport for the masses, carving for the rest of us. And so I've put a lot of emphasis on new variations of the carving game. Another new technique is one of the most exciting I've encountered in recent years—I call it "soft weight shift." This widely misunderstood technique, which I introduce in Chapter 4, is a true revelation—a true breakthrough in ease and precision. And it fits perfectly with my growing conviction that most skiers, most of the time, try too hard, work too hard.

In recent years, I have focused on a softer, more relaxed approach to extremely challenging terrain with great success. And this notion of soft skiing down hard slopes, which I summarize in Chapter 9, may well be this book's most important contribution. But I'm getting ahead of myself. We've got a whole book in front of us before we get there: a blend of classic and new techniques.

Beginners—I Haven't Forgotten You

One final note on the strategy for using this book. As its subtitle suggests, *Breakthrough on the New Skis* is aimed at intermediate skiers, at long-time skiers who have often practiced the sport for years without ever truly mastering it. That is to say, the majority of skiers, the middle of that proverbial bell-shaped curve. I wanted to jump right in and get to work with these skiers, with skiers like you. But I also know that this book will probably be read by quite a few beginners too. Rather than delaying the presentation of my main themes to my target readers by starting the book with the obligatory chapter on beginning to ski, I've tucked that chapter at the very end of the book—an extra chapter, actually an appendix .... So beginners, please don't feel ignored. Turn to this last chapter first. And then, when you've mastered my simplified set of basic skills for novices, return to Chapter 1 to start your own adventurous pursuit of expert skiing.

Good reading, good viewing, good learning, good skiing!

Part I

Expert Skiing Simplified

Understanding Expert Skiing

The Surprising Inner Logic of Modern Skiing

The sun is just blinking over the eastern horizon, a sawtooth edge of white peaks stretching off forever in our skiers' imaginations. Soon, with a creak of cables and gears, spiderweb ski lifts will start to purr toward the summits like magic carpets for skiers who have forgotten that once pioneers hiked to the top to enjoy one perfect straight run down. We're still looking for that perfect run. Experts, in tune with their skis, with the mountain, find that perfect run again and again. Many skiers find it once or twice and then it slips away. And some skiers have ridden these lifts for years without ever enjoying that perfect run. Worse, they don't know where it's hiding, how to get there, how expert skiing really works. Why? Why are some skiers better, better still, best? Why do some runs, even some turns, rise to another level?

Welcome to the big picture. This chapter is designed to lay out the basic ideas and principles we'll follow, step by step, point by point, and turn by turn, as we build expert skiing patterns through the rest of this book. Understanding expert skiing is not sufficient, in itself, to make you ski like an expert. But it helps. In particular, such understanding gives would-be experts a sense of why things work, of where they are going, and why they are practicing certain moves. It removes the voodoo from ski learning and substitutes a

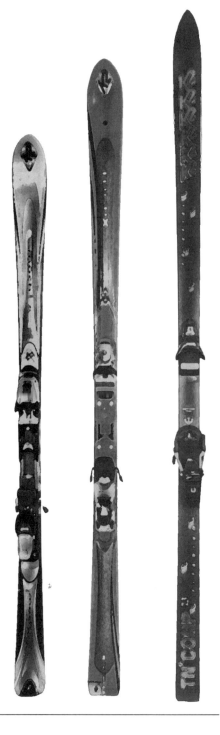

Figure 1.1 *The shape of shaped skis.* Look at the difference between old and new. It is more a difference of degree than of kind because for generations skis have been widest at the tip, narrower at the waist, and then wider again toward the tail. Here are three skis, three generations of design: (right to left) a classic ski without much sidecut; a modern shaped, or super-sidecut, ski with a much deeper side curve; and another modern ski, one of the newer carving skis whose shorter length accentuates the deep sidecut even more. And we can be sure this isn't the end of the story.

Skis have always had a sidecut, a narrower center and wider tip. Well, maybe not always, but for a long, long time. Skis from the nineteenth century, which can be seen in museums in Norway, are 90 centimeters wide at the tip, 70 centimeters wide at the center, and 80 centimeters wide at the tail. Those dimensions didn't vary all that much for more than one hundred years. In the past few years, however, skis have gotten proportionately much, much wider at the tip and proportionately much narrower at the waist, with amazing results. Of course, this curved-sided ski geometry isn't the only factor to consider in our quest to understand modern skiing. But this is the perfect place to start. So before we look at the skier's role, at the skilled skier's stance, at a skier's balance and movement patterns, let's visit a slightly more abstract subject—how our skis interact with the snow.

How Skis Turn

Two complementary factors that are designed into our skis cause them to turn on the snow. The wide tip is responsible for what skiers call "skidded" turns. The narrow center section, or waist, actually makes a ski "carve" a turn. Skidding and carving are easy-to-understand terms. In a skidded turn, the ski leaves a wide track, skidding or brushing sideways, as it moves in a more or less curved path across the snow. But in a carved turn, the ski leaves a narrow track as it "slices" around, following the pure shape of an arc, without drifting, or brushing, or skidding sideways. In real life, on the slopes, these two aspects of turning are often blurred, so that one makes a turn that is somewhat carved but also somewhat skidded—that is, there is a continuum: Turns can be either more carved or more skidded. One hundred percent pure carved turns are rather rare, although more common than they used to be. Let's see how each type of turn works.

A skidded turn is produced when the ski is twisted or pivoted at an angle to its direction of motion and tipped up on its edge—the ski is then brushing or scraping somewhat sideways across the snow. In the course of this scraping

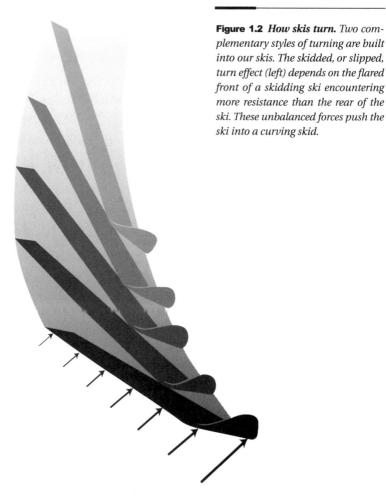

Figure 1.2 *How skis turn.* Two complementary styles of turning are built into our skis. The skidded, or slipped, turn effect (left) depends on the flared front of a skidding ski encountering more resistance than the rear of the ski. These unbalanced forces push the ski into a curving skid.

action, the wide tip of the ski will tend to bite more deeply into the snow than the rest of the ski; so friction builds up at the front of the ski while the tail, with less friction, slides out to the side, just as the rear end of a car may break loose and slide out to the side on an icy road. But at the same time, the ski continues to track more or less forward. So two movements occur at the same time: The whole ski moves forward, and the tail slips away sideways relative to the tip. The result is a wide, skidded, but nonetheless curved

The carved turn effect (below) occurs when an edged ski is bent by the skier's weight and pressed into an arc in the snow. The more this ski is edged, the more it can bend, leading to a shorter carved turn. Of course, the two turning effects can occur simultaneously, resulting in turns that are partially carved and partially slipped. In my explanations of why skis turn the way they do, I've tried to paint easy-to-visualize pictures of a very complex process. For a deeper and technically precise exploration of the physics, mechanics, and engineering of modern skis and how they turn, I recommend Ron LeMaster's terrific book The Skier's Edge.

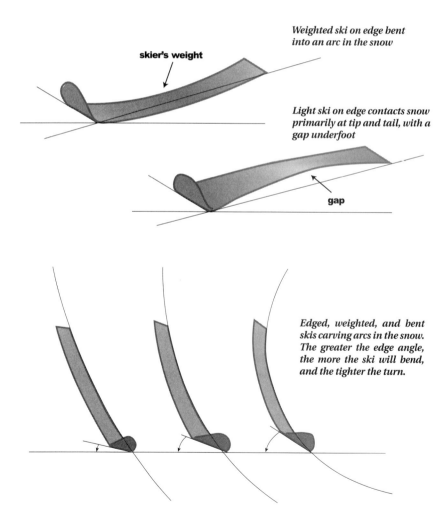

skier's weight

Weighted ski on edge bent into an arc in the snow

Light ski on edge contacts snow primarily at tip and tail, with a gap underfoot

gap

Edged, weighted, and bent skis carving arcs in the snow. The greater the edge angle, the more the ski will bend, and the tighter the turn.

Why Round Turns?

Turning, it turns out, is a lot more than just zigging and zagging your way down the hill. Of course, by turning sharply and quickly to one side or the other, you can, at least, change your direction down the mountain. You can avoid obstacles and hazards, trees, rocks, and other skiers. But turning actually has a more important function. Turning is a skier's subtlest and most effective form of speed control. And round turns, very round turns, are the secret of efficient and almost effortless speed control.

Consider this: Every time you turn your skis down the mountain, you will inevitably speed up. That's because when your skis are pointed straight down the hill, the slope of the mountain under your skis is at the maximum steepness, whereas when you are crossing the hill (or "traversing"), the angle at which your skis are sliding is not nearly so steep as when they are pointed straight down the hill. Each time you turn your skis down the hill, it is as though the slope becomes steeper underfoot and, of course, you speed up.

Even first-time beginners, making their first slow-speed turns on a gentle practice hill, can feel this brief but very real acceleration as they point or turn their skis more directly down the hill. Now a little extra speed is fine, but unless you are a dyed-in-the-wool thrill seeker, you probably don't want to go faster, and faster, and faster, from turn to turn to turn. Speeding up is okay, as long as you have a comfortable way to get rid of that extra speed when you want to. And that's exactly the role of the second half of a turn—to get rid of that extra speed you've gained in the first half of the turn, to keep things from getting out of hand.

A nice idea—speed up, slow down, speed up, slow down, with every turn. But now it's time to ask: What exactly is it that slows a skier down in the second half of each turn? Inexperienced skiers slow down by skidding and scraping their skis sideways across the snow. It's brutal and fatiguing, but it works. And that's why so many novice and intermediate skiers fall into the dreaded *twist-skid* pattern, especially on steeper slopes, throwing or twisting their skis sideways, and then scraping the snow with their edges to keep their speed down.

It's quite fatiguing to use your legs as shock absorbers in this fashion, to soak up extra speed by digging in and scraping sideways. There has to be a better way, and there is. Experienced skiers use the round shape of a smoothly arc- ing turn to reduce their speed.

It's easy. In the second half of a smooth round arc, the actual angle of the slope underfoot (or should I say, under your skis) will constantly decrease, until finally you are heading straight across the slope (where the effective slope angle will be zero). Indeed, if you continue turning, in a patient round arc, you will eventually find yourself skiing uphill—a negative slope. Thus, rounding out a turn is the same thing as skiing from a steep slope to a flat slope and, eventually, even skiing up the opposite side of a small gully. Naturally, the flatter the slope gets, the slower you'll ski. And if the slope turns uphill you'll come to a complete stop. That's exactly what happens in a pure round turn. To say it in a different way: It's the shape of the turn, the geometry of the turn, and not the sideways scraping of ski edges across the snow, that actually slows you down. And this is where we encounter the real importance of carving round turns.

Sure, carved turns look great, and they feel great too, but above all, they offer the promise of total speed control without fatiguing our leg muscles. That's why we're going to place so much emphasis on making round turns, not sharp zigzag corners, in this book—and in your adventures on the mountain. This point is so important that I really ought to say it one more time in yet another way. *The farther around the arc of the turn you ski, the slower you'll go.* Which means that experts control their speed (and slow down when they want to) not by turning harder, but by turning longer—by sticking with the arc of their turn and following it farther around the imaginary circle that their skis are drawing on the snow. To slow down, turn farther, not harder. Okay?

And one last note: Guiding your skis in a round arc doesn't mean that each turn has to be a perfect pure carve. Earlier in this chapter I said that most turns are a mixture of some skidding and some carving, and that as your skill increases, your turns will become progressively more carved and less

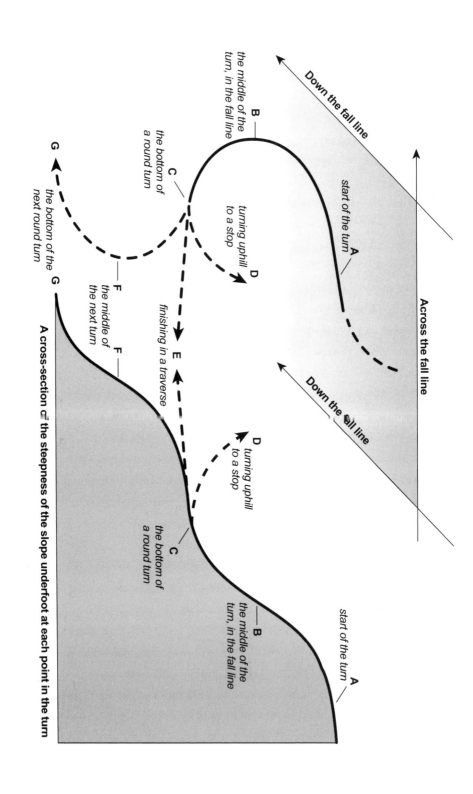

Down the fall line

Across the fall line

start of the turn

B the middle of the turn, in the fall line

C the bottom of a round turn

D turning uphill to a stop

finishing in a traverse **E**

Down the fall line

D turning uphill to a stop

C the bottom of a round turn

B the middle of the turn, in the fall line

start of the turn

A

G the bottom of the next round turn

F the middle of the next turn

G the bottom of the next round turn

F **F** the middle of the next turn

A cross-section of the steepness of the slope underfoot at each point in the turn

Figure 1.4 *The logic of round turns.*
(left) Think about the slope of the
snow underfoot as you imagine
yourself skiing the round arc shown
in this illustration. Picture how the
angle at which your skis slide over
the snow increases in steepness dur-
ing the first half of every turn and
decreases during the second half.
The way a round turn leads you
through this "flattening out" of the
slope underfoot provides a nearly
effortless and very graceful means
of speed control.

skidded. But skidding often seems like a dirty word, something to be avoided, period. So let's make a small distinction between skidding a turn and slipping a turn. From now on I'll use the term skidding only in its most negative connotation—as when skiers over-pivot their skis and they wind up skidding out sideways instead of describing a smooth arc on the snow. Slipping a turn, on the other hand, will mean that the ski is "skidding" just a bit: the tail sliding out a bit in relation to the tip but not "washing out" sideways. And I'll rephrase my point about the blending of these two modes of turning to say that most ski turns are a blend of *slipping* and *carving*. The more skilled you become, the more you will carve your turns and the less you'll slip them. But as we'll see in the following chapters, both carving and slipping turns play an important role in today's expert skiing. Both can create round turns—the round turns you need to easily and effectively control your speed down the mountain.

Modern Skis versus Earlier Skis

Before we leave the subject of skis, let me answer the obvious question that's been hanging in the air since the start of this chapter: Why do modern deep-sidecut skis work so much better than the skis of a few years ago? I've already said that modern skis (variously called "shaped" skis, "parabolic" skis, or, my favorite, "super-sidecut" skis) have significantly wider tips and, therefore, proportionally narrower waists than traditional skis used to. That means that when you roll or tilt a modern ski up on edge, it's as though there were a bigger gap between the ski and the snow underfoot. But of course, you don't just roll the ski onto an edge; you stand on it, which pushes that relatively narrower waist even farther out into the snow, creating a deeper bend in the ski. In other words, a deeper sidecut equals more bend, which equals more carving. Or, to look at it another way: Because at any given angle, a super-sidecut ski will make a deeper bend, to carve the same radius turn, you won't have to roll a modern "shaped" ski as far over on edge to make it bend and carve that turn, as you would have with an older ski.

In the past, in order to edge skis strongly enough to make them bend and carve, skiers had to use more extreme positions, more edging and more "angulation" (skiers' jargon for a body position that can increase edging), and also had to ski much faster, so that centrifugal force would support them as they tilted over to edge their skis in these extreme positions. No longer. Deep-sidecut skis have opened the door to beautiful carved turns at slower speeds—recreational speeds rather than racing speeds—with a more relaxed, upright stance than ever before. Today, with our new deep-sidecut skis, carved turns are no longer the exclusive province of bold athletic skiers, skiing very fast. They belong to all skiers.

So why didn't designers and manufacturers create such skis ten or twenty years ago? The answer is fascinating. Engineers have always known that more sidecut would produce a better-turning and easier-turning ski, but it also requires a shorter ski. Think about how a deep-sidecut ski flares outward from waist to tip. If that ski were as long as a traditional ski, then its tip would be so wide that it would become virtually unmanageable. Thus, deep-sidecut skis need to be at least 10 or 15 centimeters shorter than earlier conventional skis. And shorter skis have always felt unstable at speed. They would start to tremble and wobble and vibrate as the skier picked up speed. So super-sidecut ski design had to wait until ski manufacturers developed new methods for damping out high-speed vibrations in skis—new ways to make short skis feel like long skis at higher speeds. Virtually every modern ski builder has taken a different approach to solving this problem—from extra shock-absorbing layers, to miniature hydraulic cylinders, to a so-called piezoelectric vibration-dissipating system

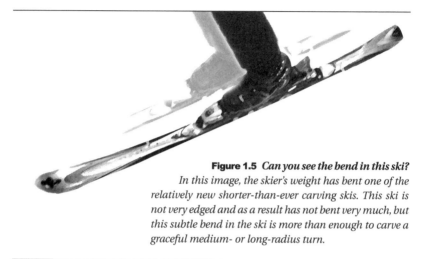

Figure 1.5 *Can you see the bend in this ski?*
In this image, the skier's weight has bent one of the relatively new shorter-than-ever carving skis. This ski is not very edged and as a result has not bent very much, but this subtle bend in the ski is more than enough to carve a graceful medium- or long-radius turn.

borrowed from the wings of jet fighter planes—and the good news is: They all work. A few years back, shaped skis were a novelty. Today they are ubiquitous, widely accepted, and widely loved. Skis nowadays are deep-sidecut skis, period.

This said, the subtleties of ski geometry are constantly changing. Every season, manufacturers tweak their designs to great effect. All-around, all-mountain, all-snow skis today have slightly wider waists than the first generation of shaped skis did, with still wider tips to compensate and maintain that all-important deep side curve. Slalom skis get shorter every season. Indeed, no one knows where this evolution will end. Perhaps it never will. From our point of view, one of the very best things about this new generation of skis is that our new super-sidecut skis don't really demand a brand new technique—although we are constantly discovering subtle new moves we can achieve with them. Classic expert ski technique still works the same way, that is to say, perfectly. *Our new skis don't really ski differently; they simply ski better.*

But they can also ski worse! By this I mean that, since these skis are shorter by design, it is even easier—all too easy—to twist them violently into a new direction and skid a very awkward turn. It's no exaggeration to say that at least half of the folks who have bought new shaped skis aren't getting the results they paid for, and hoped for, from them. Thus, the new skis can be seen as a mixed blessing: Treat them right and they will make turns that will astonish and delight you; overpower them with excess twisting and they will make the worst skidded turns you have ever experienced.

And sad to say, myths and misconceptions about shaped skis abound. Ski schools have embraced the new skis, often without a clear understanding of what they were embracing. Ski instructors, like ski journalists, are not immune to the siren song of the new. Every year ski magazines tend to look for novelties in ski technique, and so do instructors. The real question, of course, should be: *What works?* not *What's new?* So a lot of curious tales are being spun on the slopes about new ways to ski these new skis. And the beat goes on ...

All That Other Modern Gear

How about the rest of the system? Boots, bindings, and poles? Your boots are translators. They translate your wishes, and your movements, into pressures that affect the ski. And they translate the ski's movements into pressure signals you can feel through the soles of your feet, through fore and aft and lateral pressure on your shins and ankles. Boots are subtle two-way avenues of communication between skier and ski. At least they are when they fit right.

In general, ski boots are neither as high nor as stiff as they were a few years ago. And they tend to be much more comfortable. Comfort is a necessity, not an option, because any pressure points, any cramping, any foot pain or discomfort, will compromise your balance and inhibit your performance. But a comfortable pair of boots is just the beginning. Your boots, their shapes and angles and flexibility or lack of it, determine your basic stance on your skis. So it's critical to focus on *ski-boot alignment* as well as fit.

More accurately, we should talk about boot-skier alignment. Measuring and adjusting and fine-tuning skiers' alignment in their boots is a crucial art as well as a science, and few have mastered it. Very few skiers have perfectly

How Boot Alignment Works

I've been recommending custom boot alignment to my students for a long time, with great results. But what exactly is involved?

Custom boot alignment goes far beyond custom boot fitting. And although the term boot alignment is pretty common, what is really being aligned is the whole skier/ski boot/ski system. The goal, of course, is to stand in perfect functional balance over your skis, over either ski, and to be able to shift weight and pressure easily and quickly to any part of the boot and, hence, to the ski, without disturbing that balance. A worthy goal indeed. My friend Jim Lindsay of BOOTech in Aspen, the most skillful boot alignment specialist I've ever worked with, takes his time to get everything just so. An average alignment session with Jim lasts about two hours and begins with a series of very sophisticated measurements. The barefoot skier dons a pair of shorts, climbs onto a special stand, and Jim, using a set of plastic calipers and other measuring devices, records just about every angle that the foot, ankle, lower leg, and knee can make. Next, the skier stands on a computerized pressure plate and a multicolored pressure pattern appears on the monitor. There's no guesswork at this stage, not even an educated guess.

From these measurements, Jim can deduce an optimum skiing position, which differs for every skier. And then he goes about making such a position possible inside your boots. This almost always involves the building of a slightly flexible footbed, a footbed that has little in common with those routinely made in ski shops. A well-crafted footbed holds the sole of your foot in a natural, neutral, and strong position, compensating for pronation or supination. But that's only the beginning. Jim, or any other skilled boot alignment specialist, goes to

(continued on page 32)

straight, perfectly symmetrical, perfectly shaped legs. Almost everyone is a little bow-legged, or a little knock-kneed; almost everyone has an easier time balancing on one foot than the other. And that's where boot alignment comes in. Skilled boot alignment specialists can adjust and adapt the angles of your ski boots to fit the angles of your feet, ankles, and legs, so that on the slope you will find yourself standing in a balanced and neutral position over your skis. My impression is that at least half of all skiers, and probably a much larger percentage, will benefit hugely from boot alignment. It makes perfect sense to adapt your equipment to your physical structure rather than trying to overcompensate for imperfect alignment with a host of fussy little movements.

Bindings, the link between boots and skis, are your insurance policy. The safety features of ski bindings (release versus retention) are so much more sophisticated now than they were a few years ago that certain types of ski injuries have almost disappeared. Unfortunately, even the best bindings still don't seem to be very effective in preventing knee injuries. So there's room for still more R&D. Technically, bindings don't have a great influence on your ski technique. But the distance from the sole of your foot to the ski turns out to be potentially very important, so most modern bindings hold the sole of the boot somewhat higher off the ski than they used to. Skilled skiers who have bought into the "pure carving" mystique even put special plates, called risers, between their skis and bindings to lift themselves another centimeter or so off the snow. Risers seem to offer the skier additional leverage for tilting a ski over on edge and holding it there. (We'll look at risers more closely in the section on super-carving in Chapter 8.)

Finally, a few words about ski poles. I've taught lots of skiers who have unhesitatingly spent a small fortune on the latest skis, boots, and bindings but hung onto their twenty-year-old poles. Wrong. Only half in jest, I explain that their poles are their only friends and allies in this white universe (aside from their ski pro) and that when used well, poles can make all the difference between a hesitant run and a fluid run on steep, or black, terrain. In fact, poles only become truly useful, and then critical, when the skiing itself becomes very hard. I'm thinking particularly of bumps and steeps. Quick pendulumlike pole action becomes the glue that links one turn with the next, that pulls you inexorably and effortlessly straight down very steep slopes. If your poles are heavy, and most older poles are, your pole action will be slowed down just when you need it most. And you will remain skeptical about the joys of steep black-slope skiing. Super-light modern poles are an expert's secret weapon.

The Skier's Role

From the beginning I've stressed the idea that as an expert, you don't turn your skis, your skis turn you. It's true. But that doesn't mean that the skier is totally off the hook, merely a passive passenger. What does the expert skier contribute to the mix? What is the actual role of the modern skier?

As an expert skier, you have two complementary roles to play: first, staying in balance as speed, terrain, and outside forces constantly change; and second, adjusting the way your skis interact with the snow. When I say "adjusting," I want to stress that the skier sends small signals, makes small moves, applies weight or edging to one ski or the other or both in order to make something happen, in order to guide those skis down the mountain. I'm definitely not talking about pushing one's skis around, about wrestling for control of one's skis. It's almost never a question of suddenly twisting your skis into a new direction, of lifting them off the snow, of forcing them to turn. It's rather a question of subtle guiding and adjusting movements that fine-tune the skis' own built-in tendency to turn.

Balance is a big subject, and dynamic balance, balance in motion, as you slide over a changing playing field, is bigger still. But balance is more or less a reactive art: The skier reacts to changing outside forces. So let's look first at the active part of the equation: what the skier does to make something happen.

Basically, you need to trigger, or launch, your turns and then to guide them. For generations, ski teachers and ski technicians have talked about initiating turns—a fancy word for starting them. And I must say, that used to be quite a task on earlier, stiffer skis. Time was when the only way skiers could start turns was to physically lift their skis off the snow—"unweighting," we called it. So more than one generation of skiers learned to ski in a kind of *down-hup!-and-around* pattern, where the "hup" represented a strong lifting of the body to make those older, stiffer skis light enough to turn. And turn them we did, twisting the skis with strong rotary movements of the body—counterrotation, or rotation—it all boiled down to the same thing: Twist your body hard enough, and the skis would turn. No longer.

Today, expert skiers are looking for the minimum effort, the minimum motion that will get the job done. And what precisely is that job? More than anything else, starting a carved turn means getting your ski to bend into a slight arc. And that in turn generally means transferring all your weight to one ski, the "outside" ski of your new turn. *(I've thrown in an important bit of skiing jargon here. By outside ski, I mean the ski on the outside of the circle of each turn. If you're turning left, it will be your right ski; if you're turning right, it will be your left ski. Remember, talking about the outside and inside ski of each turn is not at all the same as talking about your uphill or downhill ski. Because the outside ski of a turn begins as the uphill ski, and then, as the turn finishes, it has become the downhill ski.)*

That's the key: The key to starting or launching turns is to shift your body weight to the new outside ski. This is a major theme that we'll pursue in detail and master in the coming chapters. And of course, sometimes, though rarely, we'll still have to pivot our skis, at least a bit, in the new direction of a new turn. But the more carved your turn, the less you will pivot your skis. Indeed, in a pure carved turn, you feel as though your skis are still slicing straight ahead and only slowly, gradually, progressively, do they bend and arc around. In summary, starting turns depends mainly on weight shift, with an occasional helping move—pivoting the skis slightly—thrown in only when needed.

Once the turn has started, your job is to keep it going. To make sure that

Figure 1.6 *In the middle of a turn. In this image it's easy to see why we always speak of the inside and outside ski of a turn rather than the uphill or downhill ski. We've learned that the outside ski really creates the turn through its interaction with the snow. But the inside foot and ski have an important role to play as we'll see in Chapters 2 and 3.*

your skis follow exactly the path that you had in mind. To guide the arc. And this boils down to keeping that outside ski bent and carving, keeping your weight centered on that outside ski, staying there, balanced and poised while your ski does its thing. So keeping the turn going—guiding the turn—boils down in large measure to keeping your balance with a few subtle edge adjustments down at the boot-ski-snow level. And that's really the second half of the skier's role: dynamic efficient balance. And it deserves a whole discussion.

The Skilled Skier's Stance

When skiers ask me what I've learned in the past ten years, or five years, or even over the past season, how my teaching and coaching has changed, I have a simple answer. I'm more concerned with balance now than ever before. More concerned with skiers' posture and stance. More convinced than ever that if you can stand and balance like an expert, then you can turn like an expert. I've learned that underneath multiple differences of body build, temperament, and individual skiing style, expert skiers share a sort of common approach to standing on their skis. Let's look a little closer at this skilled skier's stance:

We're standing halfway down a blue slope on a crisp January morning, looking up at a backlit field of snow, watching everything sparkle, watching skiers move as dark silhouettes down this white canvas. A good position to observe skiers' balance and stance. What do we see? Some skiers look stiff and heavy, others light and agile. Some skiers obviously care about not falling; they ski in a rock-solid but somewhat defensive position; others, the most accomplished skiers on the slope, seem totally indifferent to questions of falling or not falling. They are loose, flexible, always moving, sometimes moving just in time to keep their balance when their skis play small tricks on them. That's the first difference between average skiers and gifted skiers. Skillful skiers are always in motion, never static; less secure skiers lock up in static, sometimes almost frozen, positions. Remember a few pages ago, I was talking about dynamic balance, constantly changing balance as you adjust to a constantly changing playing field, constantly varying forces. Skilled skiers are quiet, calm, and poised but never frozen. All their joints are gently, steadily flexing and stretching as they pass over uneven terrain—and all skiing terrain is ultimately uneven, if only because the actual slope underneath your skis is becoming more steep, then flattening throughout every turn. And this dynamic stance begins with the feet.

In a sense, everything in skiing begins with the feet. Only our feet are in contact with our skis and through them with the mountain. Perhaps it isn't surprising that the biggest obstacles to developing expert balance are our ski boots—not all boots, but many that are so stiff that they don't allow any movement at all at the ankle. And stiffness here is a relative thing; a boot that I might find soft could also be too stiff for a slight, short skier who had no experience

Thanksgiving morning on Aspen Mountain, cold and windy. I wasn't going to begin teaching for another week. But here I was, skiing, of course—the proverbial busman's holiday—with my wife, Linde, on hard, early-season pack: classic marginal conditions, every skier in Colorado praying for snow. I could tell this snow was rock hard and scraped slick; I could see it, hear it, but somehow it didn't feel either hard or awkward at all. Felt great. Felt better than any start-of-the-season snow I could remember. True, I had these funny red-white-and-blue striped skis on my feet. Demos. My first ever super-sidecut skis. And yes, they had felt pretty good, maybe more than just pretty good from the very first turn. Linde, too, was skiing with an enormous grin on her face. But we didn't really realize what was going on until we headed back to the demo center on top of Aspen Mountain at noon. We turned in our K2 Fours, grabbed our regular skis, and headed down the mountain for lunch in town.

Holy smokes! In the blink of an eye, Aspen Mountain did a Dr. Jekyll and Mr. Hyde number on us. Spar Gulch suddenly turned back into an unpleasant icy chute, every turn was a struggle, our smiles disappeared under a mask of intense concentration. This was work. Too much work. When we slid to a stop by the gondola terminal, Linde kicked off her old skis—until this morning, her favorite skis of all time—and looked at me with a glint in her eye: That's it, Lito. I might as well pitch these skis in the dumpster, right here and now. I'm not going back on snow until I get my own pair of these new shaped skis. Linde doesn't exactly mince words, but that's what I'd been thinking too. First stop: truffled french fries at Ajax Tavern. Second stop: new skis. New deep-sidecut skis.

of flexing against resistance on the front of the shin. Watch average skiers from the lift the next time you go skiing. How many of them appear to have stiff, locked ankles? Too many.

The first thing I do with ski students who exhibit no ankle flex is to ask them if the top buckles of their boots are tight. They usually are. So we begin by loosening the top buckle to see if that permits the ankle to flex; often it will. This is where good balance begins. You need a fair amount of "give" (the ability to easily flex and stretch each joint) from the ankle on up—but especially at the ankle. Subtle flexing and straightening at the ankle easily moves your weight forward and back on your ski. That lets you stay right where you belong, over the ski's center, as the pitch of the slope constantly changes. After a lifetime of living and moving with flexible joints, it is totally unrealistic to expect to maintain your balance if your ski boots trap you with stiff, locked ankle joints. A carefully chosen, well-fitted, well-aligned boot (in which your foot is supported by a custom-made, nonrigid footbed) will do wonders for your balance and stance.

Moving up the body, let's pause a moment to think about your hips and your abdomen. Somewhere in this region is your center—your center of gravity—and your metaphorical center, the spot that practitioners of many Oriental martial arts and exercise systems call your *ki,* or *chi.* "Center" works for me. Skilled skiers have developed a sort of sixth sense about their center: where it is; how it moves forward down the hill; how the center, ultimately, defines your path through space; how the center moves forward and down the hill at the start of each new turn. It will take time for you to become deeply aware of your center in skiing—and in the following chapters I'll suggest some games and exercises to develop this sense of one's center that is a real part of expert balance. The role of your center in dynamic balance is nowhere more evident than in bumps. Watch a hot mogul skier, flexible as a Slinky, dropping down a steep bump run, feet and skis flexing up and down like pistons. Then take a moment to watch the skier's hips, the center. The center flows down over the bumps in a pretty straight, even line. The skier is acting around the center, from the center. But in high-level skiing your center of gravity doesn't move much, or it moves very evenly and fluidly. (We'll return to this idea in Chapters 4 and 5.)

Feet and legs are mobile and flexible; your upper body, your trunk, is not. But your arms, hands, and poles certainly are. Your hands, in particular, are very light but they are at the ends of long, flexible levers—your arms—and where you carry your hands and poles can have a terrific effect on your balance. So experts tend to spread their hands laterally and keep them ahead of their hips. Drop your hands and your center will drop back. But those intermediate skiers we've been watching from the lift generally have no particular sense of where their hands should go; they either drop them back or hug them in toward their chest. Skilled skiers tend to spread their hands for balance the way a tightrope walker does. And the comparison is a good one because a tightrope is a narrow place in space to balance on. And so is a ski. If you remember my description of why skis carve, you'll remember that it helps to put all your weight on one foot, on one ski, to bend that ski into an arc. And standing on one ski is a bit like balancing on a tightrope: a narrow base, a constant subtle adjusting of the body, fore and aft, and side to side.

So developing this kind of flexible, dynamic balance over one ski at a time will be our first step as we move from average intermediate-style skiing in the direction of real expert performance. There's simply no way you will be able to coax the best performance out of your wonderful new skis if you are stuck hunkered down on both skis in a wide stance for extra security. But that's enough theory for now. It's time to start skiing.

IN SUMMARY

- Modern skis will perform 90 percent of the work of turning for us. This built-in turning action comes from the curved sides (or sidecut) of our skis. In recent years ski manufacturers have learned how to exaggerate this sidecut, with revolutionary results.

- Two different but complementary modes of turning are built into our skis: The wide tip creates a skidded or slipped turning action, while the narrow waist of the ski allows the ski to bend into an arc and carve. Carving and slipping are often blended in the same turn.

- Very round turns, whether carved or slipped, are the secret of efficient speed control without fatigue. Expert speed control is not the result of turning harder but of turning farther around the arc.

- It's a widespread misconception that we need to edge modern super-side-cut skis more than classical skis. The opposite is true. Our new skis will carve the same radius turn with less edging than older skis—although it's also true that our skis are always on edge when we turn.

- The expert skier's role is to guide and coordinate the skis' own built-in tendency to turn. Skilled skiers do this by shifting all their weight to the outside ski and balancing over that ski through the whole arc of the turn. (There are a couple of exceptions to this rule, which we will explore in later chapters, but they are, literally, the exceptions that confirm the rule.)

- Expert skiing depends on a balanced stance, and balance begins with the feet. Foot awareness, foot comfort, and foot alignment are crucial. Most skiers need specialized boot alignment to achieve a stance that allows easy balance over one foot, one ski, at a time.

CHAPTER 2

Riding the Arc of the Turn

Coaxing a Great Curve from the Outside Ski

Lines in the snow. Curving and carving. Long graceful lines. Arcs. Thin and elegant. Lines are all skiers leave, or need to leave, behind—the only proof of our passage down the mountain. In one sense, the lines your skis leave on the snow are your signature. This is my turn. This is who I am, or was, on this particular snowy morning, on this particular run. In another sense, the lines your skis leave in the snow are like a report card: This skier gets an A, this one only a C+. It's true: The tracks of every turn tell a story. This skier can really carve. This skier was barely hanging on. Just looking at certain lines in the snow can fire a skier's admiration, a skier's imagination. It's time to start drawing some nearly perfect lines in the snow.

Now the fun part. We're going to say goodbye to average ho-hum skiing and start making changes. You're about to begin the adventure of expert skiing. Maybe you've been skiing for some time, for years and years, or maybe you only recently emerged from the ranks of novice skiers. It doesn't really matter: For skiers of all levels, the next step is exactly the same. You are about to give up the security of standing solidly on both feet, on both skis, and become a one-footed skier—metaphorically, at least, because expert skiing is a kind of dance from foot to foot, from ski to ski. And the trick is to feel comfortable, to develop a new sort of ease and comfort over one ski at a time. It's easier than you think.

Let me summarize what the transition from average to expert skiing (and incidentally, the theme of this chapter) is all about: *Learn to stand like an expert skier, and you'll be able to turn like one.* But when I say stand, I don't mean just standing there, motionless, in place, the way you stand in line at the grocery store. Standing on a moving pair of skis is a dynamic art: nothing frozen, everything supple and moving, anticipating with eyes and reflexes and ultimately with your whole body, the changing forces you are about to encounter on your ride down the mountain. When friends ask me what I've learned about skiing in recent years, I always talk about this special balance and stance. In my teaching and coaching and instructor training nowadays, I emphasize the importance of standing well far more than I ever did before. The fluid, graceful combination of posture and poise, foot-to-foot and fore-and-aft balance, that adds up to an expert's stance isn't merely important; it's essential. Most of the time, as I watch skiers slide across the slope, I can predict exactly how they will turn, just by watching the way they stand and balance on their skis. If you can discover and adopt this expert's stance, then everything else I'm going to present in this book will work rather easily. If you don't, everything else will be a struggle and may not work at all. Let's begin.

In my earlier book, *Breakthrough on Skis*, I claimed that the best-kept secret in modern skiing is that expert skiers are almost always balanced over one ski, not two. It still is! When most people look up a ski slope and watch graceful accomplished skiers skimming down the hill, they always (and quite naturally) have the impression that these skiers are standing equally on both skis and that both skis are somehow following the same path down the mountain in exactly the same way. It's an illusion, but this confusion is natural. Because it takes a slow-motion, close-up camera sequence to convincingly demonstrate the opposite: that in fact, the most skilled skiers are almost always balanced over one foot or the other, almost never on both. You can see this clearly in Fig. 2.1.

Notice how one ski, the ski on the outside of the turn, is slightly bent, into

Figure 2.1 *Riding the outside ski of a turn: one-footed balance in action. We can see how the outside ski is bent into an arc from the skier's weight and this slight arc—all but invisible as a skier streaks by on the slope—is what produces a modern carved turn. The skier's main task in a wide round turn is maintaining and refining this one-footed balance.*

an arc, because of the skier's weight. Notice how the other ski remains unflexed, showing that it's simply along for the ride but is hardly carrying any of the skier's weight. I hope you are willing to go along with this idea despite the fact that a lot of ski teachers, and ski magazine commentators and editors, have muddied the waters by claiming that the best way to utilize the new generation of shaped skis is to spread one's weight evenly across both skis. (In Chapter 8, in the section on super carving, we'll see why so many "pros" are confused on this issue.)

If you've read Chapter 1, Understanding Expert Skiing, you already have a good idea why balancing over one ski—the outside ski of each turn—is so important in modern skiing: The extra weight you transfer onto that ski helps bend it into a deeper arc, the arc your ski will follow as it carves a turn.

But I don't want you to accept anything I say about skiing on faith. The test—the only test as far as I am concerned—is how well it works. Indeed, throughout this book, I am going to propose skiing techniques and solutions that are quite different from the advice you'll get in most ski schools. I trust you to go out and try these moves and judge for yourself whether or not they work and just how well they work. If you get what seems to be a great ski tip, but somehow it doesn't change your skiing, doesn't make you ski any better, I hope you'll keep looking until you find something that really does work wonders. I hope you will adopt that same show-me attitude toward everything I propose in this book. For now, I'm going to assume I've convinced you of the value of getting comfortable over one ski, and I'll show you how to do it.

Balance and Poise on One Foot

No one can say for sure whether balance is an innate skill or whether it is a learned skill. Perhaps it's both. But the trick on skis is to utilize your full potential for balance, and in that sense I'm convinced that balance can be honed and improved. That's what you are about to do in a series of games and practice exercises that will make you more and more comfortable riding one ski.

Start, as we will often start, on a wide-open, gentle run: lots of space to move, not enough steepness to make you nervous about controlling your speed, and, I hope, no crowds of skiers to distract you. Head straight down the hill, a schuss in ski jargon, and as soon as you feel comfortable, lift one ski slightly off the snow and balance, in motion, over your other ski. Most people can do this pretty easily; they just haven't ever tried. But if you feel wobbly and insecure as you try to slide down the slope on one ski, try this: Spread your arms wider than normal; keep your hands about waist high and extended outward in front of your hips. This balancing hand-arm position should make all the difference. You will be compensating with your hands and arms for the extra lateral stability that you lost when you pulled one ski up off the snow. Look around next time you ride the chairlift: You will see less experienced skiers spread their feet and skis for balance, more experienced skiers spread their arms for balance.

I often tell my students that the best one-sentence summary of modern expert skiing is this: *Ski with your feet; balance with your hands.* And it's true. You are simply not going to become comfortable balancing over one ski at a time with your hands hanging down beside your hips. Spread your hands and keep them in front of your hips. Think of a tightrope walker or a kid balancing on a rail. Their hands are always widespread, which allows them (as it will allow you), to make subtle balance adjustments with small and subtle hand movements. Try it. You will feel quite a bit steadier as you run straight on one ski. I'm going to suggest a number of other one-footed games to help you get comfortable with this expert style of balance.

Just how much of this one-footed practice running do you need? Basically, you'll need to play around with lifting one foot completely off the snow for at least a couple of days. You won't, I hasten to add, need to devote entire days exclusively to sliding downhill on one ski; but, rather, for a couple of days, play around with one-footed skiing whenever and wherever you cross an easy section of the mountain. Catwalks, those boring flat roads that take you from one side of the mountain to another, are perfect for this kind of practice. So are beginner slopes and easy, green terrain. Don't spend all your time on such extra-easy terrain, practicing one-footed balance; it would be far too boring. In an average day of skiing, you'll cross a lot of easy slopes. Use each one to become more comfortable balancing and sliding on one ski.

I've asked you to focus on riding one ski, but actually both legs and, more precisely, both feet, have a job to do. Paradoxically, if you want to balance on your right foot and ski as you slide down a moderate slope, it is the other foot, your left foot, that has a more active role to play. Transferring your weight onto one ski is not a totally intuitive action; it's much easier and far more intuitive to focus on getting your weight *off* the other foot and ski. To balance over your right ski, you actually pull your left foot up slightly off the snow. The light foot

Figure 2.3 *Skating on skis. The very best way to develop a fluid ability to move from one ski to the other, staying balanced, poised, and ready. Skating is almost certainly the single most important exercise on your journey toward expert skiing.*

and repeat. Don't make a big deal out of skating on skis. It's just a series of long strong steps from ski to ski with your skis angled out in a slight V. If all goes well, you'll find yourself gliding forward a few extra feet on each ski with each step. The gliding part, balanced on one ski, is what makes skating useful, not just as a balance exercise but as a way of keeping your momentum up when the slope becomes too flat for easy sliding. Expert skiers are constantly skating across the most boring parts of the mountain, and soon you will too.

As you might suspect there's a little more to skating than I've just suggested. And I promise I'll fill in the blanks soon. But when I teach skiers to skate, I find it works best if they can just make a first rough attempt. Then, over the next several days, I suggest a number of refinements to make their skating more efficient. I'll try to do something similar in this book. When I return to this subject later in this chapter, I'll be a little more specific. Meanwhile: On a comfortable slope—always that friendly, comfortable slope—simply try to skate without worrying about how well you are skating.

Skating is one of a number of tricks and games I always suggest in order to make skiers feel lighter on their feet and more agile and mobile, moving from foot to foot. Initially, the whole package of boots, bindings, and skis feels not only clumsy but quite heavy, like lead weights anchoring each foot to the snow. Active, healthy people can easily lose their everyday sense of mobility when they step onto a pair of skis. I want to change that. Why shouldn't we be able to walk and step and move as easily from ski to ski as we move from foot to foot in everyday life? A good friend of mine in the Aspen Ski School has coined a great name for the tendency of skiers just to hunker down and ride along with both feet and skis glued to the snow, unable to move easily from foot to foot. He calls it the "park and ride" syndrome. Don't fall into this trap.

Here are several tricks for breaking out of this mold. When you find yourself crossing a slope in a traverse, step quickly uphill with your top ski, stand on it, and pull the other one in beside it. And repeat, stair-stepping sideways up the hill as you glide across it. Once again, the most boring spots on the mountain can provide some of the best practice opportunities. On open, rather flat slopes or on wide, level catwalks, simply step-shuffle your feet and skis from one side to the other: a sort of step-step-step to the right, followed by a step-step-step to the left. Instead of making "ski turns" you will actually be walking your skis, one after the other, toward one side of the slope and then back toward the other. It's easy. It's liberating.

I'd like you to get back in touch with all the acquired movement patterns that you have used and developed throughout a whole lifetime of stepping, walking, skipping, and running. Most of the time we spend on our feet in everyday life involves foot-to-foot movement, foot-to-foot balance, as does most of expert skiing—although in expert skiing your foot-to-foot movement is slower, smoother, and ultimately more graceful than walking along the street. (Deep powder, as we'll see later, is the important exception to this notion of skiing from foot to foot.) Mysteriously, when some people put on skis, it can seem as though all those years of walking, skipping, and running have disappeared; and many skiers seem trapped, rooted to the snow, with their weight solidly on both skis. But all the stepping games on skis that I've proposed (and particularly skating) will reconnect you with something you already know how to do well: balancing easily and gracefully over one foot.

Using One-Footed Balance in Turns

Now, the best part: not merely balancing over one ski but turning on one ski, and turning much better because of it. It's time to integrate this sense of one-footed balance into your turns.

We're going to start with long-radius turns, big turns, for a couple of reasons. Most intermediate skiers tend to make quick, pushy, overpivoted short- to medium-radius turns, corners rather than smooth round arcs. We want to break that pattern. At the same time, I want you to have more time to feel your ski bending and working for you, drawing you around that long graceful arc in the snow. A long turn will give you time to make friends with your arcing ski. Finally, to make a long turn, you'll have to calm down and slow down your movements, which, of course, makes carving more likely to happen.

As you make big wide turns, I want you to spend as much time as you can balanced over your outside ski. (You already know what I mean by "outside" ski. It's the ski on the outside of the circle you are making on the snow. If you are turning left, your right ski will be your outside ski. If you are turning right, your left ski is your outside ski.) Don't worry yet about the best way to start your turns; we'll polish that up in a while. Instead, take your time; stretch your turns out as wide, as long, as you dare. And somewhere in the middle of that

There's a moment in a skier's life when you cross an invisible line and nothing is ever the same again. Like the moment you realize you are talking in a foreign language without translating your thoughts. You're in a new space altogether. It's the moment you really make friends with your skis. Stop fighting them and start trusting them. I crossed that line years ago but I can still remember the day, the mountain, the snow, the light. Springtime in Verbier, western Switzerland, white cherry blossoms in the Vallée de Bagnes below the ski area, white cumulus clouds rubbing the tops of the peaks, the biggest mountain I'd ever imagined all around me. And an exciting season behind me. I'd spent a whole winter on skis, my first, focused 100 percent on becoming a good skier, working at it, wrestling with it, day after day, storm after storm. So much technique, so much to remember, so much to practice. I'd learned a lot, but skiing was still work.

And then on the big run below Les Ruinettes, it dawned on me, it hit me: All you have to do is start a good turn—your skis will finish it for you. Maybe I'm slow but I had never looked at it that way. That's their job—finishing the turns you start. They do it wonderfully. I checked. Yes, it was true. A small move, a small commitment, and the turn unrolls as if predestined. No, I wasn't mistaken. Thank you, skis! This was my own first breakthrough on skis, and it had only taken me all season to get there, or to realize it, or at least to put it into words. I was so delighted that I skied up to the little slopeside chalet cafe in Clambin above the village, ordered a glass of sparkling Fendant wine, and toasted my skis: Friends. Accomplices. Partners in crime. Heh, heh …

Figure 2.4 *Turning comfortably on one foot. In this image, it's clear that the skier no longer needs a wide base of support, no longer needs to be propped up on two feet, two skis. Instead, the expert skier remains comfortably balanced over the outside ski of virtually every turn.*

long turn, take the time to think about and feel the foot you are standing on. Make a special effort to put more and more and more of your weight on your outside ski: not 50/50, not 60/40, not 70 percent of your weight on the outside ski and 30 percent on the inside. No, I'm talking about *all* your weight. Stand on that ski like you mean business, and enjoy the ride.

When you stand with all your weight on your outside ski, you will immediately feel that it turns better, feels more solid, arcs around with more authority. Riding the outside ski in each turn is really the core habit, *the most basic skill* underlying all the nuances of expert skiing. It's not an option; it's fundamental—and for this reason the outside foot of a turn is often also called your stance foot, the one you stand on. You'll also find that the long round turns you make standing on the outside ski are physically easy; you aren't working as much, and you will have the definite sense that your ski is turning on its own. You're not turning; the ski is turning. But this terrific sensation depends on your willingness and ability to stay balanced over your outside ski while that ski does its thing. Moving to the outside ski is just the beginning; balancing there is what counts.

I've already mentioned the fact that weight shift at the beginning of a turn is pretty common. Skiers instinctively know it will help. But generally, before the turn has gone very far, most skiers' weight falls back onto both skis equally—dang! And, then, with weight on both skis, the beginning of a beautiful round arc turns into a messy skid. This is exactly what happens if you can't stay in balance over your outside ski and you fall back on two skis. Neither ski has enough weight on it to make it bend and grip, so both skis wind up skidding sideways instead of arcing smoothly around. (See Chapter 1 for the full explanation of this all-too-common problem.) But we're trying to head this problem off at the pass. Balancing on one ski when you turn isn't really hard; you just have to concentrate. If you can do the one-footed exercises I have proposed while going straight, then you can also balance on one ski in a turn. That's a promise. In order to concentrate on where your weight is, to develop a feel for this kind of balance and this kind of turn, it helps to have no other distractions, no worries, and especially no speed-control issues to deal with. That's why, as an instructor, I always achieve the best results on the easiest slopes. You will, too.

And as you begin to apply this new one-footed balance to turns, you will get an even better feel for something I have already mentioned: The easiest way to make one foot heavy, to shift all your weight over one ski, is simply to make the other foot light. By "make one foot light," I mean draw it gently up, out of the snow—or almost out of the snow. Try to pull your foot back from the snow, *as though you were lifting it*, although, in reality, you don't actually need to lift your foot and ski off the snow at all in order to make it light. The muscular action of *beginning* to lift your foot will do the trick even if you don't raise

Wide Track or Narrow Track?

O f all the recommendations I make in this book, none is likely to be more controversial or to raise more eyebrows in the ski-teaching establishment than my suggestion that if you really want to become an expert skier, you are going to have to abandon a wide stance. I want to explore this idea with you in detail, and I think you'll see that I have my reasons—not one but multiple reasons—for this advice.

True, I take great pains every time the subject comes up in these pages to caution you against what I consider an old-fashioned and counterproductive version of a narrow stance on skis. I don't want anyone to jam one foot next to the other or worse yet—the sin of all skiing sins—to jam one knee in behind the other. I am proposing a functional, relaxed, and dynamic narrow stance, balanced primarily on one foot with the light foot actively keeping the other ski more or less near, more or less parallel, to the ski you are standing on. But why? Why this stress on a narrow stance when most instructors, most ski schools, have been trying for years to get skiers to spread their feet and skis? And succeeding, I might add.

What we are facing here may well be, as Cool Hand Luke said in the movie, a failure to communicate. A failure to accurately describe the way the best skiers ski. Paradoxically, when we watch great skiers, like World Cup racers, making high-performance turns at high speeds, we can say that they are skiing with feet apart, but with legs relatively close together. This is not as big a contradiction as it seems. Take a look at the accompanying illustration and you will see a skier leaning in to counteract and balance the lateral forces that build up during a high-speed turn. The skier's hips are well to the inside, and the skier's legs meet the snow at an angle, not perpendicularly. This is exactly the same inward lean experienced by cyclists and motor-

Wide or narrow track? *A dynamic skier turning at pretty high speeds becomes a visual paradox: feet apart but legs together. Why? To accommodate the extreme lean needed in such turns, this skier has to flex his inside leg quite deeply to keep that inside ski light. This action of flexing one leg more than the other spreads the feet apart on the snow. But look at how closely parallel the two legs remain nonetheless. Is this skier skiing in a wide stance or a narrow one? Think about it.*

cyclists in fast turns. In this tilted-over position, the skier's inside leg needs to flex more than the outside leg, to keep weight and pressure from piling up on the inside ski. And this in turn draws the inside foot and ski away from the outside foot and ski. The two skis always have to spread apart when the skier tilts over like this. But the skier's legs themselves haven't spread. In relation to each other, the skier's legs are no farther apart than they were before the skier began to lean in to the turn. I confess this is a fiendishly tricky point to make in words, so take a careful look at the illustration above and double-check my assertion that a skier's feet can seem to be spread while the legs aren't spread at all. This is, in fact, the opposite of a wide stance.

Like most ski pros, I love watching World Cup racers. But I try to

(continued on page 60)

(continued from page 59)
see more than just how far apart their two skis are. The skis-apart phenomenon in high-level, high-speed turns that I have just described tends to produce an inaccurate visual illusion of wide-track skiing—a notion that has been widely and uncritically adopted by the ski-teaching establishment. But it ain't necessarily so.

So much for misconceptions. There's more. How about the plus side of a narrower stance? What's the advantage? A narrower stance makes it easier to shift our weight from foot to foot, from ski to ski. You can try this at home. Stand with your feet only a few inches apart and gently shift or rock from one foot to the other. Easy, right? But notice how little your body has to move. Now, spread your feet apart, say a little wider than your hips, maybe a foot or two apart. And again, shift from balance on one foot to balance on the other. Quite a difference. Notice how much more you have to move your body. In particular, how much more your hips, your center, must move from side to side. It takes a major effort, and the movement is so exaggerated that you aren't likely to arrive in a strong balanced position over the new foot. See what I mean?

That's the crux of my argument. Forget any preconceived notions about form, about looking graceful on skis. When you move easily from one position of balance to the next you are graceful—which is worth a lot more than trying to look graceful. Relatively narrow-stance skiing allows you to move effortlessly and smoothly from ski to ski. More result for less effort. Wasn't that our original goal?

Here's another game to help you feel the same movement: Stand on the flats somewhere out of the range of skier traffic and plant your two poles to either side while you do the following little two-step shuffle. Step to one side; then pull the other ski in close to the ski you have just stepped sideways—but without ever really setting it back down on the snow. Pause, breathe, and then

Figure 2.5 *Practice closing the light ski. Try this neat exercise, which I call the "two-step shuffle." Stand in place on a flat slope, step to the side, and draw your light ski in close to the ski you have just stepped onto—without, however, putting it back down on the snow. And then repeat back the other way.*

take that light ski and step it back toward its original position; stand on it and pull the other one in close. You're just stepping from side to side, and each time you step, you pull the light foot in close but never really stand on it. Like a kind of simple dance step. Step to the side ... and close. Step back ... and close. Naturally, it is the "closing" of the light ski that counts. That's why we're doing this—to develop the habit of pulling that light ski in, parallel and pretty close to the other ski. After you start to feel comfortable doing this little two-step exercise, then push off down a gentle, almost flat catwalk where speed control isn't an issue and keep on making that same series of side-to-side steps. Step to the side ... and close. Step back ... and close. Don't be surprised if you find you are making gentle turns, slow curves, down that catwalk. That's great. But what I want you to focus on is simply closing the light ski, bringing it softly and smoothly in next to the other, weighted, ski.

Why are we adjusting the skis' relation by concentrating on adjusting only the light foot and ski? It's pretty simple. If you're standing solidly on a ski, you're not going to have an easy time moving it. It's like the proverbial expression about trying to lift yourself by your own bootstraps. Without your weight pressing it into the snow, the light ski is easy to move and adjust and control, almost effortlessly, with small subtle moves of the light foot. Which is why my friend Harald Harb, one of the most gifted ski coaches in America, always refers to the light foot as the "free foot." With no weight pressing it into the snow, it really is totally free to take care of the light ski.

The Lost Arts of Skiing—Traversing and Sideslipping

In the past, ski school classes devoted an inordinate amount of time perfecting some very basic maneuvers. It was boring. And ultimately it didn't work. Novice skiers used to learn those basic maneuvers to a tee, but never really learned to ski. Eager American students and perceptive American instructors revolted against an overly formal style of instruction they had inherited from European ski schools, and a new model of ski school instruction and progress evolved, based more on a rough-and-ready approximation of overall movements than the perfection of individual maneuvers. And I must say, this new approach, today's approach, does work better. Skiers learn faster than ever and right away find they can ski more of the mountain faster and freer. But the goal of expert skiing has remained elusive, perhaps because somewhere along

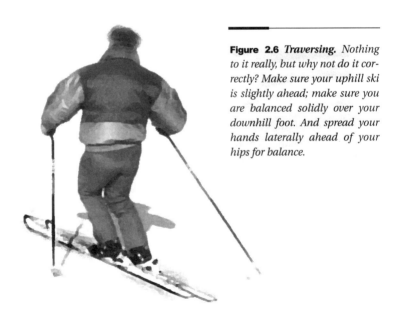

Figure 2.6 *Traversing. Nothing to it really, but why not do it correctly? Make sure your uphill ski is slightly ahead; make sure you are balanced solidly over your downhill foot. And spread your hands laterally ahead of your hips for balance.*

the line, mainstream ski-teaching threw out the baby with the bathwater. I'm thinking of two skills, two maneuvers, that aren't terribly liberating in themselves, but that are powerful practice patterns, which are hardly ever taught and certainly aren't stressed nowadays: traversing and sideslipping. Without backsliding to the bad old days, I'd like to spend a few moments on these two lost arts because I know they will reinforce your emerging expert's stance, your emerging expert's balance.

Both traversing and sideslipping involve standing well, standing poised and efficiently over your skis—and that's about it. Polish these two skills, and you will wind up polishing your turns—at least indirectly, by improving your stance. The notion of an expert stance that I have presented so far is fairly simple: You balance on one foot, on one ski, while taking care of the other light ski, controlling and adjusting its position with your light foot. This stance isn't just for turning; it's perfect for traversing.

In a traverse, you always want to weight your downhill ski. Why? As you traverse across the hill, your downhill leg is straighter and stronger. Because your uphill ski is higher, your uphill leg will be bent more than the downhill leg (and thus is far less strong). Go with the geometry of the hill and accept this strong leg/weak leg reality. Ride your lower ski across the hill and simply use your uphill foot to adjust the top ski whenever it strays. Finally, as you traverse across the hill, there are a few more details to be aware of: In a traverse, your downhill foot should feel fairly strong, or "tight," inside your boot, which will make your ski's edge grip sufficiently to hold and to track. Your uphill foot is, or should be, slightly ahead of the downhill foot (among other advantages this position prevents your ski tips from crossing). And likewise, your uphill knee should be slightly ahead, and your uphill hip should be, too. In short, the whole uphill side of your body is slightly advanced. And this in turn means that as you traverse, you wind up facing slightly downhill. I think of this as facing the future: After all, you are skiing *down* the mountain. And this slight down-the-mountain orientation of the whole body will become more and more important as you begin to ski on steeper and steeper slopes. Notice how many times I've used the word "slightly" in this description of traversing. In fact, I even hesitate to talk about your body's position at all because, in one sense, there are no real positions in skiing, only movements. But if you'll remember to slide your uphill ski slightly ahead and slightly advance the whole uphill side of your body as you traverse across the hill, you'll find that everything else works better. Spread your hands, slightly of course, for balance, and you're home free.

Traversing is terribly basic. I wouldn't even mention traversing in a chapter written for good skiers who are ready to become expert skiers, except for one thing: Most skiers today have never learned a proper traverse. Typically, to cross a ski slope from point A to point B, they just spread their feet for balance, hunker down a bit, and slide diagonally across the slope. (Remember what I said earlier: Inexperienced skiers spread their feet for balance; experts spread their hands.) And in fact, you can hone the sort of expert balance and stance I feel is so fundamental by standing well whenever you need to traverse across a slope. This is a general and very effective strategy—use the easy, almost boring parts of the mountain to focus on technique. When the going gets tough, grin and enjoy it, but when things are really easy, concentrate and build new expert habits. Polish your traversing by simply checking things out as you slide diagonally across a slope; become aware of which ski you are standing on, aware of what the light top ski is doing, aware of where your hands and poles are in space. This sort of occasional mindful attention to something as simple and basic as traversing will pay handsome dividends as you perfect carved turns.

Traversing is second cousin to sideslipping. The two skills are almost the same. One involves standing on the edge of a tracking ski, the other balancing over a ski that is no longer gripping but slipping away down the hill. Let's see how one becomes the other. Traversing is nothing more than standing with poise and balance over your downhill ski as you cross the slope—but standing on a strong, slightly tensed foot. The notion of a slightly tensed foot is important because it is this muscular tension inside your boot that really makes your ski edge grip the snow. If you simply relax that downhill foot, the edge no longer grips. Your ski will slide away, down the slope, and you will be sideslipping.

Sideslipping, the other lost art that I want to talk about, also tends to be neglected by modern ski schools. It just isn't sexy; it isn't exciting to slip sideways down a slope when people really want to push off and ski. I agree. And I don't propose that you should spend very much time sideslipping. But it is a core underlying skill that I want you to add to your bag of tricks. Sideslipping will not only reinforce your expert's stance, it will develop a sense of edging. To many, if not most skiers, edging is an on-off thing: Your skis either grip, or they don't. Black or white. Edge or release the edge. Skillful use of your skis' edges, however, will take you into a world of grays. I'd like you to develop a subtle sense of whether your edges are gripping a little, a little more, a lot, or a tad less. And there's no better way to do that than sideslipping. At the same time you'll be reinforcing your expert's stance, your balance over one ski.

I know you're convinced and ready. Let me quickly tell you how and where you should play with sideslipping. It can be boring, so don't overdo it. A few minutes a couple of times a day is plenty. Find a moderately steep groomed slope. Slide out onto that slope and stand there, facing across the hill. Take a moment to feel your downhill foot. Put your mind right down there in the boot. Is the foot tense? very tense? There's no right answer, just awareness. To increase this foot-awareness, try this simple exercise. Support yourself on your poles (remember, you are not sliding, you are just standing sideways on the hill) and close your eyes. With eyes shut, the kinesthetic awareness of your foot is increased. Try to feel your weight, the whole weight of your body, moving downward through your leg to create pressure on the sole of your downhill foot. Now, with your eyes still closed, concentrate that pressure in a line along the inside edge of your foot (where your arch is). This concentration of pressure along the edge of the foot will increase the bite, or grip, of the ski's edge. What does this feel like? Now, quickly relax your foot so that this pressure

Figure 2.7 *Sideslipping. One of the lost arts of contemporary skiing, but indispensable, nonetheless. Sideslipping reinforces balance and lets you tune in to the relative tension or relaxation in your feet, feelings that translate directly to more- or less-edged skis. Learn to make your skis sideslip by "letting go" of muscular tension in your feet, inside your boots. As always, everything begins with the feet.*

(which represents your weight) is spread evenly across the whole sole of your foot. Nine times out of ten, that ski will start to slip. That's the real mechanism of sideslipping: a softening or relaxation of the foot inside the boot. Now try this with eyes open, and let yourself slide sideways down the hill.

To sideslip slower, simply tighten your foot just a wee bit. To stop, tense your foot until the edge grips and stops you. And all the while, as you sideslip down the slope in balance over your downhill ski, your top foot is bringing the top ski along for the ride, pulling it, guiding it, to make sure that it keeps up with the ski you're really standing on. In a word, while sideslipping, you are practicing and reinforcing the basic stance you'll use in modern expert turns, balanced on one foot—in the context of sideslipping, it's always your downhill foot.

To add spice to your few moments of focused sideslipping, let me suggest a couple of other sideslipping games. Try variable-speed sideslipping: slipping continuously but constantly varying your speed by relaxing and tightening your feet, but so subtly that you don't come to a stop. Or try the falling leaf, a pattern where you sideslip forward, then backward, then forward again—like an autumn leaf falling from a maple tree—by the simple expedient of leaning a little forward in your boots, then back on your heels, then forward again. You'll discover that if your weight is precisely centered over your downhill ski, you'll sideslip straight (vertically) down the slope. And you'll discover that leaning forward just a bit while your skis are sideslipping makes your tips drop, whereas rocking backward makes the tails drop. It's no accident that I use the word "discover" here. Telling you how the ski works is one thing, but finding out for yourself is better. I think it's more important for you to feel where your weight really is than simply to know where it should be. And sideslipping is an incredible way to tune in to the subtleties of your new expert stance.

But as I said earlier, don't overdo the time you spend thinking about and playing with these two basic skills: traversing and sideslipping. Make sure they're in your repertoire and get back to skiing, real skiing, flying down wide-open, groomed runs using big, relaxed round turns. Let your skis carry you around arcs that seem like a gift, not a struggle. Feel how amazingly easy it is to turn on the outside ski. Can skiing really be this simple? Sure. But the more comfortable and efficient your stance, the easier your turns will become. For now, take a break, give yourself a few free runs, enjoy.

Narrow Your Stance (Skating Revisited)

Earlier in this chapter, I said that we would come back to skating on skis and try to polish this neat skill, which as far as I am concerned is the master exercise, the single best practice exercise for expert skiing. Now's the time. Why? Because it turns out that skating is not only a great way to practice shifting your weight from ski to ski, it's also the perfect way to train your inside foot and leg, to practice "closing" that light ski, bringing it in parallel and close to your weighted ski. In fact, reeling that light ski back in where it belongs is the secret of graceful and efficient skating on skis.

Let me talk you through skating on skis one more time—only this time we'll focus on what happens to the light ski. You push off from your left ski, striding diagonally forward onto your right ski, balancing on it, gliding over the snow. But what of that ski you've pushed off from, the ski you've left behind, so to speak? Just pull it in after you, without ever letting it touch the ground, and hold it there, parallel to the ski you are gliding on, ready to skate off on a new diagonal as soon as you slow down. And repeat. So your sequence of moves is: skate, pull the light foot in after you, skate to the other side, pull the light foot in, and so on.

If you pull that light foot in close, your next skating step will be stronger and longer. You'll be in a better position to launch your next gliding stride forward on the new ski. And of course, with every skating step or stride, you'll be practicing the key move that makes advanced parallel skiing easy. I call this move "taking care of the light ski." Don't neglect it. When skating, inexperienced skiers push off one foot and then leave it behind, like an afterthought. Now, as your skating improves, you're learning to take care of the light ski. This movement will quickly become a deep habit.

When turning, you'll do the same thing. Don't just let your light inside ski flop around passively on the snow. Instead, pull it smoothly, continuously, patiently inward toward the weighted ski, which is really doing the work of turning. This action of "closing" the light ski, easing it in toward the other ski, is really a continual happening. It's something that goes on, patiently, subtly, and persistently, all the time, throughout every turn, although actually, most skilled skiers are almost completely unaware of it. Train yourself to take care of

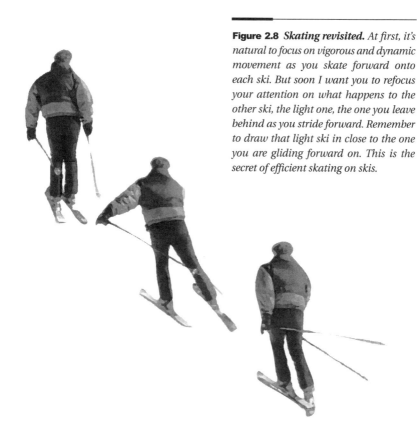

Figure 2.8 *Skating revisited.* At first, it's natural to focus on vigorous and dynamic movement as you skate forward onto each ski. But soon I want you to refocus your attention on what happens to the other ski, the light one, the one you leave behind as you stride forward. Remember to draw that light ski in close to the one you are gliding forward on. This is the secret of efficient skating on skis.

your light ski—adjusting it parallel, pulling the heel inward toward the other boot. Soon you will have the impression that your skis are simply there, parallel, right where you want them all the time.

I'd say that this subtle move, taking care of the light ski, is the main difference between skiers who are stuck in an ungainly wide-track position and others who seem to ski in a narrower, more efficient stance, almost effortlessly. You are about to join this far more efficient and far more graceful group of skiers. But before we leave this subject, let me clear up one common misconception. I constantly encourage skiers to ski with their skis comfortably close together but never jammed together, never with their skis actually touching.

There's an important difference. I talk about skiing with your feet more or less close together, or relatively close together, or simply in a narrower stance, but I'd like your two legs, feet, and skis to remain independent, to function separately. In an earlier period of skiing, people were so gung-ho about looking cool with their feet together that many skiers adopted some really counterproductive strategies in an effort to ski in a narrow stance. Some skiers would even jam their skis together and tuck one knee behind the other in an effort to keep their skis together at all costs. Of course, this is a disaster. If you were to jam your two skis together, you would lose balance, lose the independent mobility and shock-absorbing possibilities of each leg, and put yourself in a very unstable, even precarious position. Don't let this happen to you. Jamming both skis together and trying to hold them there is a bad parody of efficient expert skiing in a more or less narrow track.

On the other hand, skiing with your feet and skis more or less close together, not stuck together, offers a practical advantage. In a narrow stance you can shift from ski to ski with much less movement, much less "body English." You will feel, and you'll be, more graceful. And there's one more plus to be derived from a well-trained light inside foot. But that story can wait till the next chapter. For now, I want you to continue playing with big, lazy long-radius turns; getting your weight off the left ski to turn left; getting your weight off the right ski to turn right; and keeping that light foot under control as you enjoy those efficient round arcs, those turns that your skis are making without any help whatever from you.

More than anything else, as you begin to adopt this style of turning by balancing on the outside foot and ski, you will have a sensation of ease and comfort, of not working so hard (or at all) to make your skis turn. You feel like the lucky passenger riding a well-trained ski. You no longer wrestle your skis around the corner; you ride them in graceful round arcs. Refining and varying and fine-tuning those arcs is what we'll do in the next chapter.

IN SUMMARY

- Balance with your hands; ski with your feet. To aid balance, spread your arms laterally and keep your hands ahead of your hips.

- Weight shift is more than a momentary action. Move onto your new ski and stay there through the whole turn.

- The master exercise is skating. Skating develops dynamic weight shift and the ability to "take care" of the light ski. Pulling that light ski in parallel to the weighted ski is the secret of an expert's more or less close parallel stance.

- Moving onto the outside ski or getting off the inside ski of the turn—six of one, half a dozen of the other. But it's usually more effective to focus on the inside, or light, foot of each turn.

- Initially, use your new one-footed balance to make long-radius turns. Short turns are an invitation to overtwisting one's skis.

- Don't neglect traversing and sideslipping—unglamorous but crucial techniques. Traversing, with weight on your downhill ski, reinforces your expert skier's stance. Sideslipping develops relaxation on skis.

- Narrow your stance. Despite what many instructors will tell you, a wide stance is a recipe for disaster. Train your light, or free, foot to narrow the distance between your skis, but never jam your two skis tightly together. Independent foot and ski action is important.

Guiding the Arc of the Turn

Because Turns Come in All Sizes

You're not sure when it happened, but it happened. Your skis stopped fighting you, started cooperating. Like that classic Beatles song, you've got a ticket to ride. And ride. And ride. The roller-coaster ride of big carved turns. Such a great sensation. All your senses are wide awake. Sometimes you can feel the snow with the sole of your foot, right through all those layers of high-tech plastics. Your turns are feeling so good, you're actually calm enough to look around, look down the mountain, look across the valley as you ski. You notice rainbow refractions in the snow crystals. Damn, this place is beautiful! You can even hear the edges of your skis slicing across the snow. A gentle whispering whoosh of ski on snow, building toward the end of each turn. The snow is talking to you and it's not complaining. Turning is starting to feel as natural as walking. But how about skipping, how about running?

Slowly, we're making friends with our skis, run by run, turn by turn. It's happening. Instead of a vigorous twist to get those two pointy sticks to veer into a new direction, we've learned that as long as we stand on one, on the outside ski of our intended turn, it continues to arc around on its own. It seems to want to turn, to want to take us with it, slowly, patiently, gracefully. And while we're riding the arc of that outside ski, we've also learned to take care of its companion—the light inside ski—adjusting it with our light, free inside foot to stay parallel and not get in the way. Bravo! It feels pretty good. Almost effortless. And I can promise you that it will feel more and more effortless as we progress deeper into expert skiing.

But there's still at least one thing wrong with this picture. This sort of turn, standing on the outside ski to make it bend and then following that bend in a big circle on the snow, is altogether too passive. The arc you are making over the snow belongs to the ski; it doesn't belong to you. You didn't choose it. You wind up enjoying what the ski hands you rather than fitting the curve of your turn into the shape of the mountain, expressing yourself, your patience, your impatience, your excitement, by the kind of turn you make. That's one way to describe the subject of this chapter. We're going to play with the arc of our turn, to shape it and hone it, to fine-tune the ski's own tendency to turn to the point where our skis turn exactly as we want them to turn. As a first step, we're going to learn some easy ways to vary the size of our turns: large, medium, or small, and everything in between. But we'll begin with a few more notions about the importance of big long-radius turns.

The Mystique of Big Turns

There's no question that big turns, long-radius carved turns, are more exciting and more important in modern skiing than they ever used to be. No doubt in my mind, either, that you will learn more, faster, if you stretch your turns out and become really comfortable riding the arc of a big turn before ever trying to make short turns. But just how big is big?

Your first task is to discover the natural turning radius of your skis. What's the size of turn that has been predesigned into your skis, the size of turn that your skis will tend to make on their own? (To be technical, there's more than one answer to this question because the more your skis are on edge, the tighter a turn they will carve. But even so, there is a sort of average, natural turn that depends totally on that ski's geometry.) To discover the natural turning radius of your skis, you really have to resist the temptation to twist your feet

Figure 3.1 *The basic modern turn.* *The skier stands tall and relaxed in a long-radius turn. In turns like this, one has the strong impression that skiers are simply passengers, riding their skis in graceful arcs, not struggling to make something happen. Such turns build slowly and continuously; they are not sudden last-minute moves.*

toward the new direction. Be prepared to go straight for a while before turning. Shift your weight to your upper ski (or conversely, ease your weight off your lower ski) and wait. That's right, wait. Patience is definitely an expert skier's virtue. Inevitably, your body will start to tilt gently downhill, all your weight on your top ski will press it into a curve, the ski will start to bend and arc, and as long as you stay there, balanced over that foot, that ski will keep turning. With no other input from you, your ski will follow its natural radius, or designed-in, curve. And you'll discover that this curve is pretty big, bigger than you might have guessed.

Obviously, if the slope is steep, challenging, or scary, you're not just going to stand there and wait for a turn to materialize. Many of the most interesting discoveries on skis simply have to be made on easy, wide-open, nonthreatening slopes. Spend some time cruising these wide-open slopes, tuning in to the ease and the pleasure of making very big arcs on the snow, letting these turns happen under a weighted foot instead of forcing them to happen by twisting your feet. In a long-radius turn, not only are you not working very hard, but you also have the time and the calm to notice how well your skis are working and to feel the ski itself begin to turn. And don't be surprised that you won't really pick up a lot of extra speed from the top of the slope to the bottom. As long as you stick with each turn and ride it all the way around, your speed should stay about the same. If you pick up speed from turn to turn, that's a sure sign that you haven't arced around far enough, that you are being impatient and forgetting to complete your turns.

So far we haven't exactly broken new ground in this chapter. I simply wanted to begin by reinforcing the importance of big long-radius turns. You will learn more faster and build better, deeper habits if you don't try to make short turns for a while. Most skiers, the average skiers you'll see on any average slope, are indeed making turns that are too short, too quick. Of course, there are no absolute rules on a ski mountain. You can make your turns as short as you want to. But most skiers overpower their skis, making turns that are too short for their ability level; they treat each turn as a crisis and try to get it over with as soon as possible by cutting sharply around rather than enjoying the turn, savoring it, stretching it out, making it last. A good ski turn is a thing of beauty, and it should be savored. Long turns are your ticket to this splendid experience. Use them often. But even so, your next step is to learn to adjust your turn to the terrain and, of course, that means shortening your turns. Let's see how.

A Short Introduction to Shortening Your Turns

When most skiers try to make shorter turns, they simply overdo it. But remember, in skiing there are no prizes for exaggerating, for overacting. In fact, the best way to think about turns of varying size is to imagine that they are all long-radius turns—only some of them are sped up. That's why I am introducing our topic as "shortening your turns" rather than merely "short turns." It's a question of taking that built-in turn, the natural-radius arc, and shortening it by speeding up the ski's own tendency to turn—not, *I repeat not*, trying to turn or twist our skis harder.

Figure 3.2 *A comparison of different tracks—long turns, medium turns, and short turns. I'd like you to notice that all these turns start in a similar way, as though they were all destined to be long-radius turns. And then, progressively, the turn tightens up. In this sense a short-radius turn is really a long turn that has been shortened, not a different animal altogether.*

You're going to start your short turns as though you had all the time in the world and all the space, too—as though you were starting another big turn, and then, once that turn has begun, you're going to apply some subtle adjustments to make your ski curve around faster.

As you might suspect, there are several ways to speed up a turn and shorten its radius. And I should tell you up front, there is no right way. Rather, experts draw from their bag of tricks (their repertoire of movements) to create different sorts of shorter turns. We'll look at these moves from the simplest to the most sophisticated and from less carved to more carved arcs:

But, first, this is a good place to warn you against the "carve-at-all-costs" syndrome. It's true that experts carve most of their turns. And you too will soon be hooked on that delicious sensation of carving a ski turn. But remember my explanation in Chapter 1 about how skis turn. Our skis are designed to both carve and to slip arcs over the snow—and to do both together at the same time. In general, it's much easier to carve a long-radius turn than a short-radius turn. And that's why I've just encouraged you to spend a lot of time stretching your turns out, getting comfortable with big turns. Because it's in these long-radius turns that you will discover and master the sensation of pure carving. The idea that it's easier to carve a long turn than a short one holds true even for the most accomplished skiers, and it will hold true for you. So don't become obsessed with the goal of carving each and every turn. It can't happen. And it's not your fault. Blame it on physics.

To carve a turn the ski must first bend and then follow its bent arc over the snow. But there is a limit to how much any ski can bend. And, thus, as turns get shorter and your skis reach that limit, you will experience more skidding or slipping throughout the arc. That's definitely okay. And that's also why, as we look at ways to make our skis turn shorter and faster, I'm going to start by exploring your options for average garden-variety round turns, more or less carved, more or less slipped, but still definitely round arcs. And only then will we look at phantom edging, a wonderful, relatively new technique for shortening the radius of a pure carved turn.

Outside Leg Action to Guide a Round Turn

Generally, in the long turns I talked about earlier, you'll find yourself standing tall and relaxed over your outside ski while that ski does its thing and creates the turn. But if right in the middle of that turn, you sink down and flex forward over your turning ski, you'll find that ski suddenly turns faster. Why? The flexing/folding action makes the tip of your outside ski bite just a little more into the snow and, at the same time, sets the whole ski slightly more on edge, so that its sidecut can come into play a bit more. I've just called this move a flexing/folding action, but that description is not so very intuitive. So let's look more closely.

I'm talking about letting the leg you're standing on "give" and fold a bit. As your leg folds, your knee bends. At the same time, I want you to imagine that as your knee is bending, it's also pushing forward and inward. That is to say, as your knee flexes it pushes in the direction of the turn. A tall order? Not really.

But here's a caution. It's helpful to focus on the notion of flexing your leg *forward* into the direction of your turn. If you don't, if you simply allow your leg to bend without pushing forward, then your hips (your center of gravity) can fall backward. And if your weight does fall back, you'll wind up pushing the tails of your skis sideways in an awkward skid rather than guiding the tips into a tighter arc. However, a forward flexing of the knee, of the bending leg, will put pressure against the cuff of your ski boot, which in turn transfers pressure to the tip of your ski and to its inside edge. But this whole movement, which I'll call the "guiding action" of your outside leg, is indeed subtle. You can't really flex your leg very far before your boot stops the motion. And this flexing/folding action of your outside leg should always be progressive, not

Figure 3.3 *Shortening the turn. All I need to do is progressively, smoothly flex my outside leg forward in the direction of the turn. The ski tip bites and grips and tightens the arc of my turn. A patient subtle steering action of the foot can help too, but, please, no sudden twisting.*

Ski Tuning—How Much? How Often?

Among professional skiers it's an accepted fact of daily life on snow that no matter how good your skis are, they just won't perform right if they aren't well tuned. Many of the skiers I admire the most spend long hours patiently bent over a tuning bench, filing, scraping, repairing bases, touching up this and that, and finally waxing their skis. But, frankly, maintaining your own skis requires too big a commitment of time for most skiers. Even pros, those who enjoy working on their own skis, and who are good at it, have their limits. When early-season rocks in the snow have trashed their skis' bases and edges, even pros take their skis in to the shop for major surgery. We all have our "guy," a ski tuner and repairman that we trust absolutely, that we discuss skis and tuning and performance with and who has an arsenal of specialized ski repair and tuning equipment and years of practice using it.

So your first task, I'd say, is to find your own "guy." Ski repair technicians at ski areas are simply more experienced than their urban counterparts. So ask around at your favorite resort, find out whom the pros trust with their skis, and start building a relationship not with a ski shop, but with the shop's best ski tuner. But you'll need to be pretty savvy about what needs to be done and how often in order to keep your skis in top shape.

Let's start with the simplest aspect of ski maintenance and progress to the most complex. Waxed skis ski better. Not merely faster but better. And although I try to wax my skis every morning, I recommend that serious recreational skiers make a point of having their skis waxed at least once every ski trip. For example, once a weekend, or always at the beginning of a week-long ski vacation, and then again after a few days. Well-waxed skis are slippery enough to carry you across boring flats, and you'll find that they perform better at slow speeds too. Waxing has changed considerably in the past decade or so. Ideally, wax should be applied hot to penetrate the ski bases, then scraped thin, and polished, or "structured" (a curious bit of ski jargon that refers to brushing the waxed bases with nylon or brass bristle brushes that introduce microgrooves into the wax surface to help break up suction between ski and snow). Altogether, waxing can be a complicated and messy business. Probably better done in a ski shop, not on the kitchen counter of your snow-country condo.

After routine waxing comes "tuning." Tuning is the mechanical part: flattening and truing up the bases, getting rid of any nicks in the edges, and filing to adjust the precise angles of your edges relative to the base of the ski. This edge tuning can and really should be done to a precision of about half a degree. Of course no one can see that precisely or has that steady a hand with a file, and so special tools are used to dial in the desired angles. "Beveling" is the technical term for changing the angle of the metal edge from the obvious right-angled corner, parallel and perpendicular to the basic flat plane of the ski base. And beveling can drastically affect a ski's performance. There is no magic formula. When you take a ski in to be tuned, start with the manufacturer's recommended bevel angles. A knowledgeable ski tuner will know what that is. I always like to take new skis out of the box and try them first with no bevel at all to establish a sort of baseline image of the neutral behavior of the ski before I start tweaking it. You can probably get away with tuning your skis every eight or ten days or so. But you will need to have them worked on more often if the snow is thin and you wind up scratching your bases and dinging

(continued on page 82)

(continued from page 81)
your edges on half-hidden rocks. For just such conditions, which are pretty common during the first pre-Christmas weeks of the season, I carry a small sharpening stone in my parka pocket. At noon, I run my fingers along the edges of my skis to see if they feel rough to the touch or smooth. Sliding your fingers along the edges works better than visual inspection for rock damage. If the edge feels rough, I smooth it out by rubbing it with my small sharpening stone, held parallel to the base and then parallel to the side of the edge. (You don't need an expensive diamond sharpening stone. A $2 stone from the local hardware store will do.) A sharpening stone will remove and smooth out nicks that completely defeat a file. It will become your secret weapon for low-snow years.

And finally, if you really fall in love with a certain pair of skis—as I often do—it's nice to know that almost any damage can be repaired. Did you tear out a section of edge? Gouge an enormous hole in your plastic base? A good ski tuner can put Humpty-Dumpty together again, overnight. The basic idea, however, is incredibly simple: Take care of your skis and they'll take care of you.

jerky, smooth, not sudden. You flex the leg you're standing on and your ski turns faster. Sounds simple, and it is.

But I should also point out that this guiding action of the outside leg involves both your leg *and foot*. I mention your foot because, ultimately, every action you make to affect your skis must pass through your foot in order to reach your ski. I should also mention that when it comes to guiding the arc of a turn, it's okay to use some gentle turning (or slow-motion twisting) of your feet inside your boots. This steering action of the feet, if progressive and subtle, will also make the inside edge and the tip of your ski bite more and turn better. There may well always be a small bit of turning, or twisting, or "steering" of the feet in most turns. But there shouldn't be much.

So back to the slopes: from theory to action. To shorten your turns, you're going to apply a little more leg action by flexing down and forward into your turn, until that motion is stopped by the relative stiffness of your boot. Focus on flexing your knee in the direction you want to turn. If you are turning to the left, you start your turn, as always, balanced over your right ski. Then, to speed up that turn, flex your right leg until pressure from your right boot stops the movement. In everyday life, nothing ever pushes back against our shins, but in skiing your boots push back all the time. Don't shy away from this extra pressure against the front and inside of your shin; it's a direct way of communicating with your ski. (Pressure is okay; sharp pressure points are not, and pain from ski boots is to be avoided at all costs.) And of course in response to this pushing/folding/flexing action of your outside leg, your ski turns faster, giving you a simple and effective way to shorten turns.

Play with this approach a bit at a time. Vary your turns from *very* long, to long, to a bit shorter, to medium—shortening your skis' natural-radius turn rather than trying for a series of very short turns down the hill. (That will come later, but of course there's a trick to it.) What I'd like you to develop at this point is a feel for varying the size of your turns, for stretching them out versus tightening them up. And to do this in a smooth, comfortable way without overacting, without overpivoting your skis.

Shorter turns take a bit more energy, but not much; your skis are still doing almost all the work. You flex into these shorter turns, then stand up and relax between turns, so that you can flex again to shorten the next turn. Don't just stay in a low, flexed bottomed-out position. And it should be obvious that you are flexing both legs. One is loose and light; the other, the outside leg of each turn, feels strong and solid (it should because it is supporting all your weight). Yet both legs are cooperating, moving together, in this gentle ballet of flexing, then standing back up, then flexing again. Before long you will have substituted this new pattern for the classic intermediate's way of making a short turn—

twisting the hell out of both skis and skidding: a most ungraceful and inefficient way to ski. Far better to start a patient longer turn and speed it up by sinking down and forward over that outside ski. Such turns, which are partly carved and partly slipped, are all round turns, and they feel pretty darn good. But wouldn't it be great if we could shorten our turns in a way that would keep them carving, even reinforce the carving action of our new shaped skis? We can.

Phantom Edging to Fine-tune a Carved Turn

We've already learned—in Chapter 2—that you can often shift weight more easily by concentrating on taking your weight off the inside foot rather than focusing on shifting to the other foot. That's one important role for the inside foot: triggering and facilitating weight shift. And there's a second task that this light inside foot is eminently suited for: narrowing your stance by pulling that light inside ski inward toward the weighted turning ski. We practiced that narrowing,

Figure 3.4 *Phantom edging. This is one of the most subtle and powerful techniques for controlling the arc of your turn and especially for carving a shorter, tighter arc. Here, after lightening the inside foot (weight shift, by any other name), the skier rolls that light foot over in the air to a higher edge angle. A kind of "let's-pretend" edging with the light, free inside foot of the turn. A move that, for all its simplicity, actually controls how much the weighted foot and ski will edge.*

or "closing," movement when we worked on improving our skating on skis.

Now I'm about to introduce a third big role for the light inside foot. Overload? Not to worry. Phantom edging is a natural and easy extension of everything we've done so far with the light inside foot of our turns. But phantom edging is a little strange at first. So I am going to slow down and explain what it is and why it works so well before I suggest some practice exercises for learning this subtle expert's move.

By phantom edging, I mean rolling the inside ski of a turn over onto its edge, but not actually edging it into the snow. In terms of your action, phantom edging means rolling your light inside foot over toward the outside or little-toe side of that foot, as though you were going to edge that ski into the snow—but without ever putting any weight or pressure on it. Hence, the term phantom edging: an edging movement that creates a definite edge angle with the light inside ski, but never digs or presses that ski into the surface of the snow. Edging without edging. Make-believe edging. Let's-pretend edging. But why would you want to do this? And to what end?

Phantom edging is the darnedest move. Its effect is surprising and unexpected, although phantom edging itself is very easy to do. And here is what it accomplishes: Phantom edging with the light foot controls and adjusts the real edging of the other, weighted, foot and ski in a very powerful and effective way. If you want your turning ski—the weighted outside ski to edge more and thus to bend more and carve a tighter arc—all you need to do is increase the "make-believe" edging of your light inside foot. The phantom edging action of your light foot provokes a kind of automatic chain reaction all the way up your light leg, through your hips, and right down to the other ski—the one that is really turning. It's remarkable. It's as though by rolling your light foot over toward its little-toe side, you could easily tilt your whole body to that side. And indeed you do, but subtly, gently, just enough to produce increased edging on the other weighted ski. And we know what that does. Increased edging effectively increases the sidecut of the ski, enabling the ski to bend to a deeper arc

The voice on the phone was familiar, confident, infectiously enthusiastic: my buddy Tim Petrick from the K2 ski company. Lito, I've got some new skis I want you to try ... and you're not going to believe this, but ... they're only 167 centimeters long. Silence. Really? Really. Trust me.... I do trust Tim, and, besides, I'll try almost anything on Colorado snow. So I waited impatiently for the UPS man, tore open the cardboard box, took out a pair of these ridiculously small skis, mounted them up. And went out on the hill for one more life-changing experience. I went nuts. A new dimension opened up underfoot. Something altogether new was happening between these cunning new carving skis and the snow.

These new skis had all the qualities I've come to love and depend on in modern shaped skis— and a little more. I could tell they would turn fast and clean and make shorter than normal arcs when I rolled them up on edge. They did. But I kept expecting to run into limits, new limits, as a result of this

and, thus, carve a shorter turn—which is what we had in mind all along.

(I am indebted to my friend, Harald Harb, one of the most creative ski coaches of our time, not just for the term phantom edging, but for pointing out the importance of this subtle move. As far as I know, Harald is the first coach anywhere to focus on this phantom action of the light foot.)

In a moment I am going to propose a couple of easy exercises that you can even do at home in your socks to get you into the swing of using phantom edging. But first let me complete the picture of how we are going to use this skill out on the slopes. Initially, it may sound a bit complex. There are three separate moves you can make with your light inside foot. You can use it to pull your weight off one ski, and you can use it to ease that light ski in close to the other ski, and finally you can use it to create phantom edging and tighten up your *novel short super-sidecut geometry. I never really found them. Instead, I would look down at my skis and grin and carve a few more amazing turns. Amazing because on this latest iteration of the super-sidecut idea I was discovering that I could carve much smaller turns than ever before, but still go out and ski as fast or faster than I normally would on skis that were at least 20 centimeters longer. How, I wondered, could engineers pack so much performance into such a small package? A revolution. Another revolution, a revolution in the revolution. This was last season's revolution. It's early summer as I write this and I am asking myself: What's next? I can't even guess. Great skis are like perfect days when the gods smile, tear aside the clouds, and cover the landscape in fresh snow. When you count your blessings, remember to count your favorite skis too. And even so, I know that these brand new skis that I fell in love with last season will soon enough become tomorrow's old skis. It's hard to believe. But I've become a believer.*

carved turns. Wow, that's a lot. But of course, these aren't really three separate actions. They are going to flow together into one smooth movement of the light foot. This global action of your light foot (and ski) is a powerful expert's move. Let me talk you through it once, and then we'll set about learning phantom edging and starting to integrate it into our skiing.

Imagine that you are skiing diagonally down an open slope toward the right side of the run, and you are about to start a turn to the left. Begin by getting your weight off that left foot by simply lifting your left foot ever so slightly off the snow (so that it is skimming along, light, on the surface). Now, roll that foot over, more or less in the air, onto its little-toe edge (in a movement that physiologists call "eversion"). But, of course, you're not going to put any weight on that outside edge of your foot or ski. Almost immediately you feel your right ski begin to turn; it bends; it starts to arc around. And now all you need to do is to make your light ski keep up with that turning ski, to cooperate with it. And so, that left foot, your light or free foot, continues gently to adjust its light ski throughout the whole turn. The flow of action with that foot is: Lighten, roll over to a phantom edge, keep pulling inward to maintain a close parallel relation. Lighten, roll, pull in. Lighten, roll, pull in. Not three separate moves but one smooth continuous action—with your left foot on this left turn, with your right foot on a right turn. In a very short time, this inside-foot action can and will become a habit, something you do, naturally, without even thinking about it. But for a while, we'll continue to focus and concentrate on our inside foot. Let's practice together.

Stand up (well, actually, you can try all this after reading this paragraph) and walk into the kitchen or bathroom where you can support yourself by placing both hands on the countertop in front of you. That way you can try anything on one foot without losing your balance and toppling over. Now, lift one foot (say, your left foot), and roll your ankle out and the sole of that foot in. That is to say, tilt the sole of your foot so that it is somewhat facing your other foot. Your foot is still in the air, but if you were to put it down on the ground, you would be standing on the outside, or left, or little-toe edge of that foot. This is the movement of eversion, which is the technical heart of phantom edging.

Now, try this several times, first picking up one foot, then the other. Try to *evert* your light foot just a tiny bit, then a bit more, then a lot. You'll notice that the effort of rolling your foot over toward the outside seems to want to make your knee move to the outside too, making you a bit bowlegged. That's okay, but it's important, even crucial, to realize that this phantom edging move is a move of the foot, not the leg—as most of the really neat moves in skiing are, and for good reason.

Movements of the foot are fine motor movements. Only three areas in the body are capable of such movements: your hands, your feet, and your face. Delicate finger movements, such as writing, and all the myriad nuances of

Figure 3.5 *Phantom edging—up close.*
This sequence, with the skier simply stand-
ing in place, spotlights the foot action of
phantom edging—an eversion of the light
foot. That is to say, the ankle rolls out and
the sole of the foot rolls in, as though you
were about to stand on the outside, or little
toe, edge of your foot, although you never
really do.

facial expression depend on fine motor movements. As we consider movements higher up the arm or the leg (movements of the elbow, or knee, or hips), we enter the realm of gross motor movements, so-named not because moves of the knee, for example, are gross, but simply because muscular action in the rest of the body cannot be as subtly and precisely controlled as fine motor movements of the face, hands, and feet. Phantom edging is amazing because although it affects and controls the edging action of your whole lower body, it is actually accomplished with the light foot, and so it is a fine motor skill. And thus the amount of make-believe, or phantom, edging you use can be very precisely controlled: a smidgen more, a tad less, just the right amount.

Remember, even though it seems ass-backward to edge the foot you are *not* standing on—in the air as it were—this unreal, or phantom, edging actually creates a strong and effective parallel edging of the other, the weighted, foot, the

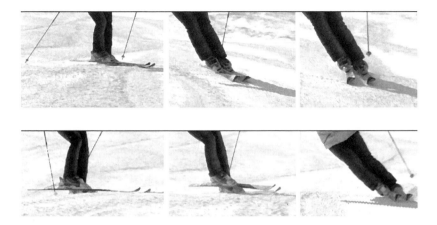

Figure 3.6 *How much phantom edging? The rule of thumb is simple: The more phantom edging you apply the tighter a curve your ski will carve. Compare these two turns, one with less and one with more phantom edging.*

foot *and ski* that you *are* standing on. It seems like voodoo. But it works great. And of course the fact that your light foot really is light makes it ever so much easier for you to fine-tune and adjust the amount of phantom edging you use. So let's use it now out on the slopes.

Start with long, lazy round turns, riding your outside ski in its natural arc. And as soon as you feel that you are stable and centered and comfortable in that turn, roll your light foot over to a bit more of a phantom edge and feel what happens. The radius of the turn shortens. The turn tightens up. But without any slipping. Your ski keeps carving—only it carves a tighter arc. And of course, we understand why: Phantom edging actually increases the real edging of your weighted outside ski. And with a higher edge angle, that ski can bend more deeply under your weight, and more bend equals more arc.

Be gentle. Take your time. Experiment. This notion of imaginary, or phantom, edging of the ski you are *not* standing on is frankly counterintuitive. Nonetheless, it's a powerful expert's technique that we want to turn into a habit. We'd like to do it often enough that it becomes a more or less automatic response to the mere thought of tightening up a turn. Honestly, when I'm free skiing for my own pleasure, I'm not aware of phantom edging. But I am doing it, unthinkingly, whenever I need to. It's very much like the idea of keeping your light ski in close to the turning ski, which we worked on in the previous chapter and that also needs to become an unthinking habit. Not surprisingly, both moves are accomplished with the light inside foot. Make friends with your unweighted inside foot, use it, and your turns will be 100 percent more effective. This strong focus on the role of the inside foot in expert skiing is one of the most exciting and effective developments in my own teaching and coaching in recent years. It is much easier to integrate and use than any amount of stress on what the outside weighted foot is doing. And it seems all of a piece. You want to turn right, so you get your weight off your right foot and ski, and with that foot free, it's no sweat to pull it inward and tilt it over in the phantom edging move. *Voilà!* a very carved arc.

And I repeat; the secret of shortening up a carved turn is simply to increase your phantom edging. More phantom edging equals a shorter carved turn. Try it.

More Carving, Better Carving

I can't very well leave the subject of guiding the arc of your turn—and guiding it as a very carved arc—without offering you a few more carving tricks, tips, techniques, small points that will enhance your skis' own built-in tendency to carve. Carving, pure carving, is, I suppose, what most distinguishes modern expert skiing from the way experts skied ten or even five years ago. Carving is easier than ever and totally delightful. It feels good: a precise and creative way of interacting with the snow, an expression of precisely honed balance. And you will quickly discover that carving a series of turns is physically less tiring than skidding each turn. Remember that in skidded turns you are using your legs as shock absorbers to soak up and dissipate extra speed, whereas in a carved turn, it's the constantly decreasing angle of your skis in the second half of each turn that really slows you down.

There are a number of ways of describing the difference between carved turns (where the ski tracks along an arc) and slipped turns (where the ski skids along an arc). One of the most interesting ways is the following description of how the skier stands in these two types of turns. In a carved turn, you need to balance solidly on the inside edge of your outside foot. But in a slipped turn, your feet are more relaxed; and you wind up standing on the whole flat sole of your foot, not on the edge of your foot. What I'm describing is the kinesthetic difference between carving and slipping turns, something you can feel in your body, in your foot.

In order to balance on the edge of your foot, that foot needs to be muscularly strong, tensed somewhat inside your boot. I often talk to my students about carving on a "tight" foot, tightening the muscles of the stance foot to make one's connection with the edge of the ski more solid. It's all of a piece, the edge of your foot, the edge of the boot, the edge of the weighted turning ski. Conversely, if you want to skid your turns, or, as I tend to call it, slip your turns a bit, you can simply relax your outside foot inside your boot, which in turn relaxes or rather releases the grip of your ski's edge on the snow.

Does this sound familiar? Have you heard this before? Indeed you have, in Chapter 2 when I discussed sideslipping. Sideslipping trains you to adjust the relative gripping and releasing of your skis' edges by how tense or how relaxed your foot is inside your boot. Same story. Only now you can use that kind of foot edging to make sure your ski edge holds in a carved arc.

But isn't there a lot more to edging than simply tensing one's foot to concentrate pressure along the edge of the foot, boot, and ski? How about angulation? Have you heard this term? If you have taken a lot of ski lessons you probably have. Instructors spend a lot of time talking about angulation, about making "angles" with your body, especially your lower body, to help hold the ski solidly on edge. Ski pros often talk about knee angulation, or hip

Figure 3.7 *Angulation happens. Often skiers and ski instructors will concentrate on tilting and angling their bodies to create just the right amount of angulation, but usually that's not necessary. Focus on the action of your feet and angulation simply happens in order to balance the external forces acting on your body in a turn. Effective angulation in turns is more of a natural reaction than a conscious action.*

angulation—pushing the knees, or hips, toward the hill and leaning out with the upper body to compensate and avoid falling over. I'd like to suggest that angulation, although a part of skiing, is much overrated. It arises naturally as a consequence of speed and the body's natural tendency to tilt in during a turn, to instinctively balance the forces that build when turning—just as a bicycle rider tilts or leans in when turning a corner at a good clip, without ever planning to do so. It just happens. Angulation, enough angulation, will just happen too if you concentrate on balancing over your outside ski as you turn. Your focus should be balancing over the outside ski, not angulating to edge that ski more.

What else can most improve the carved quality of your turns? What else will keep you from skidding and slipping your turns? Maybe the most important thing you can do is stop turning. No, I don't mean just skiing straight. Rather, I'm talking about patience, about waiting for your skis to start each new turn on their own, about not twisting or pivoting your skis at all in the direction of your coming turn, about letting them turn, not making them turn. Indeed, at the beginning of a carved turn you have the unlikely and delicious sensation that you are still moving straight ahead for a few seconds, not turning at all. And then the new turn starts to build, slowly, progressively. Let me put this last bit of advice into different words: The slower you start your turns, the less pivoting you use, the more likely you are to enjoy a real carving sensation as you complete your arc. In carved turns, less really is more.

But even though you don't do much at the start of an expert turn, you still do something. You have a key role to play, and that's the subject of our next chapter.

IN SUMMARY

- Carving long turns is your first goal. Then turn your attention to shortening the radius of your turns.

- As you start to tighten up your turns, don't rush it. Avoid sudden and excessive twisting. Even short turns should start patiently, smoothly, more or less slowly.

- Shortening the arc of our turns requires more "leg action." Folding, flexing, and guiding the outside leg of the turn applies more forward pressure and edging to the ski and speeds up its turning action on the snow.

- Phantom edging is a kind of imaginary, or fake, edging of the light inside ski. It produces a strong and very real edging of the other, weighted, outside ski. Experiment with phantom edging to shorten, or tighten up, your carved turns. In a carved turn, the higher the edge angle, the shorter the turn.

- Focus on your feet to guide your turns. Learn to ride an edged foot inside your boot. Let the carved turn build progressively underfoot. Remember, you won't be able to carve every turn. The shorter the turn, the harder it is to carve a pure arc. Some slipping can be expected, and that's okay.

CHAPTER 4

Launching Turns

Secrets of a Pure Parallel Start

It sounds, and it seems, so easy—like some Zen koan about chopping wood and carrying water. When going straight, just go straight; when turning, just turn. You've seen turns like that. Following a more skilled friend down the mountain, you shoot out onto a pretty steep slope, and suddenly your buddy peels off; no warning, no preparation, just like that. A perfect turn out of the blue. Your friend wanted to turn and just turned. But somehow you aren't quite ready to do the same thing. No, you're not quite there yet.

When going straight, just go straight; when turning, just turn. No big deal. I don't know how many times I've suggested to my students that starting parallel turns is no big deal—that the real story and the real measure of one's skill is not how you start a turn but how you keep it going, how you finish it. True, but also false. Starting turns is a big deal until you've got it wired, until you've turned technique and timing into habit, and habit into deep habit. Then indeed you simply turn and focus all your attention and your effort into making that turn a thing of beauty, carving it, guiding it, polishing, and perfecting that arc. At that point, turns just happen. But how to get there? Yes, for now, starting turns is a big deal, but it's about to get a lot easier.

Some skiers really seem to start all their turns effortlessly—with their skis perfectly and effortlessly parallel—in the damnedest situations, in the midst of gnarly bumps, on impressive double-black steeps, in moments of crisis and stress. The majority don't, and perhaps you belong to this majority: Skiers who can indeed launch parallel turns easily when the slope is friendly and groomed, when the gods are smiling. But when the terrain starts to challenge you, then you stem.

Are you familiar with this term? To stem? Most skiers are. And it's not generally a term of admiration. Stemming one's skis, even slightly, at the start of a turn, is a skier's equivalent of cheating, of copping out, of hesitating at that moment of truth, the start of a turn. Stemming simply means tilting or pushing your top ski out until it forms a V-angle with your downhill ski, thereby pointing it down the hill in the direction you want to turn a second or so before you are ready to commit your weight to it. Then with the security of knowing that your upper ski is actually pointed in the right direction, down the hill, you commit your weight to it and go. That's stemming (it's an inherited German word, and a movement that's been part of skiing seemingly from the beginning). And stemming works. It certainly isn't elegant. Or efficient. And in some situations it can get you in a lot of trouble. Yet it is almost universal. What's going on here?

Why Skiers Stem to Start Their Turns

Skiers stem to start their turns for a number of reasons. But the most important reason, I'd suggest, is that they are looking for security—something to hold on to in the slippery, fast-changing world of sliding downhill. And that something is the security of standing solidly and safely on their downhill ski while they are getting ready to turn. Let's talk ourselves through the start of a less-than-cool turn once more and pay special attention to what the skier is trying to accomplish. Let's say you are the culprit in this story, the skier who is about to stem. You are moving across the hill. Your downhill ski provides a sort of home base, a stable platform, from which you can operate. From this solid base of support, it seems easy to push or displace the top ski out to the side, up the hill a bit so that it's pointing at an angle to your direction of travel; and

Figure 4.1 *Stemming to start a turn.* *A darn good intermediate ski turn with a common flaw. This skier is late shifting his weight to his outside ski. As a result, almost unconsciously, his top foot begins to aim his top ski down the hill before any real weight shift takes place. This weight shift, when it comes, is only partial, and thus the turn finishes as a two-footed skid instead of a clean carve.*

not only have you angled that ski, but you've changed its edge. Let's say that you have stemmed, or pushed out, the right ski, preparing for a turn down the hill to the left. That stemmed right ski is now resting on its inside (left) edge. Everything is ready. You just stand on it, get your downhill ski out of the way (somehow), and you're off and turning.

What's wrong with this way of starting a turn? Why not leave well enough alone, keep on stemming, and concentrate on improving other aspects of our skiing? Of course, stemming to start a turn doesn't look as cool as just peeling off down the hill, both skis parallel, cooperating in a perfect arc. But there's more. If you stem to start your turns, the initial angle is too great; the ski turns too fast; you're more likely to skid, not carve—especially since few skiers can

We all remember great days on skis. Those easy, but I have a few memories, vivid as yesterday, of particularly trying moments on the slopes. And one of the clearest comes from my very first season as a ski instructor, or should I say, as a brand new skier trying to pass myself off as a ski instructor, to fake it, even though I barely had as many hours on my skis as my students. Somehow it worked. I didn't just survive but fell in love with both skiing and ski-teaching. Came home from Switzerland and got a job with the Squaw Valley ski school and never looked back. But that first winter in Leysin, Switzerland, was a daily adventure in insecurity. There I was, teaching gangs of cynical teenagers from an American expatriate high school how to ski, and how to ski better, when I could barely ski myself. Every maneuver I demonstrated for my classes was a gamble, a flip of the coin. Would it work? Or not? Would I make it? Or crash right there in front of all my students? I never really knew. But I almost always made it—or recovered before anyone could laugh. **>**

resist a kind of twisting rotary push off from the lower ski to the stemmed ski, adding body English in the form of muscular twisting to the angle you have already created by stemming. Bad juju, for sure. But there's more to come. Stemming the upper ski creates enormous additional problems in three important situations in advanced skiing: steeps, bumps, and powder. If you stem your skis just a little to start your turns, then as the slope steepens you will find that top ski stemming more and more. Eventually on real steeps, you will find yourself reaching way out to the side with your top ski in a vain attempt to turn faster and spend less time facing straight downhill. In bumps, if you cling to the security of your downhill ski and try to push the other one out into the start of a turn, you will push your top ski clear off the crest of the

The most nerve-racking times were when I had to demonstrate parallel turns for my more advanced students. Can this possibly work? Is this the day, the run, when I am really going to make a fool of myself? I still think that my students never knew. But to say that I was nervous is a giant understatement. I knew what I had to do: Commit myself, move into the turn, give up the security of my uphill edges gripping the snow. And hope for the best. It always worked. I never crashed in front of my class. But the experience stuck with me. I had learned, firsthand, how insecure a good turn really feels. How there are no guarantees in skiing any more than in life. How every good turn is a dare, and a risk that's always worth taking. It's still true. After so many years, so many changes in ski technique, so much fantastic evolution in equipment. Every good turn has a secret second of commitment, a point of no return. Either you make it, or you'll fall on your head. For sure. Only you never do. Some risks, it turns out, are always worth taking.

bump and into the gully or trough; that ski will drop out from underneath you, sliding away, and you will have to rescue your old downhill ski, now stuck high and dry on the top of the bump, by jerking it up off the snow and slamming it in desperately next to the one that got away. Trouble by any other name. And finally, if you rely on a stemming habit to start your turns, you will tend to use it without thinking whenever you are in deep or powder snow, just out of habit. Then, of course, you will run into a wall of snow and resistance with that ski as you try to stem it. And you'll trip and crash. So stemming to start turns isn't such a successful strategy after all. Don't let this catalog of woes become your fate. Let's get rid of this frustrating and counterproductive bad habit right now by developing a bombproof mechanism to launch pure parallel turns—without a hint of stemming.

As a first step, let me offer you another and more useful image of what stemming means. Stemming is actually late, or delayed, weight shift. And the answer to stemming, the key to a perfect parallel start to our turns, is early weight shift. But before we dive into the exciting and uncertain arena of early weight shift, let's quickly summarize the general notion of shifting weight once more. We've been discussing this for several chapters. And I know you're already aware of just how important weight shift is in modern expert skiing. I've talked repeatedly about skiing from foot to foot, from ski to ski. We know that putting all our weight on the outside ski of a turn helps to bend that ski into an arc, to make it carve. And I'm convinced that you are already doing just that, balancing 100 percent on your outside foot, your outside ski, during most of the arc of a turn. But just as in love, war, and the stock market, in skiing too, timing is everything. So far I haven't stressed the timing of your move from one foot to another. I've merely suggested that you need to find and keep your balance over that turning ski, and I know you've done so—at least most of the time. I wanted to stress getting on that outside ski and staying there as a first step in our process of mastering expert turns because of the all-too-common occurrence of what I call phony, or incomplete, weight shift, which is pretty typical of most intermediate skiing. Unskilled skiers often step, or push, or lurch over onto their outside ski for an instant as they start turns, pulling their inside ski off the snow as they do so. But this weight shift is short-lived. Such skiers never find a position of balance over that outside ski. They don't stay there and ride that ski. Instead they fall off it, back onto their old ski, sinking back into a beginner's balance situation on both feet, both skis. This sort of false weight shift is very common and leads, of course, to skidded washed out turns. And that's why, in the past two chapters, I've stressed how important it is to find a position of comfort and balance over your turning ski, to stay there through the arc. Now we're going to polish the way we get there: the action and, above all, the timing of shifting from ski to ski.

The Solution: Early Weight Shift

To put early weight shift in perspective, let's imagine you are about to turn downhill to the left. As far as your uphill ski is concerned, you have two options: You can turn your ski first and then stand on it. Or you can stand on it and then try to turn it. The first option produces a stem, or V, at the start of the turn. The second option produces a perfect pure parallel start: late weight shift versus early weight shift. These two actions, standing on a ski and turning that ski (or standing on one foot and turning that foot), are intimately related.

The reason inexperienced skiers are able to stem their top ski out in a V is precisely because they aren't standing on it, because it is therefore light and mobile, and thus can easily be twisted into a new direction first, before the skier shifts weight to it. This is what creates the dreaded stem, which inevitably condemns you to play catch-up with the other ski—yanking it in parallel to the one you have stemmed out first. The old one-two, stem-step shuffle.

But in our second case, where we step on our top, or new, outside ski first before trying to turn it, any sudden pushing or twisting or turning of that ski will be impossible—precisely because we *are* standing on it, because our weight is pinning it to the snow. In fact, if we preweight that top ski, an instant, a split second, before we want to turn, then it also proves virtually impossible to twist it suddenly into the turn because our weight anchors it in the snow.

The only possible start of a turn open to us will be a gradual, progressive start: The ski rolls slowly off its old edge, bends, and peels off into a patient round turn. In short, early weight shift—shifting to the top, soon to be outside ski of the turn, before anything else, condemns us to something like perfection as we begin our turns. It accomplishes two important goals: It prevents stemming, and it slows down the initiation of the turn, making it more likely that the ski will carve, not skid.

Figure 4.2 *Early weight shift. Down at the foot and ski level where the real destiny of every turn is played out. The crucial sequence of events is always the same: Move to the top ski first; then start your turn.*

It becomes impossible to stem out the top ski in a small V if you are already standing on it. It becomes impossible to twist your ski suddenly and excessively if you are already standing on it. Shift weight first, before you do anything else, and you won't be able to cheat at the start of your turns. It's that simple. But it's also, like so much in skiing, easier said than done. So now, assuming that I've convinced you of this important idea—or at least convinced you to try it, let's look at how we can practice and perfect early weight shift. But wait, I can hear somebody calling: How about the other ski? Sure, if you shift weight to the uphill ski before turning, you won't be able to open it in a stem. But how about the other ski, the lower ski, now your light, or free, ski? What happens to it at the start of your turn? Not to worry. That lower light ski will always, always turn at the same time as the weighted upper ski. It has to. And better yet, all the inside foot and leg action we practiced in Chapters 2 and 3 will help ensure that your light ski moves smoothly inward at the start of the turn—to stay comfortably closely parallel to the top ski as it starts the turn. All this is far easier and far more natural than you might think, and it all depends on early weight shift. So how are we going to build that habit?

Start with extra-early weight shift. Simply exaggerate for a while by shifting from ski to ski, from your lower foot to your uphill foot, not just a split second before launching your turn, but 10 or 15 feet or more before you want to turn. In this case you can feel yourself tracking forward for a moment on your new outside ski-to-be, your upper ski, well before you start to turn downhill. The rhythm and timing I'm talking about feels like this: Change feet … and … turn. That pause, that "and," is about the length of an in-drawn breath or a full beat in music—the calm before the storm of turning. Later, you'll simply change feet and go, but for now, that extra second or so that you spend poised on your new ski before turning will pay handsome dividends. You will feel more balanced as you start your turn. Your skis will peel off downhill much more slowly. You will realize that, somehow, that top ski always turns, it never gets stuck, and your confidence will soar.

But first you'll have to make peace with the idea that you are not 100 percent in charge of what happens. When intermediate skiers resort to that old twist-skid pattern, powering their skis around into a skid, there's no doubt who is in charge. The perfect start to a perfect parallel turn, however, is closer to an act of faith. You commit yourself to your new ski, and then you wait to see what will happen. There are no guarantees. Either your skis turn, or you'll fall on your head—at least that's the way it sometimes feels. But that's okay. You can grow accustomed to this delicious moment of insecurity at the start of a good turn, and you will. I promise. Remember I said that the reason that so many skiers

Figure 4.3 *Another view of early weight shift.* *Once again, the skier shifts off his down-hill ski before anything else happens. This early commitment to the top ski actually makes it impossible to stem that top ski out in the dreaded V. I jokingly say that early weight shift condemns you to parallel perfection.*

have trouble launching pure parallel turns and, instead, stem their top ski a bit was because of the extra security provided by the stable solid platform of their lower ski, a stable platform that most intermediate skiers are loath to give up. But that's just what we do when we focus on early weight shift. We're giving up that extra moment of security for a better start to our turns. And it's a fair trade.

Aside from what I've called extra-early weight shift, what else can you do to replace the late weight shift/stemming habit? My answer is that to replace one habit, you have to build a new one. And to build any new habit requires lots and lots of successful repetition. So don't challenge yourself with steep terrain while you're experimenting with early weight shift. You need to do a lot of skiing on slopes that are so comfortable, so unchallenging, that you can afford to play with new movements or, in this case, a new sense of timing for a familiar movement without any anxiety at all about whether it will work. I'd like you to shift your weight from one ski to another without even so much as a hint of twisting or turning or stemming your ski, dozens—no, hundreds—of times.

Perhaps more than anything else, the early weight shift that triggers a clean pure parallel start to your turn is a matter of belief, a confidence game. You have to feel certain, to know at a gut level, that if you shift to your uphill ski first, the result will be a good turn, a pure parallel turn. And the only way to build that confidence is repetition.

Remember too that shifting *onto* your outside ski is exactly the same as shifting *off* your inside ski. Focus on whichever pattern has worked best for you. In my experience, far more skiers achieve success in their effort to take weight off the inside ski than to put weight on the new outside ski. So let this be your mantra: *Launch a turn to the left by getting off your left foot; launch a right turn by getting off your right foot.* But focus on doing so an instant before you really want to turn—early weight shift. You'll discover that you can't be too early, but you can easily be late … and stem. Don't.

Later in this chapter, we're going to look at and practice three separate types of weight shift to start three different types of turn, but first we have one more element to add to the start of a pure parallel turn.

Going with the Flow: Crossover and Commitment

I confess: I'm guilty of oversimplification. Because in addition to early weight shift, something else needs to happen at the start of a really good parallel turn. That something is crossover. "Crossover" merely means letting your body (your center of gravity, really) move forward across your skis and down the hill as you start each new turn. This is how you will keep up with your skis as they speed up into the turn. So crossover is really a balancing move or, more accurately, a re-balancing, or maybe even pre-balancing move—a move that is very typical of the way expert skiers balance over their skis.

Earlier, when talking about an expert's stance and balance, I tried to stress that in skiing we are dealing with dynamic balance, not static balance, with constantly changing balance to cope with constantly changing forces. Nothing frozen, nothing stiff and stuck. And that's a good way to think about crossover. In essence, crossover means that you are going to start to fall over, or topple over, downhill (although that's an extreme way of putting it) at the start of your turn. You tilt down the mountain into a position of imbalance, so that a split second later, as your skis begin to turn and accelerate beneath you, you will find yourself in balance once again. You are anticipating where your balance will be a few feet, a few seconds, into the future. Here's one more image to round out your picture of crossover. By letting your body tilt forward down the hill, it's as though you were trying to get there ahead of your skis—but you never do because your skis are constantly catching up, speeding up in the first half of every turn. They wind up right underneath you, and you wind up in perfect balance over them. Sound good? I thought so.

And, also, by "crossing over" your skis, by moving your body down the hill, to the inside of the coming turn, you will be doing something else important—changing the edges of your skis!

Figure 4.4 *Crossover—the rest of the story. In addition to early weight shift, crossover completes the task of launching a good parallel turn. Crossover really means moving, or tilting downhill, toward the center of the new turn. Crossover represents real commitment: The skier moving smoothly and irrevocably across the skis into the coming turn.*

Now this is beginning to sound pretty technical, so I'd like to ask you to do something with me right now to visualize the edges of your skis in a turn. In a moment, I want you to put this book down and hold your two hands in front of you, fingers extended away from you, palms down. Now, pretend that these two hands are your two skis and move them in the air, keeping your hands parallel, in a series of S-curves from side to side that represent ski turns. I'm certain that without even thinking about it, you will bank or tilt your two hands in the air as you do so—as though they were edging into imaginary snow on each imaginary turn. (Everyone seems to do this without prompting.) So now let's make a few more of these imaginary turns in the air but this time, watch your hands. Notice how your hands roll to a new "edge" each time you bank them back toward the other direction. Likewise, to start a new turn on the snow, your skis must roll off their old edges and tilt up on their new inside edges.

Figure 4.5 *Edge change. It happens in every downhill turn, but generally a skier doesn't need to think about edge change. Crossover does it for us. As we lean or move forward and down the hill into our new turn, our skis roll smoothly from one set of edges to the other.*

For example, suppose you want to turn downhill to the left. In this case, the right, or uphill, edges of your skis are gripping the snow (that's what lets you cut across the hill). But as you start your new turn down the mountain, those skis will have to release their grip on the snow, flatten out, and then roll on over to the other set of edges, the downhill edges, which will quickly become the inside edges of your new turn. This is what we mean by changing edges. (See Fig. 4.5 for a close-up view of this edge change.) And in fact, it happens in every turn, whether you know it or not, whether you think about it or not. But our focus right now is to see how we can facilitate this subtle but crucial move.

That's where crossover comes in. On a gentle slope, it really seems as though your skis change edges by themselves, but the steeper the slope becomes, the more you have to commit your body down the hill in order to facilitate this edge change, to make it happen. In other words, the steeper the slope, the more crossover we need and use. Remember the definition of crossover? It's simply letting your body—above all, your hips, your center—move smoothly across your skis, down the hill, and into the new turn. Going with the flow. Not hanging back. Very much like a controlled slow-motion fall into the turn, a fall that never falls very far because, of course, your skis instantly catch up to you, and you find yourself balanced perfectly once more against the outside ski of your new turn.

Crossover is not such a big deal. Yes, it's a real movement that the most gifted skiers make instinctively, and the rest of us need to learn and practice. Crossover is a smooth and subtle and hard to see movement—almost more of a feeling than a normal athletic movement. Just a sense of tipping forward in space. But it's part of every good turn, and you should certainly practice it and thereby strengthen and improve the start of all your turns.

Here are several practice games that will give you a feeling for crossover. Try "the thousand steps." On an easy slope just start walking in place as you slide diagonally down the hill: step, step, step, step ... And then try to step your way around the corner, walking a turn (step, step, step ...) instead of sliding it or carving it. You will discover that your skis don't really want to come around until you tilt your body in the direction you want them to go—then it's easy. This exercise doesn't represent good skiing. It isn't. But it will underline the importance of committing your body to any turn.

Another intriguing game, a little harder than the thousand steps, is to try to start a turn down the hill from a traverse on the top, or uphill, ski. This feels most unnatural, but it's worth trying. Slide across the hill in a traverse and lift your lower ski off the snow a little. (This is the exact opposite of a normal traverse

Figure 4.6 *The thousand steps. In this exercise for developing the feel of crossover, the skier simply starts stepping, as if walking, from ski to ski, and tries to walk and step around the corner. We quickly discover that we can step-step-step forever, but nothing will happen until we tilt our bodies in the direction we want to turn.*

Figure 4.7 *Turning off the top ski: another great crossover exercise. Lift your lower ski off the snow and traverse across the hill on your top ski. From this position, try to turn down the mountain. Awkward, for sure. But you will find that if you tilt your body downhill, it works. A not-so-subtle version of crossover.*

where your weight is mostly on that lower ski.) Now, from this strange position, standing only on your top ski, try to start a turn down the hill. You can do it, but you'll find that until you tilt your body down the hill, nothing happens. Your ski stays stuck on its upper edge. Yet as soon as you commit yourself and lean downhill—a very unnatural feeling, as though you were going to fall over—then your ski turns. Do this a couple of times only, just to prove that you can, and focus on how your body needs to tilt to commit itself to the turn. And then relax and go skiing.

Once you've tried these demonstration games that I have proposed, how are you going to integrate crossover in regular turns, in your regular skiing? There's no black-and-white answer to this question, but of course I have a few more tricks in my bag. The first thing is to identify and embrace that sensation of commitment, of moving forward down the hill to enter the new turn. I stress commitment because actually there is a point of no return in a pure parallel turn, a moment when you are no longer safely in balance, when if the turn doesn't happen, you're going to fall over—but remember, you never do. Even so, this sensation is unnerving at first. You have to say to yourself: "Wow, this is amazing! I'm 'losing my balance' only to find it again." Trust me. This sensation is actually delightful. It's like a secret plot you enter into with your skis. A high-wire act in which your well-trained skis are your safety net. Because they will always catch up to you, you will always wind up in balance over your turning ski. And, of course, you will feel this delicious sensation of momentary insecurity more on steeper slopes. Crossover is virtually invisible on flatish slopes, and it's scarcely needed, or noticeable, until the hill steepens.

Pay attention, too, to the sequence of moves at the start of a pure parallel turn. I introduced early weight shift first, and only then did I mention crossover. And that's the way it has to happen on the hill. You shift to the top ski, the one that is going to be on the outside of your coming turn, and only then do you start your crossover, your tilt down the hill. Shift feet, then go. Change weight, then tilt. If—heaven forfend—you were to tilt or move your body down the hill first, it would just load up your downhill ski and make weight shift that much harder and slower. So again, the rhythm, the timing of a strong parallel start is: *Shift weight; then commit to the turn.*

Here's a crossover image that I love to have my students play with. On a wide-open but moderately pitched slope (neither flat nor steep) make a series of medium-large turns. At the start of each turn, as soon as you have shifted to the upper, outside, ski move your hips across the skis as though you were going to brace them on an invisible pillow of air just down the hill. Before starting this run, reach down with both hands and touch your hips. Move them a bit, close your eyes, and feel where your hips really are in space. This will help you crossover with a crucial part of your body, your center. So as you turn left,

Time for New Skis?
Try, Then Buy, or Maybe Rent

A few years ago you could ask skiing friends: Have you tried those new skis yet? Whaddaya think? Now virtually all skiers, even beginners, are skiing on shaped, or deep-sidecut, skis. They are ubiquitous. That's all you'll find in ski shops, and what I've called classic-design skis are rapidly going the way of 8-track tape cassettes. Fine—so you've either purchased modern shaped skis, or you are about to. And I hope this book has only reinforced the notion that a great pair of skis can do wonders for you. How do you find that great pair of skis?

Not all skis, even among the most modern marvels of ski engineering, are created equal. And even among the best of them some skis are more suitable for certain skiers, for their temperament and their technique. Those who march into a ski shop and buy the skis that their best friend has recommended will almost certainly wind up with inappropriate skis. Don't do it. Try before you buy is an absolute rule with modern skis. Yes, they all have deep sidecuts but the geometry varies, and a ski's personality, strengths, and weaknesses are derived from much more than just the curve of its sidecut. Flex, torsional stiffness, vibration absorbing or dampening characteristics, and a host of other factors all interact to give each ski a unique feel.

Fortunately, in recent years the ski industry has reorganized itself around the concept of renting high-performance demo skis. Well-cared for, well-tuned skis, representing the very latest design innovations, are now available at almost every ski area. Take advantage of this offering to ski at least two or three different models for at least a half day each before committing yourself to a certain ski. It's an important choice. All skis work. Some will work better than others, and believe me, you will be able to feel the difference. If you don't fall in love with these new beauties underfoot, why bother to buy them?

And I'll go one step further and ask again: Why bother to buy new skis anyway? There are, of course, many reasons, most revolving around convenience and familiarity: bindings that are always adjusted to your boots; skis that are well-tuned because you had them tuned last Thursday; and the comfort of knowing just how your skis will respond to a given move, a given edge angle. Because you've been there before, often. But I'd like to suggest that if you aren't able to ski more than a total of two weeks every season, you should consider simply renting high-performance demo skis rather than buying your own. Ski design nowadays is so exciting, so innovative, and changes so quickly that you may be better off, experientially as well as financially, to simply rent the latest model top-quality demo skis every year. Give it a thought. Tomorrow, today's skis will become yesterday's skis.

imagine you are moving your left hip in until it is supported by some invisible force that props you up as you turn. And likewise on right turns: Take your weight off your right ski and move your right hip across the skis to the inside of your new turn, as though there was something there to lean on. (That something, that invisible pillow of air, is actually centrifugal force building up from the turning action of your skis.) This is a strange image, but it works for a lot of my students and seems to make crossover feel a little more real.

And here's a last tip to integrate crossover into your everyday repertoire of skiing movements: Use your hands. Remember my one-sentence oversimplification of modern skiing: Ski with your feet; balance with your hands. Well, it holds true in spades at the start of a turn. Early weight shift, of course, involves your feet, involves shifting from foot to foot. But your body, and your center, tends to follow what you do with your hands. So if you are carrying your hands in what I think of as the normal home-base balancing position—spread laterally and ahead of your hips—then it should be easy to simply reach both hands a little farther ahead and down the hill as soon as you have shifted to your new ski. Right now, you are probably sitting down, reading this book. So put the book down in front of you and spread your hands out in that skier's balancing position (elbows away from your sides, hands spread and extended). Now reach your hands forward about six inches or so. Do you feel how this small gesture pulls you forward in your chair or on the couch? How it tilts your torso slightly forward? That's it. Only the slightest beginning of a movement down the hill with both hands and your crossover will simply happen. Conversely, if you let your hands drop back by your hips your body will stay back, and you will wind up "in the back seat" as your skis start to turn instead of going with them.

That's all there is to crossover: Going with your skis, going with the flow. Committing yourself, body and soul—and center of gravity to the new turn, after your early weight shift. Don't put the cart before the horse. Early weight shift is still the secret of an easy strong parallel start. And now, it's time to refine our notions of weight shift just a little bit more. Because it turns out that there are at least three very different ways in which expert skiers move from ski to ski, three different flavors of weight shift that each have their advantages in different situations. But remember this. *There's no best way of shifting from ski to ski.* Experts use whatever feels best for the circumstances they find themselves in. But I'd like you to become comfortable with each one of these different ways of shifting weight—to practice them and to see what their advantages are in different turns. So we'll look at each flavor of weight shift separately, bearing in mind that the one thing that doesn't change is the importance of early weight shift. First shift weight, then turn.

Active Weight Shift—By Skating and Stepping

It's time to take another look at our old friend: skating on skis. I call skating the master exercise for modern expert skiing because good skating contains so many of the key elements of good turns. We've already practiced skating to focus on weight shift, active weight shift, pushing off from one ski to balance on the other. And later we polished our skating by focusing on the role of the light foot, the one you pushed off of, the one you left behind. And through skating, we learned to take care of that light foot and ski, pulling it in toward the other foot, closing it parallel with the weighted ski (but not really putting it back down on the snow). Now we're going to use skating steps to start turns, and as we do so, we will be reinforcing the notions of early weight shift and gradual progressive edge change.

All I'd like you to do—on a rather gentle slope, please—is to start skating straight down the hill. And then skate slower and slower. That is to say, skate onto your new foot, pull the old ski back in, and hesitate an extra moment before skating back to the other side. Stretch out each skating step. Glide as long as possible on each step, and then some. The rhythm is: Skate … and wait; skate … and wait. It's easy. Nothing you haven't done before. What happens when you hesitate and wait between skating strides, when you ride that weighted ski a little farther than normal? You guessed it. Your ski begins to turn. Not a fast turn. Not a tight turn. But a slow steady carving arc. More like the beginning of a carved turn than a whole, complete turn. But a turn, nonetheless.

Let's go through one skating cycle in detail to see what's happening. Imagine you're standing on your left ski ready to skate off onto your right ski. As you do so, you are actually pushing off vigorously from the edge of your left foot. So we can already see that edges have a role to play in skating. Now you are balancing on that right ski, gliding forward. You pull your left foot and ski all the way in until your two boots are close together, and slowly, deliberately, without rushing it, you prepare to skate off once more to the other side onto your left ski. But how exactly does your body get ready for that next step? Without thinking about it, without planning it consciously, you are starting to lean and tilt to the left—getting set to push off the left edge of your right ski.

Figure 4.8 *Active weight shift: skating into a turn.* *One of the most dynamic and active ways to launch a turn. Skating into a carved turn, or a series of curved turns, is exhilarating and better yet, you absolutely can't cheat. Skating into a parallel turn reinforces all the key expert skills: early weight shift, taking care of the light ski, commitment of the body in the direction of the turn. A basic move in your repertoire of advanced techniques.*

And if this sounds a bit like the crossover action we've just covered, well, it is. So in essence you are now standing a little more on the inside edge of your weighted gliding ski, your weighted foot. So the curved ski edge engages the snow and slowly, gently, begins to arc. A moment later it's time, and you vigorously push off that ski into another skating step. The beauty of what I've just described in detail is that it always happens by itself without the skier really thinking about it or working at it. You simply skate … and wait, skate … and hesitate. And you will experience these arcs that are nothing other than the beginnings of long, patient carved turns. And while you play with this sort of hesitation-skating you will be reinforcing a number of expert habits: early weight shift, inside foot and leg action, and the sort of progressive rolling to a new edge that comes with efficient crossover.

Now let's do better. Once you feel comfortable with this pattern of skating into the beginnings of a carved turn, simply reduce the size of your skating step. So instead of the usual vigorous forward stride onto your new ski, you simply step onto it smartly and decisively but not so dramatically. And at the same time as you reduce the size of your skating step to a mere step, I want you to pause longer, in balance on your new ski, and let that beginning of a turn stretch out into more of a full arc. In short, you are going to let your sequence of skating steps blend smoothly into a sequence of carved turns. But you are still stepping to a new ski each time, to the new outside ski of the coming turn.

Figure 4.9 *Active weight shift: stepping into a turn. Just like skating into a turn, only less so. The movement of skating forward has been reduced to a subtle step, but it's still there, still visible, still effective. The difference between skating and stepping into a turn is a matter of degree, not of kind.*

And you are stepping forward onto that ski, moving forward with it, not twisting it, not stemming it into a new turn. Bravo. You've got it: efficient early weight transfer (because the skating or stepping happens well before the turn begins); good balance over the new outside ski; and enough patience to let the turn develop and build. Sounds like a winning recipe for a long carved turn. At least for one kind of turn.

I describe this kind of turn as a turn with *active weight shift*. And it is indeed very active. You can feel the energy of this stepping, or skating, movement that carries you from ski to ski. Someone watching you can see you clearly stepping from foot to foot. The movement is all out there in the open. No secrets. Active weight shift.

And it makes a helluva good turn. A dynamite turn. Although, on reflection, we have to admit that this vigorous active stepping from ski to ski does take a certain amount of effort. These aren't particularly lazy or mellow turns. So we realize that although such carved turns with active weight shift are wonderful at reinforcing some good expert habits and even better at helping us to eliminate any old twisting, stemming movements at the start of our turns, they aren't universal all-purpose turns to be used in every situation. Where would a very skilled skier choose to turn with such active weight shift?

Turns with active weight shift, stepping or skating to the new outside ski, are perfect on open gentle slopes where you want to keep your speed up or even increase your speed. Of course, on gentler slopes, if you regress and fall back into an earlier twist-skid pattern or stem your outside ski at an angle, instead of letting it simply carve forward into the new arc, then your skis will turn too sharply, will skid and brake. And it will be harder to maintain speed and maintain a smooth flow of turns. But skating forward into each turn can keep your speed up and sets up a perfect carve that avoids scraping and braking—altogether a wonderful way to ski down wide-open, groomed easy slopes.

Stepping and skating turns can help you maintain your speed in a NASTAR race course too. But we'll go into that in more detail in Chapter 8. Turning with active weight shift, by stepping or skating to the new ski, is also a wonderful way of warming up on a cold morning. The very physicality of these stepping movements will get your blood flowing and set you up for a great day on skis. Typically, I do a lot of skating and stepping on my first run or runs of the day. It feels good and it warms me up (muscularly and thermally). Try it, you'll like it. But don't place an absolute value on stepping actively from ski to ski to start your turns. Instead, I'd like you to visualize a whole spectrum of weight shift options that expert skiers can choose and use, from very active and obvious to very quiet and subtle. Somewhere in the middle of this spectrum is our next weight shift option.

Weight Shift by Lightening One Ski: For Carving on Hard Snow

Heads or tails of the same coin. Six of one or half a dozen of the other. Shifting your weight onto the outside ski, or taking your weight off the inside ski. I've been at great pains to stress that these two ways of looking at weight shift really accomplish the same thing. But for the skier, the feeling, the focus, and emphasis are certainly different. And in my experience, I have found that lightening the inside foot of an upcoming turn seems an easier and more intuitive task for a majority of skiers. Easier, that is, than actively stepping to the outside ski as we practiced in the previous section. So that's what we are going to touch on next—what I call *weight shift by lightening one ski*. Not vigorously active, not quietly passive, but somewhere in between.

Not to worry; this is nothing new. I'm pretty sure you have been using this very effective middle-of-the-road sort of weight shift for some time now. Remember my earlier instructions, in Chapter 2, to turn left, get off your left foot; to turn right, get off your right foot. Of course, life is always a little more complex than your ski coach lets on, so the whole story might better be expressed as: to turn left, get off your left foot, and stay off it. In this sort of weight shift, skiers lift or pull their inside ski off the snow—sometimes actually lifting it visibly off the surface of the snow, and sometimes lifting or pulling it up

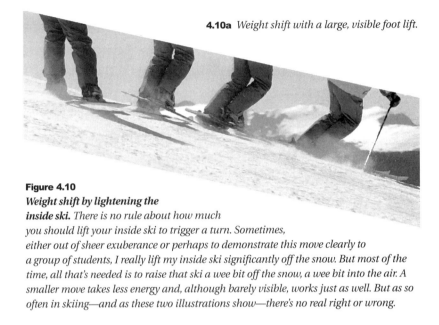

4.10a *Weight shift with a large, visible foot lift.*

Figure 4.10
Weight shift by lightening the
inside ski. *There is no rule about how much
you should lift your inside ski to trigger a turn. Sometimes,
either out of sheer exuberance or perhaps to demonstrate this move clearly to
a group of students, I really lift my inside ski significantly off the snow. But most of the
time, all that's needed is to raise that ski a wee bit off the snow, a wee bit into the air. A
smaller move takes less energy and, although barely visible, works just as well. But as so
often in skiing—and as these two illustrations show—there's no real right or wrong.*

4.10b *Weight shift with a small, almost visible foot lift.*

so deftly and subtly that the light foot and ski hardly moves but simply skims
along, weightless, perhaps a tiny fraction of an inch above the snow (virtually off
the snow but not way off the snow). Again, there is a spectrum of possibilities.

Typically, when skiers first play with this sort of inside-out weight shift,
getting off one ski rather than moving onto the other ski, they overdo it, lifting
that ski right up off the snow. I do this often to show my students clearly what's
going on, to make it very obvious just where my weight really is. And as I've

said before, there's no right or wrong here. Only remember, once you have taken your weight off that inside ski, it won't get any lighter if you lift it higher off the snow.

I know you are going to use this style of weight shift a lot. But our rule about *early* weight shift still applies. Get off your downhill ski ... then turn. Do it first. Do it early. Weight shift by lightening the inside ski has a number of advantages: It takes much less effort and energy than stepping or skating. The movement can be small, almost invisible. And best of all, it sets you up perfectly to use phantom edging to control the arc of a carved turn. I'm sure you haven't forgotten phantom edging, my surprising and surprisingly effective technique for adjusting the radius of pure carved turns (introduced in Chapter 3). Phantom edging consists of rolling the light foot over in space, as though you were trying to edge the little-toe edge (or outside edge) of your foot and ski; only you never really press that ski into the snow. We learned that this sort of make-believe edging action of the light foot actually causes—and controls—a real edging movement of your active weighted foot and ski. A mysterious cause and effect link that helps us fine-tune the arcs of our carved turns. The more phantom edging of the light foot, the more real edging of the weighted foot, and the faster your outside ski will carve.

As it happens, launching your turns by pulling your weight off one foot sets that foot up perfectly for phantom edging. As a result, this is the way I almost always tend to turn on hard or icy snow where subtle edge control and real carving are both important and difficult.

Let's visualize such a turn on a very hard slope: Say you're about to carve a turn to the right. You start things by easing the heel of your right foot up, a little off the snow. (I mention the heel because by focusing on the heel of your foot, you'll keep your weight moving forward; but should you try to lift the toe of your boot to lighten that ski, your weight would fall back.) In the same smooth motion, as your right foot comes gently up off the snow, you begin to roll it over toward its outside edge, toward its little-toe edge. And that's all there is to it. Your turn is launched, and you keep it together by applying more, or less, phantom edging to carve a tighter, or a looser, turn. And you'll notice that we never even mentioned, or thought about, twisting or turning our feet. This turn, like all good carved turns, begins slowly. As we pull our weight off our right foot, our body begins to tip over to the right (naturally, because we've just eliminated our support on that side). And the ski we are left standing on, our left ski, begins to roll over to its new inside edge and, at the same time, to bend under our weight. This slowly bending edge pulls us forward into the turn—a carved start, not a sudden pivot. I should simply stress that although I've mentioned two skills, weight shift by lightening one foot and phantom edging by rolling that foot over, I don't have the sensation of two separate movements. It's all one continuous smooth action of the inside foot, lightening and rolling over to a phantom edge. In a deeper sense, I guess, almost everything in expert skiing is one continuous smooth motion, although often we need to break individual motions down and practice them in isolation.

The sort of weight shift I've just described is a much less energetic way of starting turns than by skating or by stepping. But it's still early weight shift. This kind of weight shift is a natural invitation to experiment with phantom edging. For many expert-level skiers, this sort of weight shift becomes a home-base technique for triggering or launching medium-radius turns on medium steep slopes. It's the ideal way to carve a series of big signature S-curves down freshly groomed blue slopes early in the morning. And it's even more effective as a way of starting medium- to long-radius turns on very hard or icy snow. Weight shift by lightening the inside ski is a good way of accessing and activating all your carving skills. The slicker the snow surface, the more likely I am to start my turns this way. Yet this sort of weight shift is far from a universal solution for starting turns in all situations, especially on steeps. So there's one more weight shift option that I need to share with you, which will round out your expert's bag of tricks for launching turns.

Soft Weight Shift: The Subtlest Secret of Expert Skiing

You look up and spot a remarkable skier cruising down the slope. You know she's a great skier because you saw her earlier on a double-black-diamond run, skimming over giant man-eating bumps as though they were a groomed playground. But now you're baffled. How on earth is she turning? She's simply turning, or rather her skis are, and you can't see any particular actions, any special technique, no stepping, no weight shift, no nothing, just perfect parallel turns, both skis tipping and turning together, by some kind of mysterious remote control.

I know you've seen skiers like this one. Skiers so polished and so subtle in their technique that it's far from obvious what is triggering their turns, what's keeping them going. Now it's time to pull aside the veil and introduce you to the most enjoyable and the most mysterious form of weight shift I know. And very useful too, I hasten to add. I'm talking about passive, or soft, weight shift—or, to say it another way, weight shift through relaxation. Fortunately, it's a lot easier to describe, or to do, than it is to see because this subtle form of weight shift, perfect for steep slopes, for very short turns, for some bumps, and for lazy relaxed cruising too, is all but invisible. Are you ready?

Let's step back from the action of turning for a minute and visualize ourselves just traversing diagonally down and across a groomed slope. We've already learned that in a traverse, most of your weight should be carried by your downhill ski, foot, and leg. And I'm sure you're doing just that now in your mind's eye. But how can skiers support all their weight on one leg? The answer is simple: by tensing the muscles in that leg and foot. I don't mean making your leg stiff and rigid with muscle tension, but still a certain amount of muscle tension is needed to give your leg the structural integrity, the relative rigidity, that it needs to support your weight. We're going to start, as we often do, not with the whole leg but with the foot. With a little practice, perhaps while you are sitting reading this chapter, you will be able to feel the difference between tensing the muscles in your foot and relaxing them. But first, in our imagination, let's return to our easy diagonal descent. Instead of traversing straight across the hill, picture yourself heading diagonally downward at about 45 degrees on a rather easy slope. Let's say you're moving toward the right side of the slope, so most of your weight will be on your downhill or left ski, and I want you to feel how strong and tight your left foot has to be in order to support all that weight. Now, in order to start an easy turn, I'm going to ask you to suddenly relax your left foot inside your boot—to let it go limp and soft. And see what happens. This is a tough one because it always seems easier to do something active than to simply let go. But I know you can do it.

Here's another example of what I am talking about. Take one hand and hold it in the air in front of you, all fingers extended. Tense that hand so that all the fingers are stiff, almost bent backward by muscle tension. Now count to three as you hold your hand very tight, and on the count of three, let go of all

Figure 4.11a *Soft weight shift to start a turn. Soft weight shift is really weight shift through relaxation of the inside foot and leg. This subtle way of shifting from ski to ski is surely the most difficult form of weight shift to observe, but perhaps the easiest to do. It's certainly one of the most liberating and versatile ways of starting a turn. Instead of an active shift of the body's weight from ski to ski, one has the impression that the body's weight flows smoothly and effortlessly to the new ski, just by relaxing your inside foot and leg. In the close-up, we can see that the light, inside ski virtually never leaves the snow.*

that tension. Let your hand and fingers flop around like those of a rag doll. That's what I want you to feel in your boot.

If I demonstrate this on a ski slope, traversing down the hill on my down-hill ski and then simply relaxing that downhill foot to trigger a turn, my students can't see me do anything at all, but they will see my two skis begin to turn; that sudden relaxation of the tight downhill foot allows all my weight to simply flow over to my other foot, which, so to speak, catches me and keeps me from collapsing totally. The same thing will happen when you try this—on a green slope first, please. You slide across the slope, standing mostly on your downhill foot, then you relax that foot completely, suddenly, totally, letting your foot go limp and squishy inside the boot (like a rag doll's foot), and voilà, your skis start to turn because this relaxation is just a subtle form of weight shift. I generally refer to it as *soft weight shift*.

Soft weight shift, or weight shift through relaxation, is very special and very versatile. Lots of expert skiers use it most of the time. And the fact that it is so hard to spot, to observe and understand, at least from the outside, has led many ski schools and many ski instructors to assert that a lot of the best skiers aren't shifting weight at all, but actually skiing balanced equally on both skis. Wrong! We'll investigate soft weight shift and its multiple variations in detail, and I'll suggest a number of practice patterns to make it your own. But let me point out another curious aspect of this gentle, all-but-invisible form of weight shift. It can be used in a wide range of skiing situations to trigger or launch some very different kinds of turns, from long, lazy, almost effortless cruising turns to quick, tight short-radius turns on scary steep slopes, to turns through dense bumps.

We're going to start, as we so often do, at the more laid-back end of this spectrum. I want you to use soft weight shift to make the laziest, easiest turns you've ever made. Not high-speed turns at first. Not dashing turns. Not even pure carved turns, although they will definitely be round arcs. I'm talking about the sort of lazy laid-back turns that you might want to do on the last run of the day, skiing with friends, not pushing it, watching the last sunshine light up clouds on distant peaks with pink and gold alpenglow. Late afternoon turns. Just quietly riding your skis in effortless arcs. Start each turn by completely relaxing one foot, letting it go soft and squishy, so to speak, inside your boot. Let go with the left foot … and a left turn begins. Let go with your right foot … and turn right. Do this for at least a couple of runs, and file this kind of weight shift through relaxation away in the back of your skier's consciousness as probably the easiest, most effortless way you have ever started turns.

But there's more to this story of soft weight shift. Starting a turn by merely relaxing your inside foot only works when the slope is not very steep and when you can afford to take quite a bit of time to come around. Steeper slopes demand shorter more dynamic turns; you just don't want to linger in the fall line, picking up speed. So now, to use soft weight shift more dynamically, we're going to bring the entire inside (or downhill) leg into play at the start of the turn, not just the foot. Yet we still want to trigger these turns by relaxing, by letting go. This time let's imagine that you are approaching a sort of drop-off on the slope, the beginnings of a bump perhaps or just a steep section. Suppose your left leg is your downhill leg, so naturally you want to launch a turn down the slope to your left. First, become aware of just how tight, how relatively strong and tense, your downhill leg has to be to hold you up against the pull of gravity. And then, when you reach the spot you've chosen, simply allow that whole left leg to collapse—by releasing all the muscle tension in it. Wham—an easy short turn.

I use a variety of words to describe this action, or should I say this anti-action, of the downhill foot and leg: collapsing, folding, flexing out of the way, giving, letting go.… It all adds up to the same thing. When you suddenly let all the muscle tension in that inside foot *and leg* drain away, you are no longer supporting yourself or holding yourself up with that downhill leg. Effortlessly, automatically, your weight winds up on the other leg, foot, and ski. Effortlessly, and rather quickly too, your skis begin to turn down the hill. This whole-leg version of soft weight shift is certainly trickier than simply launching a lazy

Figure 4.11b *Soft weight shift to start a turn.*

slow turn by relaxing your inside foot. But it is still weight shift through relaxation, soft weight shift. And it works wonders.

You will feel several things when this move works. Soft weight shift is very smooth, very supple. Although it happens quickly, there are no sudden, jerky movements to disturb your balance. Your skis tend to hug the snow, and this will be wonderfully important in mogul, or bump, skiing. And this sort of soft weight shift can also trigger a faster shorter-radius turn than anything we have tried yet. It really opens the door to very short turns.

To get the most out of this subtle form of weight shift, you can refine it in several ways. On steeper slopes, to start shorter turns, become conscious that your inside leg isn't merely giving, or flexing, or folding up, it's actually folding out of the way; that is to say, if you are turning to the right, you let your right leg give and as it folds up slightly, your right knee will move out of the way, downhill to the right—making room for your outside ski and leg to come around faster. Likewise, as you start a short turn to the left with this complete soft weight shift, you have the impression that your left knee is softly folding to the left, getting out of the way. What makes this whole business work is your ability to relax the muscles in one leg, not the other, in one foot, not the other. Differential relaxation.

It takes a while to get a handle on this feeling of differential relaxation, to develop a sort of sixth-sense awareness of which leg is working and which leg is relaxing. But it's worth the effort, or should I say, the lack of effort, because you will have the impression that these are the easiest turns you have ever made. And they are. By the way, no one watching you start turns with soft weight shift, no one looking down from the chairlift, will be able to see that you are really shifting from ski to ski, from foot to foot. These turns give the visual impression that a skier is standing equally on both skis. But we know we're not. Let's just keep this as our secret.

Putting It All Together

Perhaps you have a final question about these multiple variations on a theme of shifting weight. You should. The obvious question is: How do I know when to use which form of weight shift? I think this is a very good question, indeed.

When really skilled experts dance down the mountain, they are definitely not thinking about which technique to use on the next turn or the next pitch. In a wonderful sense, they aren't really thinking consciously at all, at least not about skiing, but rather are reacting and responding to the changing mountain in front of them. Although we need to practice these discrete forms of weight shift separately, focusing on how each one works, when we are free skiing they just tend to happen, as needed.

Sure, from time to time you may need to give yourself a little reminder: Oh, oh, I'm slipping out a bit on this icy snow. How about a little more phantom edging? Or perhaps on the steeps, you'll notice that you're lifting your inside foot up off the snow, which is causing balance problems, so you'll refocus for a moment on soft weight shift to make your skis hug the snow. But, generally, with experience, you will find yourself using different types of weight shift without even thinking about it, depending largely on your mood, on how active or how lazy you feel on any given run.

The one notion that doesn't change, that runs like a thread through expert turns of all sorts, is early weight shift: Change feet, change skis, at the start of your turn, not partway around the corner. Shift weight a split second before the start of your turn, before anything else happens. Move to the new ski, and then enjoy the ride. A glorious ride to be sure. We've learned to carve turns, all kinds of turns on our amazing shaped skis. And now, thanks to early weight shift, you can launch a bombproof parallel turn wherever and whenever you want to. But we still need one more new skill before the picture is perfect, a new pattern that will let us link very short turns straight down the slope, straight down the fall line. This pattern is called anticipation, and we'll master it in the next chapter.

IN SUMMARY

• Many skiers pivot their top ski first into a slight V to start their turn and are forced into all sorts of shenanigans to make the inside ski catch up. This "stem" is caused by late weight shift: turning the top ski before standing on it.

• To eliminate the stem and start each turn in a pure parallel fashion, all you need is early weight shift—moving to your top (soon to be your outside) ski before your turn begins. It's all in the timing: Change feet, then turn.

• Crossover helps too. Let your whole body tilt forward and down the hill once you've committed to your top ski. The sequence is always: early weight shift, then crossover.

• Weight shift is the key to efficient expert turns on packed slopes, but it comes in different flavors. Experiment and play with and practice each of the following main forms of weight shift:

Active weight shift: visibly, dynamically, and energetically stepping to the top or outside ski. Skating is the master exercise for practicing this sort of weight shift. Active weight shift is great for warming up on cold mornings, for accelerating into turns, for expressing energy and exuberance on skis.

Weight shift by lightening one ski: "inside-out" weight shift. Instead of stepping to your new ski, simply pull your weight off your old ski. It's not necessary to lift, or pull, this ski high up off the snow—an inch, a centimeter, will do. Light is light. Lightening your downhill foot to trigger a downhill turn frees that light foot to adjust your edging with a phantom move. Weight shift by lightening the inside ski is particularly effective for starting carved turns on icy slopes.

Soft weight shift through relaxation: the most versatile and subtle form of weight shift depends on selectively releasing muscular tension in your downhill foot to trigger a new turn. A totally relaxed foot can't support your weight, which literally flows over to the other ski, your new outside ski. On steeper slopes, relax not only your lower foot but your whole lower leg. Relaxing and folding your downhill leg will trigger a faster and shorter turn. Soft weight shift is the easiest way to launch a parallel turn and also a powerful option in challenging conditions. Soft weight shift is a widely misunderstood technique because it doesn't look as though you are really shifting from foot to foot. Soft weight shift may be virtually invisible, but weight shift it is. Don't neglect this one!

Linking Short Turns

How to Tame Steeper Slopes

Steep, steeper, steepest. There's a common misconception floating around that expert skiers are only happy eating double-black-diamond slopes for breakfast—that if you're really good, all you care about is skiing right at your limits and beyond. But of course, it ain't necessarily so. Still, steep slopes happen. Happen even to skiers who'd rather avoid them, who don't have a supercharged passion for challenge and difficulty. Happen to everyone. Wouldn't it be great, at least, to feel at home on steeper slopes? To drop over the edge without hesitation. To tighten your turns, almost effortlessly, from long lazy arcs into short rhythmic pendulumlike pivots, and leave your signature with a flourish on a slope most skiers can't handle. To arrive at the bottom still smiling, exhilarated, not even out of breath. A graduation of sorts. A skiing milestone. A confirmation.

Carved turns work on a skier's spirit like strong drugs. They are intoxicating, addictive. It would be easy just to say: "Okay, now I can really carve—that makes me an expert," and leave it at that. Almost, but not quite. There's one more river to cross to reach Jordan, one more situation that separates experts from average skiers, and that's steep terrain, really steep terrain. I'd like to devote this chapter to getting you over this last hurdle, to mastering a very special skiing pattern for taming steeper and steeper slopes—linked short turns.

Generally speaking, carved turns tend to be medium- to long-radius arcs.

Our skis need some time to bend, some extra time and space, to pull us around that perfect circle on the snow. But on very steep slopes, we don't have that free time or space, because on the steeps, long turns would create too much acceleration. On a very steep slope, no one really wants to linger in the fall line, gathering more and more speed from one turn to the next, accelerating toward an inevitable crisis. Instead, our basic tool for keeping it together on the steeps is to link a series of continuous short turns straight down the hill (or straight down the fall line in skiing jargon). Short linked turns are a perfect recipe for keeping the lid on your speed and thus for negotiating steep slopes—or narrow slopes, or any number of other particularly challenging situations.

In an earlier era, short linked turns were considered *the* hallmark of expert skiing. "Short swing" and "wedel," as the two main styles of linked short turns were then called, used to be universal skiers' goals, what expert skiing was all about. And then came carving. Today, expert skiers typically spend more time carving longer turns—slicing big and satisfying carved arcs down snowy mountainsides—than they do making small and staccato check turns down tight chutes and steep faces or wiggling decorative little arcs along groomed catwalks. It's not because they have somehow lost the knack of linking short tight turns, but simply because large carved arcs on our modern skis are so seductive, so satisfying.

I understand. I too have fallen in love with carved turns, and these days I tend to spend more time carving long arcs than I do making short turns and looking for steeper steeps. But it's all relative. The steeps are still there, waiting and challenging, and so are bumps, which also demand short turns. And it's certainly still true today that you can't call yourself an expert skier until you can ski it all … with a smile on your face. So on we go, to deal with short linked turns, the last big step in our expert skiing apprenticeship.

But first, a small caveat: When done well, short linked turns look effortless, and they very nearly are. Learning to link short turns, however, is anything but.

I almost think of these short linked turns as a kind of separate sport within the larger sport of skiing—they have their own patterns, their own learning curve, their own moves and mystique: a separate endeavor. And sure enough, as soon as you start working on the mysteries of dynamic anticipation—which is the technical key to efficient short turns—you will probably feel like a beginner all over again. All your grace and poise will fly out the window, and you'll have to put it back together turn by turn by turn. But forewarned is forearmed; so don't get discouraged, and soon we'll be dancing down the steeps together with smoothly linked short turns.

Flowing Down the Mountain: The Importance of Continuous Turns

Before we zero in on the special challenge of short turns and how to link them into long fluid chains, let's spend a moment exploring the general notion of linking turns—any and all turns. After all, that's precisely what expert skiers do. Have you noticed? The most skilled skiers on the slope, the ones you truly admire, are always turning. They seldom go straight across the slope from point A to point B and then turn. Instead, they are always somewhere in the process of linking two arcs, blending one round arc smoothly into the next, one turn into the next. Their turning motion is so smooth and so continuous that there is almost never a frozen or static moment between turns. It's almost hard to see for sure where one turn stops and the next begins. This way of skiing is far more graceful and rhythmic than the alternative—going straight, turning, going straight again, then turning again. As we'll see, it's also technically easier to turn continuously. So I'm going to ask you to make this a conscious goal: to transform every run into a long series of continuous turns—continuous linked S-shapes—to make continuous turning a habit.

Obviously, it wouldn't be very satisfying to make hundreds of pushy little corners all the way down the mountain run after run. So most of the time, you will be stretching your turns out, one really big arc blending into another really big arc, with variations in the size and speed of your turns as the terrain and

Figure 5.1 *Continuous turns: the real hallmark of expert skiing.* Why go straight between turns when linking one arc, smoothly and inevitably, to the next is so much more graceful and so much more efficient?

134

your mood suggest. Stand at the top of a long and, I hope, uncrowded slope, and give yourself a sort of assignment: Ski all the way to the bottom of this slope in ten big turns, or a dozen, or however many you want, with no traverses, no straight-line sections to break the rhythm. At first you'll need to concentrate, to remind yourself to keep on turning, to stretch each turn out, farther and farther, until there's nothing left and it's time to shift weight and launch the next turn. Don't rush it. Even though the long-term goal of this chapter is to link exciting, dashing short turns, we're going to get there slowly and patiently. And I promise you that this pattern of always turning, of continuous turning (rather than going straight between turns) is such a graceful and satisfying way of skiing that it will quickly become your preferred approach to any slope.

What you are really doing here is finding your own rhythm. The first image I used in the first chapter of this book was to compare expert skiing to dancing. This image isn't merely a flight of fancy; it's grounded in technique, in movement patterns—above all, in that sense of rhythm and rhythmic movement that both skiing and dancing share. Skiing too means moving rhythmically through space—only the space we are lucky enough to move through is the tilted side of a mountain, our white ballroom. And nothing reinforces the rhythmic quality of good skiing like continuous turning. Look around you on the slopes from the chair. Am I right? The very best skiers you spot will be tracing continuous S-shapes down the mountain all the time. You should too.

But there are endless different rhythms, endless different dances, in life and on skis. Sometimes I'm tempted to compare big sensuous carved turns to a waltz and short turns, especially short turns through bumps, to jazz dancing. The comparison is imperfect, but you can see what I'm getting at. There is no correct or best rhythm on skis; you need to develop your own—your own different rhythms, not one single rhythm. A pattern emerges that is typical of all skilled skiing, all expert skiing, and that pattern is one of continuous fluid movement with no dead spots, no frozen moments, no frozen positions. In other words, in effective expert skiing you are always doing *something*, even if it seems to be in slow motion. The underlying pattern continues: Turn, then turn back; turn, then return; ride one ski, then ride the other; turn, then turn again. And this continuity, this flow of turning movement, is a pattern that repeats itself also in the skier's body: Your legs, for example, are either smoothly flexing or stretching back out, but never frozen in one position.

Let me share a couple of exercises to reinforce this pattern of continuous movement. Do you remember when I asked you, in Chapter 3, to do a sort of side-step shuffle down an easy catwalk? Step to the side and close your free ski, moving it in toward the weighted ski; then step back to the other side and close the new free ski? And as you repeated this simple step-step, step-step pattern down that catwalk, your skis began to turn slightly from side to side. Let's do it again, only this time as you pull your light ski in close to your weighted ski, I'd like you to sink down flexing your legs somewhat more than usual. Now the pattern is: Step, close your light ski and flex, step back, close your light ski and flex, and so on. As before, your skis will begin to turn back and forth with each step. (This is more like a series of turn beginnings than complete turns.) But the extra flexing/folding action I'm asking you to add will smooth out these mini-turns. You will feel more graceful, more rhythmic, more supple. Because you are constantly moving up and down—flexing as you pull that light ski in, then stretching taller as you step back to the other side—you will never experience any sudden overload of pressure on your skis. Your skis will make these mini-arcs in a smoother, rounder, and more dynamic way than before.

Our main idea is that a skier's body should never be stuck in one position, even for an instant, but should always be moving, if only gently. And something else interesting happens. We know already that as you flex your legs into a turn, your ski tip will bite more deeply into the snow and your skis will come around faster. That's exactly what happens when you increase the progressive flexing of your legs through a sequence of turns. The result:

Spring comes slowly in the high High Sierra. The snow doesn't seem to visibly melt but simply changes, and changes, and changes into ever more perfect corn. Eventually the lifts close, and the ski season comes to an end more from lack of interest than lack of snow. But before that happens, it's time to put your skis on your shoulder and hike. We walk up the ridge above Siberia to the flattop summit of the Palisades and look out over a white no-man's land between Squaw Valley and nearby Alpine Meadows: the undeveloped semiwilderness of the Five Lakes Basin. The back side. The Sun Bowl. It's steep. Late-morning snow just starting to soften into spring velvet. Easy edging. Steep and smooth but safe. No rocks, no cliffs, just a long way down.

I start slowly: slide, edge, pivot, repeat. Steep enough to get slightly more than 100 percent attention. But it feels good, better in fact with each successful turn, and a few hundred feet below the top I start to lighten up and enjoy the whole experience. An underlying rhythm to these turns begins to establish itself. I become aware of a rhythmic soundtrack: the near silence of a quick pivot, the growing gritty whoooosh of edges scraping and biting at the same time, something like a crunch of snow at the end of each turn, and silence once more as my flexed, wound-up skis are released down the hill again. The rhythm has taken over, conscious and unconscious: turn and … turn back … and … turn back … and … It is totally compelling. I have lost the will, or even the ability, to vary my turns. Each turn triggers its mirror image. I have become a human pendulum. Tick tock, tick tock. Turn return. Turn return. Time stops. I am lost inside the pulsing rhythm of anticipated short turns. They carry me on like a river, hundreds and hundreds of feet on down the Sun

(continued on page 138)

(continued from page 137)
Bowl until at last we run out of steepness, the mountain and I.

Ten minutes later, tucking into a spring picnic of cheese and sala-mi and Beaujolais on a smooth granite slab beside one of the still- *frozen Five Lakes, I look back up at the Sun Bowl and can just make out my long zipper of tracks from the very top. The hypnotic magic of linked turns still repeating its steady rhythm in my memory. Even today. So many years later.*

Your turns inevitably become quicker, shorter, and more fluid.

Explore this possibility: Start by skiing down a long, easy slope linking long, easy turns. No problem, right? Then, progressively with each succeeding turn, I'd like you to flex deeper, and deeper, and deeper. Actually both legs are "giving" and flexing forward, but it's your outside leg, the one you are truly standing on, that gets the job done. And what precisely is that job? Why shortening your turns, of course. So I'm really asking you to increase the flexing of your outside leg, but steadily and progressively, from turn to turn. If you deepen your flexing follow-through on each turn, by the time you reach the bottom of the slope your turns will be half the size they were at the top or less. Remember, we're not yet thinking of super short turns, but rather of progressively shortening a series of turns. The ability to shorten up your turns, whenever you want, will give you a delicious sense of increased control.

Notice that I have been talking about *shortening* your turns rather than making short turns. This is an all-important distinction. When most skiers decide to make short turns, they start each turn by twisting their skis suddenly and powerfully in an effort to get them to the other side as fast as possible. A more sophisticated expert approach is to treat almost all turns the same and realize that a short turn is simply a long turn in which the turning action of the skis is sped up by effective leg action. Let me say this once more: A short turn is not a different animal; it's a normal turn in which the skis simply arc around faster. And that means that the difference is not in how you start a short turn, but in how you guide it and finish it.

A Short Digression About Poles

Now it's time for a break in the action. We need to talk about our ski poles for a minute. Alert readers may have noticed that until this moment, I've avoided all mention of our poles. I did this for a reason. Whenever ski pros suggest that their students use their poles, it seems as though this new focus distracts attention from the feet and skis—where the real action is—and things start to fall apart. Besides, until you're ready for linked short turns, there is no technical reason to do anything special with your poles. But we're almost there, so let's bring these interesting tools into play. For starters, I'm going to ask you to use your poles to mark out the rhythm of successive continuous turns.

Stand on your skis on some flat spot without sliding. You can do this at home too. Hold your arms, hands, and poles in their normal position: spread laterally for balance, slightly ahead of your hips, at just about waist level or a little above. Now, using only wrist action, play around with your poles, flicking first one, then the other forward, *without* swinging your arms at all. That's it: flick, flick, flick, reaching the tip of your pole forward, but only with hand and wrist action. This is the way experts plant, or tap, or touch their poles on the snow at the start of many, actually almost all, turns. To tell the truth, in most cases we do this only out of habit (although it's a very good habit) rather than necessity. For easy long-radius turns there is almost nothing to be gained by doing anything at all with one's poles. But in short turns and on steep slopes, poles do have a critical role to play. To start with, this constant reaching, reaching, reaching, with the tips of your poles helps maintain the rhythm of a series of linked or continuous turns. (And I'll add another more important reason to use your poles in a few pages.)

Figure 5.2 *Dynamic anticipation.*
The perfect recipe for linking short turns straight down the mountain. Here it's clear that the skier's body is facing and, more importantly, moving straight down the hill, and only the skis, feet, and legs are turning from side to side. The skier's torso is all but motionless whether viewed from above or below.

Don't think me redundant if I add that you want to be sure to mark the start of a right turn by tapping your right pole into the snow. Mark the start of a left turn with your left pole. This shouldn't be too confusing: Tap the left pole, make the left ski light, and turn left. Tap the right pole, make the right ski light, and turn right. It's all of a piece. What I'm describing is pretty basic, simply "pole action 101." In a while our pole action will become much more precise, much more purposeful.

Your main concern right now, however, is not to worry about your poles; your main task at this point is to focus on making your turns more continuous, more rhythmic, every run, every weekend, every ski trip. As much as possible, banish straight lines, banish straight traverses between turns, from your skiing.

Live your ski life as a celebration of linked and blended curves. Continuous nonstop turning forms a background pattern against which we are going to start working on a very special new technique for making and linking short turns—dynamic anticipation.

Dynamic Anticipation: The Secret of Linking Short Turns

The special mechanism, or movement pattern, that experts use for linking short turns is pretty tricky. I call this special pattern dynamic anticipation. It is not one simple movement; it's certainly not just a position that the skier assumes. Rather, dynamic anticipation is an integrated movement pattern that involves the whole body, from feet to hips to hands and poles, and everything in between.

I'm going to tackle dynamic anticipation in two parts. First, in this section, I am simply going to describe *how* experts link short turns, how dynamic anticipation looks, and feels, and works. I want to give you as clear a mental movie as possible of this cunning expert skiing pattern. Then, in the next section, I'll lay out a practical sequence of exercises and practice patterns for getting there, a way for you to make this essential and far-from-obvious expert skill your own. Right now, take a deep breath and let's begin to build our mental picture of short turns with dynamic anticipation:

You've paused at the side of a steep black trail, and while you're catching your breath, a dazzling skier comes into sight—linking short arcs down the slope with the deftness of a Zen calligrapher connecting black brushstrokes down a scroll of white rice paper. You look closer. And you realize you are watching a visual paradox: motion and stillness in the same picture. In these short turns you can observe a lot of rapid action and, at the same time, a lot of calm and quiet. Skis, feet, and legs are pivoting and turning together rapidly from side to side in a rhythmic pendulumlike motion beneath the skier's torso. But that torso isn't turning at all; it's virtually motionless. From the waist up, actually from the hips up, this dashing skier's body is scarcely moving—not motionless in a stiff or frozen sense, but instead traveling smoothly in a straight line down the hill, seemingly unconnected and uninvolved with the back-and-forth turning action of legs, feet, and skis down below.

From the hips up, our dashing expert skier seems totally relaxed, quiet, and comfortable, definitely enjoying the ride, but certainly not working at it. Perhaps the only sure sign that this skier is really involved with the short turns that are happening down at the snow level is a big grin. That, plus active hands that keep flicking the ski poles down the hill to mark the start of each new turn—tick, tock, tick, tock, like a metronome. This is the classic short-turn pattern: *active feet and skis, turning back and forth beneath a quiet, relaxed upper body.*

This image is so very important that I'd like to express it once more in a slightly different way. *The feet and skis are turning, but the skier is not.* The skier seems to be going straight, looking and moving straight down the hill. Each time the two skis finish one short arc and pivot back downhill, it's as though the skier has gotten there first. The skier's body—by facing and moving straight down the hill—seems to be already halfway around each new turn. The skier's body is "anticipating" each coming turn. Like the echo of a line from a T. S. Eliot poem, our expert skier, linking short arcs straight down the fall line, seems to be the still center of a turning world.

There's a lot of efficiency and logic to this style of skiing as well as dash and excitement. It makes sense. Short turns aren't only short; they're also quick, and when you link them together without a pause, they are very, very quick indeed. Most of us have a sense of how long it takes to count seconds: One thousand one, one thousand two, one thousand three, and so forth. Consider this: In a series of short linked turns, expert skiers often find themselves making one new turn every second or every two seconds if they're feeling lazy. That's quite quick. And there simply isn't enough time for skiers to turn their bodies (their upper bodies or torsos) from side to side, from right to left and back, every second or two. There isn't enough time or enough energy.

Your torso, from hips to shoulders (plus your arms and head, of course), accounts for about two thirds of your total weight. For many adults, that easily adds up to 100 pounds, roughly the weight of a sack of Portland cement. Have you ever tried to pick up a sack of cement? Brutal. Now imagine that you were running down a sidewalk with a sack of cement in your arms, zigzagging your way around parking meters like a slalom racer. And on top of everything, imagine that you had to twist that sack of cement, first to the right, then to the left, at each change of direction. I don't think you could do it. Likewise on skis, skiers do not have enough strength or enough time to twist their body first right, then left, then back, with every short turn in a series of tight turns. It's simply too much work. By the same token, it's a far easier task simply to turn your lower body—your feet and legs. They are so much lighter, so much more flexible, so much quicker.

You can see that the pattern I am talking about—turning with active feet beneath a quiet upper body—isn't really a choice; it's a necessity. This way of linking short turns *exclusively with lower body action* has been around for a long time. Surprisingly, instructors have never been able to agree 100 percent on what's going on in such turns. Indeed, instructors and coaches haven't even been able to agree on what to call this all-important skiing pattern. It has been called upper-lower body separation, or upper-lower body opposition, or countering, or most often anticipation. The word *anticipation* seems

143

appropriate because the skier's body, which looks like it is facing across the skis and down the hill, appears to be anticipating the coming pivoting action of the skis. Fair enough. But there's a lot more to this skiing pattern than just facing downhill. In fact, a common misconception is that anticipation implies actively twisting your body downhill first, just before the skis follow. Wrong. The torso is not the active player here. Your trunk stays quiet, almost motionless. Why? Because it is simply too much work to move or twist the heavy upper body with every turn. Instead, it's the feet and legs that are active.

As the feet and legs turn back and forth beneath the torso, muscle tension is built up and then released into the next turn. This build-up and release of tension occurs in a lot of different sports and is sometimes called a "windup-and-release" movement. Baseball pitchers wind up before hurling the ball toward home plate. Both tennis players and golfers use a backstroke before delivering a power stroke. It's the same principle: The windup movement stretches the muscles that will be used a second later, and as a result these muscles contract more powerfully, more efficiently. Indeed, it's this windup-and-release mechanism that makes short linked ski turns almost automatic—almost effortless. Let's look even closer.

Imagine that you're finishing a short turn to the left. Your legs are flexed, and you're applying smooth forward and inward guiding pressures to your skis (especially to your outside ski); perhaps you're even using some phantom edging. No matter what your mix of movements, your skis (especially your outside ski) are biting into the snow and coming around rapidly beneath you. In fact, your feet and skis are turning a lot faster than you are. That's because your upper body, being heavier, has more inertia than your legs and skis. And also because the muscular connections between your torso and your legs are quite relaxed, so that in a sense you are uncoupled, or unconnected, from your feet and legs.

Meanwhile, as your skis continue to bite and arc around toward the left—but you don't—something fascinating happens. A kind of twisting tension, or

Figure 5.3 *Turning with dynamic anticipation: a closer look. As the skier finishes one turn to the left, tension is building between skis and lower body and the heavier, more stable mass of the torso. This tension can be released into the new turn, with our familiar weight shift and crossover, and the skier experiences an unwinding of the skis in the direction of the new turn.*

torsion, builds between your upper and lower body, between your hips and your legs. You feel wound up against yourself. Your legs and skis are now aimed across the hill while your body is still aimed more or less down the hill. This is far from a normal anatomical position. So now, if you can simply release your skis' grip on the snow, then your whole lower body—skis, feet, and legs—will want to come back where it belongs, to realign itself beneath your torso. You will feel as though your skis are unwinding beneath you, turning back toward the fall line *on their own*. Or maybe I should say, "re-turning" on their own, pivoting back down the hill on their own. A wonderful sensation. Such turning action feels like a gift, a free start to the next turn, and so it is.

In all this the skier has only a small helping role to play. All you need to trigger this unwinding action is to release your skis' grip on the snow—and really it's only your outside, downhill, ski that's weighted and gripping—at the end of your short turn. And while you're at it, shift your weight to the soon-to-be new outside ski. It's easily done, especially if you've begun to develop a good feel for what I've called soft weight shift (review the end of Chapter 4 if this term doesn't ring a bell). Easily done because both tasks—releasing the ski to turn and shifting weight—are best accomplished simultaneously by letting go with the muscles of your downhill foot and leg. No longer supported on the downhill side, your body begins to tilt or lean, or "topple over," down the hill, and this in turn flattens your skis so they can unwind back beneath you while your weight settles smoothly onto the new outside ski—the one that is about to dominate and guide you around out of the fall line to finish this new turn. It sounds complicated but it isn't because the whole complex pattern is triggered effortlessly by the letting go, folding, or collapsing of the downhill leg. Soft weight shift really works.

And that's almost the whole picture of how effortless short turns work: tension building up at the end of one arc that can be released into the next. Your skis turning out of the fall line only to return down the hill beneath you. But there is one more technical point I need to underline—pole action—and how it helps us to link short turns.

Picture again the end of one short turn with your skis aimed more or less across the hill while your upper body is aimed more or less down the hill. You want your skis, feet, and legs to unwind down the hill, toward the fall line, into the coming turn. Since you are all wound up, you know your body is going to straighten out, come back to center. But just what part of you is going to unwind? Feet or trunk? What is to prevent your upper body from unwinding until you are facing across the hill as your skis are? The answer is simple: your pole. If at the end of one short turn, you make a vigorous and decisive pole plant straight down the hill and really support yourself on that pole for a second or two, you will find your upper body blocked, or anchored, or held fast, by this pole plant. Such a pole plant guarantees that your upper body will continue to face downhill and this, in turn, guarantees that all the unwinding action will take place at the foot and snow level—exactly what we had in mind. To tell the truth, this is the first important, technically critical use of our poles that we have made so far in this book or in skiing in general. A decisive, well-timed, and well-aimed pole plant holds your upper body momentarily in that all-important anticipated position, so that your skis can then follow you down the hill. This is the free start to a short turn we've been talking about.

But let me remind you that we're not really interested in separate turns—no matter how elegant, efficient, and easy—but in linked turns: a series, a succession, a chain of turns; a rhythmic alternation of turns—turning pressure, then release and pivot back; turning pressure, then release and pivot back; wind up, then unwind; turn, then return. Again and again and again.

This whole pattern, wind up and unwind, turn and return, is what I mean when I talk about dynamic anticipation. I got discouraged with all the conflicting interpretations of the term *anticipation* and decided I needed an expression that would underline the back-and-forth interaction of a skier's upper and lower body. There's a lot more to it than just facing down the mountain in the direction of the new turn (which, it seems to me, would be a sort of passive anticipation of the next turn). There's a constant alternation of lower body action and reaction while the skier (in particular, the skier's *center*) keeps moving down the mountain—a special case of the crossover we discussed in Chapter 4. So actually the entire pattern—not just the back-and-forth turning action of the feet under the skier—is active and dynamic. We don't merely anticipate the coming turn by facing the direction in which we want our skis

All Techniques Are Possible: How to Choose?

Skiing is an open-ended sport. There is just no right way to ski. No best way to ski. No one is keeping score. In a ski race the fastest skier is the best, sure, but most of us aren't ski racers. And the vast majority of ski runs can be judged, if they must be judged, only by the personal satisfaction, the pleasure of the skier. You may have noticed: There are a lot of different ideas about ski technique out there and a lot of different techniques. Maybe you've already had the experience of one instructor telling you one thing, only to have this advice contradicted the next weekend by a different instructor at a different ski school. Long-time skiers can surely remember earlier ski techniques that were once all the rage. There was the Arlberg technique, and reverse shoulder, and rotation. Some ski schools stressed something called up-unweighting to help you turn while others made a big deal out of down-unweighting. And today unweighting is seldom even mentioned. In this book, for example, I am sharing with you my own interpretation of the best of modern skiing, but I can't pretend that the turns I love and teach are the only turns one can make on skis.

I'll go even further and admit that all techniques are possible. I can make very good turns with my weight on the outside ski. But I can also make damn good turns with my weight on both skis. With enough practice, you can too. So how to chose? How to know? And how to decide what technical path you should follow on your own personal skiing adventure?

Trust your first impressions, your reactions, your own judgment. If a new set of moves feels good, it probably is. If a new turn feels efficient and graceful, it probably is. But look for something more than merely minimal success, something more than just being able to turn without falling. I suggest that optimum technique should feel easy, but also efficient and relaxed. If one style of skiing leaves you less fatigued after a long run, there's probably a reason. And that's a good enough reason to stick with that style of skiing, even though another style of turning got you down the same run without crashing. You are looking for poise and balance, for ease and efficiency. For legs that don't feel sore at the end of a long day's skiing. For a style of turning that gives you options and choices, that lets you turn at will, almost effortlessly, in all kinds of situations, lets you easily vary the radius of each turn, and easily control your speed. I'm pretty convinced that the simple movement patterns I'm stressing in this book will do all that and more. But don't be surprised if someone says: Hey, that's not the way. Try it my way. And why not? But make up your own mind about what works best, easiest, most naturally and gracefully. And zero in on your own home-base technique. Just because a certain move or turn or technique is possible doesn't mean it will help you ski better. All techniques are possible, but not all techniques will carry you to that next level. You can feel the difference. Trust your feelings.

to turn, but by moving, and tilting, and committing ourselves in that direction—anticipation, certainly, but dynamic anticipation. From now on, whenever I mention anticipation, or an anticipated position, or skiing with anticipation, or a movement of anticipation, you'll know I'm referring to this whole integrated pattern.

If this all sounds a bit complex, well, it is. I confess that linking short turns with dynamic anticipation is the single most complex aspect of expert skiing that I am going to present in this book. That's why I'm spending so much time on it. And why I've tried to describe it in such detail. Stick with it. Be patient;

above all, be patient with yourself. I know you can master linking short turns with dynamic anticipation. But you can't do it in a single day. Nonetheless, this sensational style of skiing is the key that will open up the most challenging expert terrain on the mountain, steep black and double-black slopes. Now, I think it's time to start practicing.

Tackling Dynamic Anticipation

I've just said that you can't master short turns with anticipation in a day. In my experience it usually takes about a week and never less than three days, even working with a skilled coach. The reason it takes so long to absorb this pattern is that it involves not one movement but several—in particular, it involves the coordination of lower body and upper body action. While your feet (and legs) are finishing one turn, your upper body is preparing the next one; you're already reaching down the mountain with the hand and pole that will trigger the next turn. It's a bit like the trick of rubbing your tummy and patting your head at the same time. (In fact, the only harder skill I've ever tried to teach is an Eskimo roll when one capsizes a kayak. That skill too involves upper-lower body coordination but is complicated by the fact that you are upside down under water.)

But let's not dwell on how tricky dynamic anticipation is. Let's just do it. And we'll start by getting used to turning our feet and skis without moving our upper body. You can even begin, right now, as you read this book, by trying a simple exercise while sitting on the edge of a table. Sit on the table, so your legs are dangling free, just clear of the floor, and hold the edge of the table with your hands. Now, without moving your body at all, simply move and steer your two feet in a semicircular motion from side to side beneath you—as though you were guiding very small S-shaped turns exclusively with your feet. This is not a practice pattern for real skiing but merely a demonstration of how well you can move your feet without involving the rest of your body. I often ask my students to make this same move while riding up the mountain in a chairlift—

just move your feet in small curves from one side to the other for a preview of how dynamic anticipation (active feet beneath a quiet body) feels.

Why is this little foot exercise so easy, whereas putting dynamic anticipation to work in our skiing is often so challenging? The reason is that when you are just sitting, experimenting with your feet, you are probably very relaxed. However, when most skiers tackle the challenge of linked short turns, they are anything but relaxed. Let me say it differently: *In linked short turns, the big problem is excess muscle tension, and the key to success is a loose relaxed body.* Why? Simple. The anticipated style of short turns depends on different parts of your body doing different things at the same time; and for this to happen easily, these different body segments—legs and trunk, for example—must be connected by loose flexible joints. But when you tense the muscles around any joint—ankle, knee, hip—or indeed the muscles in any part of your body, you tend to lock yourself into what I think of as a rigid one-piece construction.

Physiologists describe this state as one of muscular co-contraction, a state in which both the flexor and extensor muscles that articulate a given joint are pulling against each other. Muscular co-contraction inhibits the free movement around a joint or prevents it altogether. To feel the effect, try this: Hold your arm out in front of you, make a fist, and at the same time tighten your whole arm. In this state, with your whole arm still tense, bend your arm until your fist touches your shoulder—an awkward slow movement, right? Now extend your arm again, but this time, make sure that the entire arm and hand are as relaxed as possible and quickly flex your elbow so your hand touches your shoulder. Quite a difference. This sort of easy movement where one is no longer fighting one's own tense muscles is referred to as ballistic movement. All efficient sports movements are to some extent ballistic movements—that is to say, the muscles responsible for getting the job done are not fighting with other tense muscles. And so it is with short linked turns. Any excess muscle tension will make it harder for the legs to rotate freely beneath your trunk. When the body is tense, it tends to turn as one massive unit.

'd in on the small of the back as the area where excess ...on would have the biggest impact, effectively blocking or cancel-ing out any independent upper-lower body action. It's still true. I still think that a relaxed lower back is essential if you hope to link short turns with dynamic anticipation. But in the last few seasons, I've become convinced that not only the lower back but the skier's entire body has to be pretty loose and relaxed for dynamic anticipation really to work. And this observation holds true in all those situations where short linked turns are a must: steeps, bumps, narrow chutes, steep powder—the full spectrum of challenging terrain.

Unfortunately, it's counterintuitive for skiers to relax in situations that seem particularly challenging, demanding, almost threatening. Counterintu-itive, but necessary. And together we're going to train ourselves to loosen up, to lighten up, whenever we begin to play with short turns. The way we're going to do this is with sideslipping. No, not just straight sideslipping, a bor-ing though necessary skill, but by using the feel and flavor of sideslipping in a series of exercises and technical games meant to build up the pattern of starting short turns with anticipation. Sideslipping really means letting go of the mountain. Sideslipping is actually an exercise in applied relaxation on skis. Remember when I first introduced sideslipping in Chapter 2, I stressed that the best way to make it happen was to relax your feet inside your boots, letting the foot go soft and limp, which in turn releases the grip of the ski's edge. Now I'm going to ask you to do the same thing: Relax from the feet up in a series of practice maneuvers that will build the habit of dynamic antici-pation. In the same sense that skating is the master exercise for practicing carved turns, sideslipping may be the master skill for short turns. (If this ref-erence to sideslipping doesn't jog your memory, if you skipped over this neat maneuver, do take a minute and go back and review pages 65 through 67 in Chapter 2.)

Now let's start building our short-turn pattern with a few hockey stops. Hockey stops are simple. They are named after the way hockey skaters skid

Figure 5.4 *A hockey stop. A simple exercise in turning the feet and skis without turning the whole body. Relax, pivot both skis, and skid to a stop.*

quickly to a stop by turning their skates sideways. That's exactly what we're going to do with our skis: Pivot them quickly sideways and skid to a stop. But what makes this move easy is that just as I start twisting both skis sideways, I relax both feet and legs, sinking or flexing down a little to make sure my legs and feet aren't tense. This pretty much guarantees that once I have pivoted my skis crosswise they will continue to slide straight down the slope and that they won't catch and shoot off across the hill. And that's all there is to hockey stops. Sink, relax, twist both skis sideways, and slide to a stop. If all goes well, only your feet, skis, and to some extent your legs will pivot across the hill, but your body will remain facing down the hill.

Your first hockey stops, however, won't be perfect. Probably, as you twist your skis across the hill, say to the left, you'll find that your body will tend to swing around to the left too, at least a bit. How can we change this? How can we keep your torso facing and moving straight downhill as your skis turn sideways? It's okay to literally hold your body facing downhill, at least the first few times you try a hockey stop. Little by little, you will simply relax and allow your trunk to continue facing downhill. It also helps to spread your hands a little wider apart than normal. This tends to quiet your upper body, to make it turn less when your feet turn. Have you ever watched figure skaters start a fast spin? Typically they pull their arms in close to the body to spin faster and, then, to stop that spinning, skaters extend their arms. I remember something similar in my high school physics class—the piano stool experiment: A student would sit on a rotating piano stool. As she extended her legs or feet, the stool would turn more slowly; but when she pulled her arms and legs in toward the center, the piano stool turned faster. Same on skis. It has to do with the inertia of rotation, and without getting any more technical, I can tell you that as you extend your arms away from your body, your trunk seems to have more rotational inertia, so it turns more slowly—just what we want. So one rule of thumb for skiing with anticipation, whether in the form of hockey stop exercises or actual short turns, is to always spread your hands out from your body a bit more than usual. This seems to anchor your body in space and prevents it from following your skis around the corner. Keep your hands close in, "in your pockets," as it were, and your body always tends to rotate around with your feet and skis.

But hockey stops, although useful in an emergency (when someone trips and falls in front of you on a catwalk, for example), are merely exercises, practice patterns, to develop what we can call upper-lower body independence. Real turns are something else, so let's move on. Our next step takes us halfway to linked short turns. We are going to practice what I call linked pivot slips— very similar to hockey stops but smoother, softer, and more continuous. Start

Figure 5.5 *Hockey stops and pivot slips. These two practice maneuvers are really the same. Link some hockey stops together and we call them linked pivot slips. The basic idea is simple: Twist your feet and skis vigorously beneath your body and slide. Not a round turn but a way to practice turning both feet and skis without turning the upper body.*

straight down the hill, then pivot your skis sideways just like a hockey stop, and slide a bit with loose relaxed feet. But before you have lost too much speed, put your downhill pole in for balance and support, and pivot your two skis back again to the other side, and keep sliding. And repeat. A series of softer, gentler hockey stops, if you will, in which you turn your skis first to one side, then to the other, without ever turning your body from side to side—at least that's what we hope will happen. This pattern—linked pivot slips—is much closer to short linked turns than to individual hockey stops.

Are linked pivot slips easy for you? If so, bravo. But if not, chances are that your lower back is too tense. To experience skiing with anticipation we need to "disconnect" our upper body from our legs, and this means relaxing the whole area from waist through hips and, particularly, our lower back. I'm talking about the hollow of your back, right above your hips. This is where a lot of the muscular connections between legs, thighs, and torso are located. So you'll find that if you can relax your lower back, your torso will be much less affected by movements of your legs.

Figure 5.6 *Feel the difference a relaxed back can make. Tighten your back against your hand or fist. Then suddenly relax the tension. Hips drop and shoulders slump a bit. This relaxed position will greatly facilitate turning with anticipation.*

Try this nifty experiment to see what I am talking about. Stand up (you can even do this at home without skis or boots) and place the back of one hand against the small of your back. Now tighten your back so that you feel your back muscles pushing against your hand. That's it! Do this really hard, so that you feel strong pressure between the small of your back and your hand. Hold that pressure a moment longer than you want to, almost till it hurts, and then, suddenly, relax. Whew.… Feels good. But at the same time, you probably noticed that your whole upper body slumps a bit: your shoulders round out, your hips drop, you sag a bit. That is exactly the loose, relaxed posture that is going to make upper and lower body independence a reality. By relaxing your lower back more than usual, you will be able to float along, unmoved and uninvolved by the muscular action of your legs and feet, guiding your skis. The opposite of a relaxed lower back—excess muscle tension in this area—is often visible in the form of a "hollow" back, which occurs when skiers stick their rear ends out while simultaneously pulling back elbows and shoulders. This hollow, or sway-backed, posture is a dead giveaway of excess muscle tension on skis. A relaxed lower back leads to an altogether different posture (see Fig. 5.6). Relaxing your lower back is an important idea, and one that really works. In this slightly slumped down, and much more relaxed posture, you will find that your hockey stops, and your pivot slips, and ultimately your short turns work much better, that only your feet and skis turn but your torso doesn't.

I said that linked pivot slips will bring you much closer to short linked turns than individual hockey stops will. And our next practice pattern, pre-turns, will bring us closer still. Remember, our goal now is not so much to make great individual turns, but to coordinate the linking of turns. That's what dynamic anticipation is really all about—not turning per se, but the easy transition between two turns. Not just how to start a short turn, but the way in which the end of one turn can actually launch the next one—the way a good short turn can wind you up and then release you like a coiled spring into a new turn. But inevitably, we will focus more on how we end one turn than on how we start the following turn. If we can finish a short turn just right, then the new turn simply happens. The tail end of our turn is the action, and the new turn merely the reaction.

Preturns and Practice

Since it is the "anticipated" tail end of one turn that "winds us up" for an easy entry into the following turn, I propose that we take that *tail end* of a short turn out of context and practice it by itself, as a kind of uphill hook, or separate uphill turn. Doing this will help us develop the "anticipated" quality we bring to the tail end of a short turn without having to deal with the moment of truth when we actually turn downhill (especially on a steep slope). This special practice pattern—the tail end of one short turn, taken out of context—is called a *preturn*. Once this separate preturn becomes comfortable, it will be easy to integrate it into real continuous old runs and enjoy the result effortlessly linked short turns. (By the way, preturns are seldom practiced in typical ski school settings. They are unglamorous; they demand far more patience than most instructors or most students are willing to commit. But they work wonders.)

Let's start with a few garden-variety, run-of-the-mill uphill turns. But I do want to ask you to make these simple uphill turns in a very relaxed way. Zoom diagonally down and across the hill in a traverse, and then relax your feet and flex your legs to start an easy turn up the hill, in the same direction, to a stop. Careful not to overtwist your feet as you make these uphill turns. If you simply relax your feet in a traverse, you will feel your skis start to slip a bit. Then you can flex forward into the front of your boots (especially your downhill boot, of course) to make your ski tips bite and pull you around up the hill. So far nothing new. Just a basic uphill turn, also called an uphill christie.

But now we'll begin to make a very special kind of uphill christie, introducing the full anticipation pattern in a couple of easy steps. Pick a target—say, a certain tree on the other side of the slope—and aim yourself and your skis toward that target as you push off. Then while you turn your skis up the hill to stop, make sure to keep your torso, your head, and your arms facing that target. Initially, it may take a muscular effort to keep your body from turning, but soon you will be able to do so simply by relaxing, relaxing all the muscular connections that tie your trunk to your legs (don't forget that relaxed lower back).

After a few successes, add the next element: your pole. Do it subtly. If you simply advance the tip of your downhill pole with wrist action while you turn up the hill, you'll find that that downhill pole plants itself neatly in the snow when you come to a stop. Because your upper body hasn't turned uphill with your skis, because you are still facing more or less down the slope, you wind up planting your pole in the snow well below your skis. Easy: a simple, almost automatic pole plant in line with your original direction of sliding. And it feels good, reassuring, something solid to support yourself on if you need to—and you will on steeper slopes. Now, when you come to a stop, take a moment and check out the relative alignment of your body and your skis. It should be similar to what you see in Fig. 5.7. Do you feel a little "wound up," or "twisted against yourself"? You should. Your skis, feet, and legs have all turned up the hill, while the rest of you is still aimed more down the hill. Soon this opposition, or twist, between upper and lower body will work to our advantage, pulling our skis back down the hill into the next turn. But for now, congratulations. You've made your first preturn.

Now, let's use our preturns to experience that almost automatic start, that almost automatic pivoting return toward the fall line that characterizes skiing with dynamic anticipation. Like this: Push off down and across the hill with a little more speed than before. Make another preturn, but this time don't turn all the way uphill to a stop. Instead, just as you start to turn up the hill, just as you start to feel that twist build between legs and torso, plant your pole and shift your weight to the top ski. What happens? Your skis begin to pivot back down the hill—on their own. As you shift to the top ski, releasing the turning pressure on your downhill ski, what's left to keep those skis aimed up the hill?

Figure 5.7 *A preturn to a stop. Feet and skis turn up the hill, but the skier's body doesn't turn and ends up still facing down the mountain, across the skis. A good preturn ends with a solid pole plant as you stop.*

Nothing. They unwind back beneath your torso, realigning with your body, with the direction in which you were originally moving. You have just experienced a gift—the automatic free start to a new turn, as your skis re-turn, or realign, themselves under your anticipated upper body.

You don't have to complete this turn. Instead you can fire off a series of preturn maneuvers across the slope—a nifty practice pattern called a garland (in this case, a preturn garland because a garland is any practice exercise repeated across the hill). From a medium steep traverse you can arc uphill, then shift weight, and pivot back to your original traverse direction: arc up, pivot back, arc up, pivot back. Can you feel the alternation of action and reaction, windup and release? I bet you can. It's not important to do these preturns perfectly; just do them. Again, it may take several days of playing with this sensation for it to feel right, feel comfortable, and natural. Don't wear yourself out by practicing too hard. Do a few preturns, turning uphill, then pivoting back.

Then relax and ski a fun run or two. And after a while, return to a little more pre-turn practice.

We're not quite through with preturns. There's more to come. But I want to remind you that preturns are only a helpful step along the path. Our goal lies elsewhere, not in separate preturns but in dynamic continuously linked turns. Let's make a few exciting turns, right now, using our preturn pattern as a springboard. You're going to love this sensation.

Once more, zoom down and across the slope fairly fast. Start a preturn up the hill. Feel your skis begin to "wind up" beneath you but before you lose very much speed, plant your downhill pole and shift to your top ski. And this time, as you do so, let your body keep moving forward down the hill. It's this extra move, this extra commitment (that we already know by the name of crossover), that makes the difference, and instead of merely unwinding back to their original traverse direction, your skis will peel off in a complete turn, a very special turn—special in the sense that you will have the strong impression

Figure 5.8 *Using a preturn to launch an effortless parallel turn. A long smooth preturn results in a long smooth turn; a short snappy preturn produces a short snappy turn. Action equals reaction. But don't forget, preturns are a practice move, not an end in themselves.*

that your skis have entered the turn by themselves—that you didn't do it. That's the result of the unwinding from the wound-up, or twisted-against-yourself position, at the end of your preturn.

In one sense, it's no big deal to start an easy turn. For some time (and some chapters) now, your turns have been quite easy to start. But they have generally been longer carved arcs, and you have tried to start them slowly and progressively. This time, however, you will have noticed that your skis come back into the fall line rather quickly because what's really happening is that

Figure 5.9 *How much anticipation is enough? In these two illustrations, we can compare two turns launched or triggered with different amounts of anticipation. In the first photo (left), slight anticipation leads to a slight pivoting, or unwinding, of the skis—a good recipe for a medium-radius turn. But in the second (right), a far more anticipated position produces far more (and faster) unwinding of the legs and skis. And a much shorter turn results.*

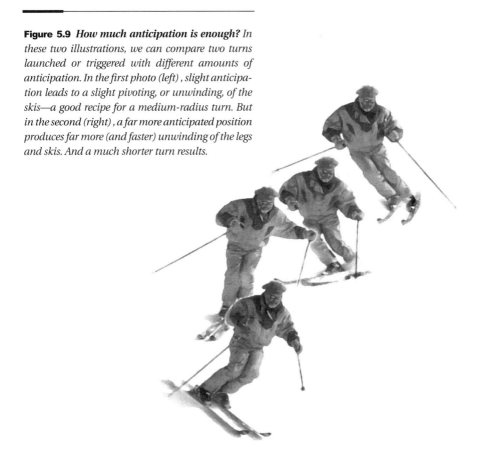

your feet and legs are pivoting all the way back to where they belong, lined up with your hips and your torso, which are aimed more or less down the hill. So you experience an effortless start to your turn through the "unwinding" of your lower body, and a pretty fast start too, appropriate to a short turn.

This leads us to an interesting point: The greater your anticipation, the faster this initial pivoting, or unwinding, of the skis, the faster you will enter the turn. And, of course, that is part of the secret of really short turns. When I say "more anticipation" or "less anticipation," I'm talking about how far across your skis you are facing, how far your upper body is aimed down the hill. If your torso were aimed only slightly across your skis, then your skis would pivot back only slightly down the hill at the start of the coming turn. But if your body is really facing directly down the hill at that critical moment when one turn ends and the next begins, why then your skis will unwind, or re-turn, all the way until they too are aimed straight down the hill. No matter how much anticipation you use (no matter how far across your skis you are facing at the end of your preturn or at the end of your previous turn), you will still reap the reward, a "free" initial pivoting of those skis down the hill into your next turn. Your skis, in short, will follow you down the hill. Frankly, this free initial pivoting is only really useful for short turns and for steep slopes. When we are cruising down open terrain in big carved arcs, we don't exactly want our skis to pivot rapidly down the hill. We would much prefer them to peel off into the new arc, slowly, patiently, progressively. But for short turns, and for those extra steep slopes where short turns are a necessity, anticipation is a must. And a well-executed preturn gives you the anticipation you need. Remember to make your preturns as soft and relaxed as you can. And note too that a given-sized preturn provides you with just the anticipation you need to make a downhill turn of the same size. That is to say, a very short preturn sets you up for a very short turn while a medium short preturn sets you up for a medium short turn, and so on.

I hope you will play around with this mode of triggering turns for a while: Preturn, shift weight, and turn back down the hill; preturn, shift weight, and turn back down the hill. An intriguing sensation. But we're still not 100 percent there. Because these are still more or less individual turns. And our ultimate goal is nothing less than a fluid sequence of turns—a linked chain of turns. And for this, separate preturns are not what we need.

When you watch expert skiers dance down steep slopes, you almost never see them make preturns, at least not separate preturns. In action, in real life skiing, the tail end of one turn functions exactly like a preturn to set you up, to wind you up, for the next turn. Remember: Our preturn is nothing more than the transition between two dynamic more or less short turns that has been taken out of context so that we can practice and feel the sensation of windup and release, turn and return. It's a great way of practicing, but not the way we want to ski.

Instead, let's try to recapture and reexperience this preturn effect as we continue turning down the slope. Start with a series of medium short turns. Only the first turn will be launched by a preturn. Head straight down the slope and make a positive snappy preturn to the left. As turning pressure starts to build underfoot, let your downhill pole virtually plant itself, and with a little support from it, shift to your top ski and voilà, both skis pivot back down the hill—almost on their own. Now the fun part. Keep it going! Press and steer and flex your outside leg as usual, riding that ski around, out of the fall line, completing this turn to the right. And once again, before you've gone too far, a pole plant and weight shift will trigger the next automatic return. That same old preturn-return sensation—only now, the end of a full turn has worked like a preturn to set you up, wind you up, for the following turn. And so on. You just keep turning. Keep on using the strong finish of one turn to trigger the following turn. That's the very essence of linking turns with dynamic anticipation, using the end of one turn to start the next.

When linking short turns, expert skiers really focus on how they finish turns, not how they start them. This is a fascinating point, worth underlining. When average intermediate skiers find themselves on a steep slope where they know they need to make short turns just to survive, they often get their priorities backward. They make a big muscular effort at the start of each turn and leave the finish, the tail end of the turn, to chance and fate. We are doing the exact opposite. We have, in essence, turned the intermediate skier's concerns inside out. Ultimately, we stop worrying about the start of each turn; we know our skis will turn back down the hill. It's a given. We concentrate most of our attention and most of our effort on a strong finish. As our skis come around to one side, our upper body is already preparing the next turn by continuing to face and move straight down the hill. We continue reaching straight down the hill with the next pole. And when enough twist has built up between legs, feet, and skis, on the one hand, and our torso, on the other, we can relax and let our skis pivot back down the hill. Note the difference between *letting* your skis start a turn and *forcing* them to turn. When skilled skiers link short turns straight down the fall line, they work the end of each turn and then relax into the beginning of the next turn. A great pattern: action-reaction, turn-return, wind up-unwind. Our situation now is the exact opposite of that of the nervous intermediate who is worried about whether or not those skis will actually turn. We *know* they're going to turn. And we are willing to let them do their thing.

What Now? Integrating the Short Turn Pattern

Now that we have a strong mental image of linking turns with anticipation, now that we have done some preliminary exercises like hockey stops and linked pivot-slips, and, finally, now that we have practiced enough preturns to get the feeling that our skis can complete a turn while our upper bodies move straight down the hill—what next? We need a strategy that will help us integrate and own this style of skiing, turn it from a new sensation into something natural, automatic.

Our strategy will be twofold. First, we are simply going to start linking shorter turns as often as possible, on groomed but not yet terribly steep slopes, confident that repetition will smooth things out, will polish the picture. The other half of our strategy will be to continue to refine preturns. Sorry. I know preturns are not much fun in themselves. Yet these strange uphill turns (in which skis, feet, and legs turn uphill while the skier's torso does not) are still the absolute best exercise for coordinating upper and lower body action in short turns. And there is a way to make preturns less dull and achieve a lot of preturn practice in a very short pitch. I'm talking about preturn garlands.

A preturn garland is nothing more than a series of preturns across the slope. In this case, the reaction phase simply brings your skis back to their

Figure 5.10 *Preturn garlands. Garlands are nothing more than exercises repeated across the hill. In this case: a preturn followed by just the start of a turn that quickly turns back into another preturn in the same direction. The advantage: lots of practice in a short space and time. An ideal way to reinforce strong new habits.*

original traverse line. So the pattern is: Arc up, pivot back, arc up, pivot back, all the way across the hill. The advantage of such garlands lies in the great number of repetitions that you can achieve in a short time and in very little vertical drop. A sort of concentrated and distilled practice session. Do such a garland—this series of "anticipated" turn beginnings—across the hill in one direction, then make a complete turn, and repeat your garland back in the other direction. Now that the basic pattern is there, concentrate on triggering your preturns with a relaxing folding action of the legs—the looser and softer your steering and controlling action, the less your upper body will turn, the more solid your anticipation. And I can promise you: The better your preturn garlands, the more effortless and efficient your linked short turns will become.

Figure 5.11 *The evolution of short turns on super-sidecut skis.* Every season, skilled skiers are learning how to make their short linked turns more and more carved by slowing down their entry into each arc and using higher edge angles. Very short and very carved turns are still more of a goal than a reality on the slopes.

And of course, that's the real payoff: just turning, turning continuously, flowing effortlessly from short turn to short turn. As you build more and more relaxation and looseness into your linked short turns, I want you to notice that even without consciously deciding to, you are probably using what I called soft weight shift as you move from one turn to the next. You relax your outside foot at the end of each turn and feel your weight flow comfortably, inevitably, onto the new outside ski. It just happens. Your turning skis hug the snow. There's no need and, ultimately, no time to step vigorously to the new ski when you're linking short turns or to lift the inside ski off the snow. Linked short turns are rhythmic, rapid, and altogether delightful. Stay loose, light, quick. And enjoy. It's taken a while, you've paid your dues, you've acquired a whole new skiing pattern. A major breakthrough.

Modern Short Swing: The Evolution of Short Turns

Long-radius turns have always been flowing and graceful, and today our easy carving super-sidecut skis make them more graceful than ever. Short turns in contrast often used to seem staccato, almost jerky, dynamic certainly but not necessarily graceful. But it doesn't have to be that way. Once again, our new skis have changed the rules and the nature of the game. As ski design continues to improve, as our shaped, or super-sidecut, skis get progressively shorter and softer in flex, it is becoming ever easier to carve turns—even, to some extent, when we make short turns.

Generally, there is a limit to how much or how deeply a ski can bend, and beyond that limit, you are going to slip your turns, not carve them. As you link shorter and shorter turns, you will soon reach that limit, and you will find yourself skidding or more exactly slipping through the arc of each short turn. Not to worry, this is completely normal, inevitable. But even when you find yourself slipping rather than carving in short turns, you still want those turns to be pretty round. Remember it's the round shape of a turn, not the force with which you turn, that gives you positive speed control on a steep slope.

Figure 5.12 *Doing it.* *Continuous short turns, linked together with dynamic anticipation—the goal of this chapter. Here the separate preturn has disappeared and, instead, the tail end of each turn acts just like a preturn to build up a twisting tension that can easily be released into the new turn. The end of one turn creates the next one.*

In the old days, athletic, jerky short turns were all the rage: Skiers hopped and heel-pushed their skis from side to side. It was effective but always a little awkward. Nowadays, experts try to round out even their shortest turns. It's all part of letting your skis do the work for you. And as always, the key to round turns is not to overdo the start, or "launching," phase of each turn. Let your skis return beneath you; don't force them. As a rule of thumb, I'd say that even in the shortest of turns, you don't want to twist your skis across the fall line. Your skis will pivot down the hill until they are once again lined up with your hips and trunk. That's all you need. Be prepared to ride and guide your skis through the second half of the turn with a certain amount of patience and finesse. Don't rush it. If you get too excited and twist or pivot your skis too hard, too far, then you'll feel the tails of your skis skid out. Instead, even in the shortest turns, let your skis simply unwind beneath you, balance on your outside ski, and ride it around; don't force it. Even in the shortest linked turns, or should I say especially in the shortest linked turns, a round track is a sign of mastery. And of course, round turns always feel great.

Short turns too, when well done, always feel great. They are a paradox, inside and out. Short turns are athletic and relaxed at the same time. The skis and feet are active; the skier's body isn't. Above all, linked short turns and the dynamic anticipation that makes them possible open the door to mastering the biggest challenge in modern skiing—bumps, or moguls. And that's what we'll look at next.

IN SUMMARY

- Expert skiers are always turning: Continuous turns are more graceful and efficient than individual turns separated by traverses. The trick to continuous turns is continuous, smooth, rhythmic motion—no frozen, static, dead moments during which the skier simply waits.

- In this age of carved turns on super-sidecut skis, fall-line skiing with linked short-radius turns is no longer as important as it once was. But linked short turns are essential for handling bumps and steeps where nothing else works.

- A special movement pattern comes into play when a skier links very short turns straight down the hill: dynamic anticipation (active skis, feet, and legs turning back and forth beneath a relatively quiet, un-turning upper body). As the skis finish one turn, the body appears to be already facing and moving down the hill, "anticipating" the next turn.

- More than anything, dynamic anticipation depends on relaxation. The muscular connections between torso and legs need to remain loose and flexible. Such relaxation allows the feet and skis to turn freely without twisting the skier's body from side to side.

- The best way to practice linking short turns with dynamic anticipation is to take the tail end of one turn out of context and practice it separately as a preturn. You can practice preturns separately or link them together as preturn garlands across the slope. In real skiing, one almost never sees separate preturns; instead, the end of one short turn acts just like a preturn to launch the next short turn.

- Short turns with anticipation create a pattern of action and reaction: turning, then returning; winding up the legs beneath one's body, then allowing them to unwind into the coming turn—a constant alternation. The end of one turn is the action; the start of the next turn, the reaction.

Part II

Bumps and Powder Simplified

CHAPTER 6

Making Friends with Bumps

The Challenge That Won't Go Away

Mean moguls have terrorized skiers as long as I can remember. It's time to declare a truce. Time to take some time and figure this one out. Because bump skiing can be as aesthetic as anything this side of two feet of champagne powder. Rising and falling, slipping and snaking through and between and around these frozen standing waves on the slope. A salsa rhythm pulsing in your head. Watching your skis—your very own skis!—arc over a crest, dive into a deep man-eating gully, only to rise again, phoenixlike over the next miniature mountain of a mogul ... and knowing that everything is okay, that nothing bad can happen to you, that you belong here against all odds. It's enough to make you smile, grin like a Cheshire cat, whoop with delight. What? Hasn't happened yet? I promise: It's about to.

Bumps are always there. You can avoid trails and runs with bumps; you can ski around most bumpy areas on the mountain. But as a modern skier, you can't really get away from bumps or from the challenge they represent. Why not make friends with bumps? You already have the technical skiing skills you need. Making your peace with bumps and the next step, enjoying bumps, is mostly a matter of strategy and timing.

Bumps are sometimes called moguls, although in more than thirty years of professional skiing I have yet to figure out where the word "mogul" comes

Figure 6.1 *Real moguls, real bumps.* This head-on view of a mogul field shows the rhythmic but always slightly irregular pattern of real-life bumps. In reality, every bump is a little different. And some are really weird.

from. The reason moguls exist is because any hump, any natural high spot, on a groomed ski slope facilitates turning. Such high spots serve as pivot points where skiers can easily pivot their skis into a new direction with less friction from the snow. As a result most skiers, consciously or unconsciously, tend to make their turns on high spots on the snow. Then the repeated passage of turning and skidding skis over the same spot, scrapes away ever more snow, transforming that high spot into a bump. That's how moguls are formed. Skiers make them while looking for easier turns. And yet, as moguls grow and spread and deepen with the continuous passage of skiers, they turn from allies to enemies. I'm sure you know exactly what I mean.

Moguls are always a challenge, a major challenge for all skiers, at all skill levels. No, not just *a* major challenge, but *the* major challenge—for most ski instructors too. Bumps are a bugaboo, period. A tiny minority of skiers actually enjoys skiing bumps—I certainly do—and I'm pretty sure I can help you join their ranks.

Mogul skiing isn't nearly as aesthetic as powder skiing, of course, but the satisfaction of turning these minefields into playgrounds is immense. I've often compared skiing to a dance with the mountain. Pursuing this metaphor, I'd compare powder skiing to a dreamlike waltz, and mogul skiing to fast-paced jazz dancing. But of all the various breakthroughs I propose in this book, making friends with moguls may well be the most satisfying. It's quite an accomplishment.

Super-Sidecut Skis and Bumps

But before we dive into the bumps (metaphorically speaking), I want to tell you that your modern shaped skis are going to make your life a lot easier in moguls. Why? It's true that, in one sense, we don't absolutely need the deep sidecut of a modern ski to make turns through the bumps because the curved shape of our turn will be created by the curved shape of each bump and its gully, not by the sidecut of our skis. And sure enough, top-level mogul competitors, right up to those in the Olympics, tend to use skis with less side-cut than racers in any other discipline. But for the rest of us, who are skiing bumps for pleasure and not against a stopwatch, today's super-sidecut skis offer two very terrific advantages. First, because they are significantly shorter than traditional skis, they fit much more easily into the limited space between tight bumps. They are easier to maneuver in such close quarters. Equally important, modern skis give one a greater sense of security in the bumps because of how quickly they can turn. You can feel confident that if a tight turn-finish is needed (in the limited space between bumps), then it will be easy to throw one in. Nowadays, I can ski a straighter and braver line through the moguls than I used to simply because I know that when the need arises, I can turn my deep sidecut skis on a dime. Paradoxically, since quick, snappy turn-finishes are always an option, I tend not to turn as much. So you can con-gratulate yourself on being a modern skier. You've got the right stuff on your feet. Bumps have never been easier—although easier is all too relative.

Why Are Bumps So Difficult?

What makes bumps so hard to ski? Bumps pose a number of problems: quick-ness and timing, balance in changing terrain, finding a good line, and, of course, speed control. On second thought, there may be only one—speed con-trol. If we were able to ski bumps more slowly, then everything would become easier. Because what actually flusters most skiers in bumps is that their skis run away with them. It's happened to you, I'm sure. It happens to everyone. You make one bump turn, you're okay; you make another one and suddenly your skis speed up. It feels like they are shooting right out from under you, and before you know it you're racing across the slope, hitting the moguls like so many speed bumps, and wondering how to slow down. Sound familiar?

I've enjoyed bump skiing for years, and when I had surgery to repair a broken anterior cruciate ligament in my knee some years ago, I realized I had to become a smoother and more efficient bumps skier if I wanted to continue enjoying moguls. I did. But my real education in bump skiing, in what makes it either impossibly hard or invitingly easy, has been my five-day intensive ski courses in Aspen. These courses attract wonderfully motivated students, and predictably, the most advanced among them are really keen to master moguls. They've given me a wonderful opportunity to focus and refine and modify my approach to bump skiing. To a person, the biggest problem these very advanced skiers face in bumps is that of speed control, the runaway skis syndrome I described above. A secondary but very real problem is the difficulty most skiers experience trying to get both skis to turn at the same time in bumps. Even when there's no trace of a stem on normal slopes, it can come back to haunt you in bumps with a one-two, step-step action at the top of a mogul that guarantees trouble. In this chapter I'm going to share the solutions I've worked out for both these problems. And I can almost guarantee that if you can handle short linked turns with anticipation (the focus of our previous chapter), then your bump adventures will be a success.

But to return to our number one question—why are bumps so hard?—I want to repeat that the main obstacle to making friends with bumps is speed control, or its lack. The problem is almost universal, and so is the answer. I've learned that if I can offer skiers a way to ski slowly through moguls, then all the other technical elements will fall into place. Ultimately, you will be able to ski bumps just as fast as you desire or dare. But first things first.

I'm going to spill the beans and tell all, give away the punch line as it were, right here at the start of this chapter. The reason your skis tend to accelerate out from under you in bumps is almost always an excess of muscular tension. And the solution is simple: sideslipping. These two bald assertions definitely demand an explanation.

Let's start with my observation that most skiers are too tense in the bumps. It's hard not to be tense. To less-experienced skiers every bump turn looks like a crisis, so they treat it like one. A self-fulfilling prophecy. These skiers make strong, powerful, more or less sudden moves to start their skis turning around the bump, and suddenly their edges "rail in," and "catch" in the snow. Then they discover that in bumps, a strongly edged ski can only track ahead in a straight line, accelerating all the way.

What's going on here? In bumps we are always on the brink of having too much edging. Imagine yourself standing on the steep flank of a mogul. Your body is more or less vertical, your skis more or less horizontal, but because the angle of the snow on the flank of the bump is very steep, you'll notice that your skis have an extreme edge angle to the snow. You didn't edge them; the steep slope creates this high edge angle. So, with skis already edged much more than normal, all it takes is a little bit of extra tension in your foot to make those edges grab and "rail in" and shoot your skis forward. Since any sudden tension, in any part of your body, gets transmitted right down through the kinetic chain to your feet and boots, we can see that excess muscle tension is the culprit making our skis catch and shoot out from under us. There you are, hanging on for dear life in the back seat.

Remember Pogo, that adorable fuzzy little cartoon character? Pogo once said, "We have seen the enemy and he is us." And that's doubly true in bumps. Any sudden, last-minute, tense or jerky movements will cause your skis to overedge and run away, triggering the full catastrophe. If we could somehow stay more relaxed in the bumps, we'd have a much better chance of keeping it together, rounding out our turns, and slowing down. But how on earth are we to do this?

Bumps are damn hard, awkward, even scary. It's easy to think that we have to psych ourselves up for a real struggle, to be strong and athletic just to survive in moguls. Wrong. In fact, that's the problem. But because relaxing, and especially relaxing in a tough situation, is so nonintuitive, we need a trick, a helper. And that trick is sideslipping. As I suggest this, I can almost hear certain eager and ambitious skiers groan and complain: I don't want to *sideslip* bumps, I want to *ski* them! Trust me, you will—better than you thought was possible. But I want to make sure you can sideslip them first. For several reasons.

Bumps are like old friends. You put up with a lot because they are your bumps; you know them. It's as if you grew up together, went to school together. And in a sense you did. Moguls are living things: They change, grow, change, keep growing, get tougher, change and keep changing. From day to day. And also from season to season. Our favorite ski mountains and their bumps keep evolving, just as we do as skiers.

Originally, I picked up my passion for bumps at Squaw Valley and saw the moguls there change as skis and techniques and skiers changed. Once upon a time, I remember, giant bumps on the West Face of KT-22 were an invitation to long round turns on 215-cm skis, but only a few years later, miniature cliffs had closed out these sweeping mogul lines. But one adapts. I adapted and kept on bumping. Loving it.

Moving to Telluride in the 1970s exposed me to new bump shapes, new skiers with new styles, new tricks, quicker feet, and ever-shorter skis. Gnarly and relentless, Telluride bumps turned me into a Telluride bump skier. Sort of. Great training, at any rate. When I visited other Colorado ski areas, the bumps always seemed forgiving by comparison. Then, just when I thought I was getting somewhere as a bump skier, Pronto, the most challenging bump run at Vail, brought me back to reality. In all the seasons I taught at Vail, I never made one perfect run down Pronto. But I kept trying. Enjoying each crisis. Today my newest, shortest skis are rewriting all my bump scenarios. Tough bumps are less tough, and it isn't because I'm getting any tougher, or quicker, or braver. Shorter shaped skis work like time machines, transporting us back to an era of widely spaced, beautifully shaped moguls. There's always a line. You always slip through the tightest spots. And, yes, I think bumps are getting better again. I'm sure of it.

Figure 6.2 *The basic bump turn. This is a pattern we will pursue and develop throughout this chapter: an anticipated start on the crest of the bump; a slow patient arcing turn around the bump; and a delayed finish below the bump itself.*

First and foremost, sideslipping really is a special form of relaxing, relaxing your feet in a very specific ski-technical sense. It's a kind of relaxation you can practice and access whenever you need to as opposed to the more nebulous notion of simply ordering your body to calm down, which almost never works. Additionally, while you're sideslipping, your skis are brushing over the snow, which adds friction that helps slow you down. And finally, as you sideslip through moguls, with loose, relaxed feet, your skis are much more likely to follow the rounded shapes in the terrain; and your turns will actually fit the bumpy terrain better.

But what about carving? And edges? Not to worry. The bumps themselves (and their gullies) will guide our skis in more or less round arcs. I view this as a liberating insight: In moguls we don't need to edge our skis in order to make turns. It's not the skis' sidecut that makes them arc around as it does on a smooth packed slope, but rather the rounded shape of the bump. A well-waxed two-by-four would probably turn almost as well. The main task of the bump skier, or would-be bump skier, is to relax, slip, and maintain good balance while the bumps themselves determine the skis' path. Sounds good. But of course, it will take us a while to get there.

Since the whole game of bump skiing is so complex, I'm going to break easy and relaxed bump skiing into several parts, which we'll tackle separately, step by step. To start we'll look at individual turns: exactly where and how to trigger your bump turns, how to control your speed once the turn has started, how to ski a line that lets you finish your turns in the right place. And only then will we go on to put individual turns together into long satisfying bump runs.

Both Skis Together: Starting Bump Turns

Often my students ask me: Should I turn over the top of the bump? Or go around the bump? The best answer is: Do both. In fact, there's a general pattern that works well in all kinds of bumps, from baby minibumps to giant Jaws-sized moguls. You do indeed start your turn on or near the top of the bump, but then

Figure 6.3 *Where to turn? As a skier passes over the crest or highest spot on a bump, there is a magic moment—magic split second would be more like it— when the skis are only touching the snow underfoot. Tips and tails are in the air. Reduced friction makes this the perfect place, and the perfect moment, to start a bump turn.*

you allow your skis to follow the contour of that bump down into the gully that wraps around it. Your turn finishes beneath the bump itself, often right against the top of the next mogul below, and you're ready to do it all over again. But now, we want to figure out the best way to start your bump turns.

I'm pretty sure you've been starting your turns on the top, or crest, of bumps, even without anyone suggesting it. It's obvious. But look closer. Picture yourself just standing (not moving or sliding) on the very crest of a big rounded bump—I mean standing with your two feet smack on the top of this bump. Clearly both the tips and the tails of your skis will be sticking out in space. Only a small area of the ski under your boot will be in contact with the snow. Fine. This means that with almost no effort, you can gently, lightly, swivel or pivot or rock your feet from side to side. And your skis, freed from the grip and friction of the snow, will also pivot easily, mostly in the air. This same easy pivoting of both skis—only a few degrees, not a big twist—is what starts your bump turn. To take advantage of this magic spot, this free pivot point, all you have to do is make your move just as your feet pass over the high point, or crest, of each bump. It's particularly appropriate to talk about your *feet* here, and not your skis, because your skis, even the shortest, modern, super-sidecut skis, are quite long compared to the shape of a single bump—so that different parts of your skis (tips, bindings, tails) can be over different parts of the bump at the same moment. As usual, your feet are where the action is.

Your feet, and only your feet, have the job of starting a bump turn. All it takes is a nudge, a small movement of both feet as you pass over the crest of the bump and your skis will respond effortlessly. It's all a matter of timing. Do it there. Right there! Right on the crest. And not one or two or three feet past the top of that bump.

To make sure you start each bump turn at the right moment, on the right spot, just mark that spot with your downhill pole—with wrist action, please, and not by swinging your arm. Simply tap the tip of your pole on the very crest of the bump, and at the same moment, as gently, as subtly as you dare, twist both feet down the hill.

Does this sound like heresy? Like unusual, maybe even contradictory, advice? It should because for many chapters now, I've been encouraging you *not* simply to twist your skis into a new direction but instead to shift your weight onto your new outside ski and to ride that ski as it bends and arcs its way into a turn. Bumps, however, are more than just a bit different. Instead of relying on ski design to create the arc of our turn, in moguls all we do is to encourage our skis to follow the round shape of the bump and its gully. The shape of our turn is already there, inscribed in the snow, below us. If we can only get our skis started turning, that rounded shape will take over and guide our skis around the bump. Neat. (Earlier in this book I said that one of the key themes in expert skiing was that instead of turning our skis, we want to let our skis turn us. This is similar. Skilled bump skiers allow the curved, rounded shape of bumps and their gullies to do the turning for them.)

But it doesn't always work. All too often skiers arrive on top of a bump and before they know it, without ever intending to stem, they find that one foot and ski is reaching out—in V-shaped stem!—into the gully, while the other foot seems stuck there on top of the bump. The turn more or less starts, but the skier has to jerk the inside ski up out of the snow and slam it back in beside the ski that started all the trouble ... and hang on. I'm pretty sure most skiers have experienced this. Have you? It is your body betraying you, playing for safety, trying to guarantee a turn at all costs, and guaranteeing a bad one. Because in bumps, either both skis turn together, or you're in big trouble. What's really going on here is a classic case of late weight shift, a stem christie, for sure. And this sort of stemmed one-ski start has a way of appearing in the bumps, even long after all your turns on smooth slopes are perfectly parallel. It's the past coming back to haunt you. Let's look at this problem of starting the turn in detail:

Our nervous skier arrives at the top of a bump standing on the downhill ski. In a sort of automatic response, the top foot starts reaching out and turning, but since that top foot and ski are light, they get away, they turn and drop off the top of the bump into the gully. But the skier is left behind, high and dry, with all the weight still on that inside ski that now has to be jerked out of the snow to catch up. Stem christie starts are never very elegant, but in bumps they are an unmitigated disaster.

Your job is to figure out a way to make both skis begin each bump turn together—this is essential. Because in such rapidly changing terrain, if one ski gets away on its own, you will feel that your skis and feet are working against each other. And you'll totally out of balance. However, in my experience there is no best way to guarantee that both skis pivot into a bump turn together. At least there is no best way for every skier. So I'm going to suggest several different approaches, and you can figure out which one works best for you.

The first and potentially easiest way to start a bump turn is simply to turn both feet, a few degrees, down the hill—not across the fall line, just a bit downhill. What of weight shift? Don't worry, you'll probably wind up on your outside ski anyway, and you don't need strong weight transfer in bumps because you don't have to bend the edge of your ski into an arc: Remember, the bump is making the turn for you. But if this is a difficult image or an awkward move for you, try this: Go back to early weight shift; make sure you are standing on your uphill ski before you start to guide it around that bump and into the gully. Or, to accomplish the same end, play with that terrific soft weight shift move that we met first at the end of Chapter 4. To make a right turn around a bump, just collapse or fold your right leg as you reach the crest of that bump. As long as you aren't standing on your inside ski at the moment the turn begins, you will discover that both skis turn together. And if both skis start down the hill together, that means they will encounter the same terrain at the same time and give you a better ride.

To experiment with different ways of making both skis turn together in bumps, you need bumps, a field of moguls, but—please—make sure they are easy, small, and well-rounded bumps. No big frozen Volkswagen-sized bumps. No sharp and cliffy bumps. Baby practice bumps, are in order—"bimps," as my friend Tim Petrick used to call them. Once you've located your field of practice bimps, see what you can do, focusing exclusively on turning both skis at the same time. Talk to yourself if you have to; remind yourself of your goal; whisper. Now, as you slide over an easy bump, try to guide both boots, both skis, together into an easy turn—easy because this practice bump slope should be so low-angle that speed control isn't an issue.

Even so, you may have noticed that something is missing in my description of how we are going to get both skis to turn together on a bump. How about anticipation? That windup and release mechanism we spent so much time on in the previous chapter? Remember that pattern in which the upper body is already moving down the hill, already halfway around the turn, as the feet begin to follow it? Doesn't that make sense in bumps too? Of course it does. And the more anticipation you can bring to the bumps, the better your turns will be. Remember, I've only been talking about guiding both feet into the turn together. And that too is another way of talking about anticipation: the feet actively

Figure 6.4 *The anticipated start of a mogul turn. In a position of maximum anticipation, with the upper body facing straight down the hill, only the feet and skis need to pivot downhill and around the bump. It's as though the skier's body was already halfway around the turn even before it starts.*

turning beneath a quiet, stable upper body. So if you can face, and look, and move straight down the hill at the start of each bump turn, so much the better. But I still want you to concentrate on your feet, on getting both feet, both skis to turn at the same time. Because if we mess up the start of a bump turn with a stem, by turning one foot before the other, nothing can save it.

But I trust you. And I trust you to solve this all-too-common hang-up at the beginning of a mogul turn. As soon as your skis start cooperating and pivoting together on top of the bumps, we can go on to deal with a bigger challenge: speed control.

Speed Control in Bumps

Even when your skis don't catch and shoot across the hill from the sort of excess muscle tension I described earlier, speed control is still a big issue in mogul skiing. That's because every bump turn, even a perfect one, begins with a rush of acceleration. The angle of the snow changes so abruptly from the relatively flat top of a bump to its steep sides and gully, that each time you turn your skis downhill over a bump you experience real acceleration. This sudden acceleration is an inevitable part of every bump turn; the bigger and steeper the bumps, the faster your skis will accelerate underneath you at the start of each turn. It's disconcerting, but it's part of the mogul game. In addition, many skiers wind up fighting a kind of runaway-skis syndrome at the start of these turns. The skis are running away due to overedging, which in turn is due to excess muscle tension. It's easy to compound the problem by tensing up even more as you feel your skis getting away from you.

Luckily, we have an all-purpose strategy for developing efficient, easy speed control in bumps, a strategy that will initially help you to ski bumps slowly, but eventually will let you ski bumps at any speed you find comfortable. There are two parts to my approach. The first involves sideslipping, and the second focuses on the line that we take around and through the bumps, a line that will give us room to slow down by finishing our turns. Let's get started.

And to get started we'll need slightly bigger bumps, not bimps any more but bumps that are not too big either—real bumps. Not to worry, we won't attack this new slope headlong. Instead I'm going to ask you to humor me and sideslip all the way down through this bump field without turning. It's not as easy as you might think, but it's a lot easier than turning on every bump. Stand in a relaxed and anticipated position as you do this—your torso facing more or less down the hill, hands spread, downhill pole ready, just as though you were about to turn. Now relax your feet, release your edges, and slide. Use some finesse to guide your sideslipping skis around awkward spots in the bumps, but keep sliding. And try not to feel silly. It may look as though you found these bumps too hard and are just trying to bail out in one piece. Don't worry, no one is watching. I simply want to get you used to sideslipping in a new and strange situation. It isn't hard. (We discussed sideslipping at length in Chapter 2, if you need a review.)

Next, I'd like to ask you to ski this somewhat more serious mogul slope as a series of *pivots* (on top of each bump) and *slips* (letting your skis slide smoothly down to the next bump crest). Pivot-slips are a hot tip for making friends with bumps. We already practiced them on smooth groomed steeps in Chapter 5—from an anticipated body position, plant your pole, pivot your skis, and slide … and repeat. Now, it turns out that if you try this in bumps—pivoting on the crest of each bump—you won't really wind up just sideslipping down the hill to the next bump. Instead, the curved shapes of the bumps take over, and although slipping, your skis tend to slip in more or less round turns. Often, working through this pattern with students, I'll ask my group to watch me make a series of pivots and sideslips at very slow speed through some serious bumps. "No way," my students often say. "You weren't sideslipping at all; you were turning." Not exactly. The bumps were actually turning my slipping skis for me. I want you to play with this pattern for a while—pivoting both skis and sideslipping. You will find it is not altogether ungraceful, and above all, you will have the impression of really being in control, of really having a lot of extra time between bumps. This is just about the slowest way you can ease down through the bumps, and it provides a good base for better turns. Pivot and slip . . . pivot and slip …

Now, as soon as your comfort level rises, thanks to our little sideslipping game, I want you to ease back toward more rounded turns. It's easy. Just start your turns more slowly (still pivoting your feet, but just barely) and let your skis slip around the bump in a slow arc rather than drifting sideways. In short, use all the same movements, but more gently: the same but less—less turning, less of a conscious effort to sideslip. Keep guiding your skis with very relaxed feet, so that you still wind up sideslipping quite a bit. Brushing your turns, smearing your turns, slipping your turns, never biting in with your edges. Letting your skis slip around each bump, not forcing them. Remember, don't rush it. Don't hurry. Start the turn, let it go. Start the turn, let it go …

Already, because your legs and feet are more relaxed, because your skis

Figure 6.5 *Sideslipping through bumps. This is a great way to loosen up in moguls. If you buy my idea that excessive muscular tension is the biggest obstacle to easy mogul skiing, then it follows that any maneuver that will help you relax in bumps will improve your bump experience. Sideslipping is nothing more than applied relaxation. Sideslip a bit through bumps and watch your mogul skiing come together.*

are slipping not edging, you'll find you are skiing these bumps more slowly, more in control. But there's more.

I want to focus on your line now, the line your skis take around each bump. Sideslipping helps us control our speed, but we learned long ago that skiing a round line is a more efficient way of slowing down—slowing down by means of turn shape rather than by scraping the snow. And bumps are no exception. But there just isn't very much space in a tight mogul field. So the trick is finding a way to fit a round turn into the anything-but-round geometry of most bumps.

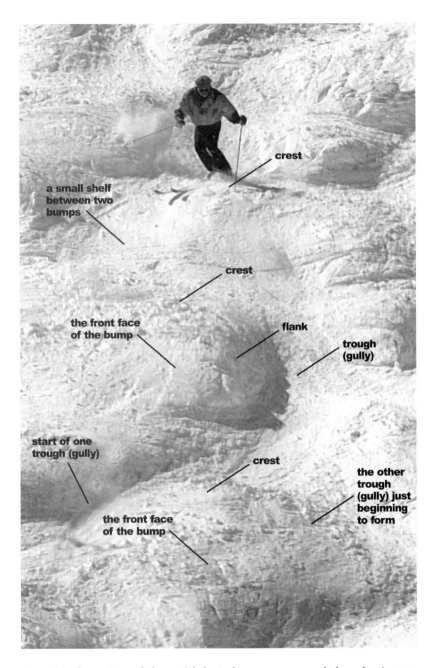

Figure 6.6 *The anatomy of a bump. It helps to share a common vocabulary when it comes to bumps. Here we can see the crest of the bump, the flank on either side of the bump, the front face of the bump, the trough that wraps around the bump on both sides, and the short shelf, or smooth section, below the bump, leading to new bumps down the hill.*

Like snowflakes, every bump is different. But generally, beneath the bump itself, the gullies widen out and we usually find a little extra room in the form of a slanted shelf of snow leading to the crest of the next bump down the hill. (Painting a perfect picture of an average bump in words is quite a challenge, so look at Fig. 6.6 to make sure we share the same mental image of a modern mogul.) And this extra space below the bump is crucial if we want to round out the tail end of our bump turns and scrub off some of the extra speed we picked up at the start of the turn. Skilled bump skiers start their turns in a relatively slow, relaxed manner—they're in no hurry to twist their skis across the fall line. They take a slower, rounder path than average skiers do. And they end this round path underneath the mogul itself—the only place where there's enough room for a strong turn finish. This is exactly the line that we are going to practice skiing now, a line that has a big part to play in controlling our speed in bumps.

Bump skiing seems so challenging, so quick and athletic, that my description of turning slowly around bumps may seem a little odd, a little out of place. But it's all relative. I really want to encourage you to turn as slowly and progressively as possible around each bump. Maybe the key word here is "progressive." Whatever you do, don't put all your turning effort into the very start of your bump turns. Stretch the curve of your turns out so that they finish below the bump, not halfway down the bump but completely below it. Our goal is a "delayed" finish to our bump turn—delayed, at least, until you have dropped down below the gully—until you finally have enough room to do something, to complete your turn. And this is where your shaped, or deepsidecut, ski will really shine. All that's needed is a slight flexing, a steering/tipping movement of the foot, and, presto, that modern ski can whip around in a flash, and you've lost all that excess speed.

And that's all we need to control our speed in moguls: a combination of relaxed feet and soft edging—sideslipping—and an intelligent line that leads around the bump and finishes beneath it: a good dose of basic bump skiing theory—how and where to start our bump turns, how to control our speed in the bumps. Now we need to go out and do it. But before we start practicing, I'd like to emphasize that I've really been talking about bump skiing for the rest of us—relaxed bump skiing, bump skiing for everyman and everywoman—not bump skiing for heroes. Because not all bump skiers want to slow down. In mogul competitions, each run is timed and greater speed is a plus. Young competitive bump skiers never round out their turns beneath each bump. They ski as straight and as fast a line as possible with fiendish grins on their faces. They can't get enough speed.

Not me. Not most skiers. I'm neither quick enough, strong enough, or daring enough to ski moguls at top speed. Being able to slow down, to maintain a relaxed and steady pace through challenging bumps, has been a must for me and for my students over the years. The key to this positive speed control, as we have seen, is twofold. One part involves following a comfortable line, wrapping your turn around the bump, and finding space beneath it to complete that turn. The other part is to avoid edging your skis, to let them slip smoothly and softly through the bumps. Remember that the shape of your turn is already right there in front of you, carved out of the slope in the shape of the bump and its gully. If you can simply maintain your balance and relax your feet, your skis will follow this curved line.

The moral of the story: In bumps, less is more. Excess turning, excess tension, and excess edging are the problem. The solution: Relax and turn less, and the bump will do it for you—I promise. Above all, relax your feet. In bumps, I want your skis to brush the snow smoothly rather than bite into it. Slip, don't try to carve. Your turns will still be round and elegant, and your skis won't run away from you. Now let's put these ideas into action.

Beyond Basics: Hot Tips for Better Bump Turns

I hope you'll start practicing on extremely easy bumps. It's humbling for any ski pro to admit that sometimes perfect, friendly terrain can be the best instructor of all, but it's true. And nowhere truer than in bumps. Motivated instructors are constantly searching their mountains for bumps that are perfect for practice and learning, for introductory bumps. Alas, those rare fields of bumps that are ideal for learning—not too steep, with smallish, rounded, and rhythmic moguls—tend not to last very long. They grow steeper and more challenging with the daily passage of skiers, or an eager-beaver mountain grooming crew flattens them back into a textbook corduroy slope. So keep your eyes peeled, or ask an instructor or a local: Where can I find the best easy practice bumps on this mountain? It's important to up the ante progressively. At each stage, keep looking for moguls that are just a wee bit harder than bumps you already find comfortable. And start skiing them.

I am going to suggest several different mogul moves, different tactics that you can focus your attention on while you ski bumps. But don't make the mistake of trying to remember or concentrate on everything I suggest all at once. If you are like me, in the thick of the mogul action, you won't be able to concentrate on more than one technical element at a time.

Start slowly. Slide up to your first bump with very little speed. You really don't need any speed because you have a lot of anticipation, right? More than anything else, anticipation (the subject of our previous chapter) is what allows me to relax at the start of a bump turn. Initially, I recommended a small foot-pivoting action to get you going at the top of each baby bump. But as the bumps get bigger and more serious, anticipation and the unwinding, or return to center from an anticipated position, is what will pull your skis effortlessly into each new bump turn. How much anticipation? Total anticipation. The max. In real moguls, your upper body should already be facing straight down the hill, straight down the fall line, as you start to turn. To be sure you stay as anticipated as possible, simply reach and plant your downhill pole straight down the hill below you, even further down the hill than normal. And then lean on it. Support yourself on this pole for a brief instant as you tilt forward, down the hill, and allow your feet to pivot, or return back, beneath you. Your

goal should be a truly relaxed start to each turn, letting your skis turn back down the hill more than forcing them to turn.

Go on. Play with this idea. Experiment to see how little you have to do to get your skis to pivot patiently down the hill and into the gully, provided your body is already facing that direction. The slower you're moving as you approach the crest of your bump, the easier the whole business will seem.

Next, work on your pole action. I'd like to

Figure 6.7 *Pole action in bumps: reaching for the next turn. Use wrist action to reach rapidly with the new pole (the pole on the outside of your turn) toward the next bump down the slope. This forward flick of the pole is not an option but a must in serious moguls. It keeps you anticipated, moves you forward, keeps you over your skis, and readies you, physically and psychologically, for the next turn.*

share a bump skier's trick with you now, one that will pull everything together. It's not enough just to plant your downhill pole and support yourself on it as you start your bump turn. Your other hand and pole, the one on the outside of the coming turn, also has a big job to do. As soon as you feel your ski tips begin to turn, I want you to flick the point of this outside pole ahead, ahead of your hand and down the hill. (Look at Fig. 6.7 to see how fast that outside pole moves ahead and down the hill.)

It's as though you are already reaching down the mountain for your next turn well before your skis have finished the current one. The tip of your outside pole is preceding you, leading you down the hill, toward the next bump and your next turn. This forward reaching/flicking of the outside hand and pole accomplishes several things at once. By reaching straight down the fall line (never across the hill), you make sure that you stay anticipated, that your body continues to move straight down the mountain and doesn't swing around with your skis, to face across the slope.

Reaching strongly downhill also moves or tilts your whole body—and your center of gravity—down the mountain. And this guarantees that you will keep up with your skis as they accelerate down the steep flank of the bump. This simple hand/pole action really rebalances you forward. If you forget to reach down the hill, and leave your outside hand parked by your hip as you turn, you will experience the definite sensation of being left back on your heels, of your skis running out from underneath you. Don't let this happen. Reach. And reach. And reach again.

Another point: In bumps, try to keep your feet and skis together. In Chapter 1, I warned you against jamming your feet and skis together, and I stressed that independent leg action is a hallmark of modern skiing. True enough. Yet bumps are almost an exception to this rule. Skilled bump skiers always keep their feet close together. Why? Mainly so that their two skis will encounter the same shapes as they slide through the moguls. If you ski moguls in a wide stance, one ski can climb up the side of a bump while the other dives down into a trough. You can imagine the problem. But in a narrow stance, both skis will float up and down over the same shapes at the same time—a lot easier to deal with.

And there's a bonus in maintaining a narrower-than-normal stance in bumps. With your legs close together, you won't be able to make overly powerful twisting movements when you turn (it's as though one leg blocks the rotation of the other). As a result, you will wind up starting and guiding your bump turns with smaller, gentler foot and leg movements. It's very easy to overpower your skis in a wide-track stance. Indeed, we'll find that a narrower-than-normal stance is ideal for both kinds of skiing we're exploring in this section of this book—bumps and powder.

Finally, pay attention to your feet. Often you should feel that only your feet are actively turning, that only your feet are skiing, that only your feet are guiding your skis around each bump. I'm tempted to call this effect "super anticipation." Instead of active legs beneath a quiet body, you experience only active feet, way down there on the snow. Do you remember my little exercise in which you sat on the edge of a table and moved your dangling feet in small semicircles? Try it again now, on the chairlift, between bump runs, just to tune in to the sensation of moving only your feet. As you sit on the chairlift and make small turning motions with feet and skis, you'll notice that your upper legs, your thighs, aren't moving at all (at least not visibly). All the action takes place below your knees—and so it is in the bumps. Your feet are light and quick. Foot action, coupled with the shape of the bump, is all that's needed to guide your skis through a field of moguls.

That's our next challenge: to string separate bump turns together into complete bump runs, great bump runs. It won't take long before your individual bump turns, at least some of them, start to feel pretty good. We've developed a pattern that really works. The same dynamic anticipation that let us link short turns on smooth groomed slopes is now helping us to link turns in the bumps. As we finish one turn below a bump, we arrive at the top of the next bump wound up for the next turn. A good anticipated pole plant stabilizes us, and we can let our skis unwind back down the hill around the next bump. It's a now-familiar story: the end of one turn setting us up for the next one. Your feet are relaxed so your skis never rail in and run away from you; you slip from bump to bump. And your best turns follow the basic pattern for easy bump skiing: a slow, patient anticipated start leading to a strong delayed finish below the bump—a pattern we are about to use to create some amazing bump runs.

Putting Together Continuous Bump Runs

A few good bump turns are one thing; a long flowing continuous run right down through a whole mogul field is an altogether larger achievement. Bump skiing is not about choosing your bump; it's more about accepting what the slope offers. After each turn, the next one is right there, waiting for you, and the next, and the next. That kind of continuous bump skiing is our goal, and it is well within your reach. The quick pole action we practiced above is one part of the package; another equally important part is developing a sense of the best line, or path, through a big field of bumps.

Let's start by admitting how tangled and confused a bump run looks when viewed from above. Line? What line? All you see is a confusion of bumps, all sizes and shapes. Not to worry: Experts build their great bump runs a few moguls at a time. And you can too. First figure out where to start. You can see where the first few turns will take you. And from that point on you just take things as they come—with very few big choices but a couple of options, nonetheless, about how you'll ski from bump to bump, turn to turn. Most of your options involve choosing just where you'll exit each bump turn. Let's look closer.

Once you've mastered the anticipated start, the beginning, or launching, phase of your turns doesn't seem so important any more. It always works. Your skis always unwind down the hill. More and more you focus your attention on the end phase, or exit, of your turn. And in continuous bump runs the exit of each turn becomes critical. Why dive over a mogul into a trough if that gully closes out in an ugly trap, an awkward minicliff, or a sudden shelf? I'm always looking at the bottom of the bump, asking myself where I'm going, and what will happen to me when I get there. And you should too.

The best bumps, or at least the ones that are easiest to handle, offer us lots of space to round out and finish our turns. If there isn't enough space we can sometimes make more space by turning a little wider around the bump, curving past the small chopped-off walls that are sometimes produced when

Figure 6.8a *Different lines through the bumps*

Figure 6.8b *The long exit from a bump, stretching the turn out.*

unskilled skiers slam back into the same bump they have turned on. Looking at the bottom of the bump tells you where you are going next. Generally there are two possibilities: one fast, one slow. And your ability to use either the fast exit or the slow exit from a bump turn will help you craft a long bump run just to your liking: fast or slow or in-between.

First, the fast exit: If you stood on top of a bump and rolled a beach ball over the crest and down into the gully, what would the beach ball do? It would

Figures 6.8a-c *Different lines through the bumps. Basically, I distinguish two different paths around the average bump—what I call the short line and the long line, or sometimes, the short exit from a bump and the long exit. The short exit involves turning back down the hill at the very first opportunity while the long line, or long exit, involves wrapping the turn all the way around the bump and then climbing up and over the next bump to the side. Of course, you can mix and match long and short lines through a mogul field and craft a run just to your liking.*

roll around the bump, following the curve of the gully, and then it would drop right down into the mouth of the first gully below. That's the fastest line, and that's what I call the short exit, or fast exit, from a bump turn. The idea for a skier, not a beach ball, is to drop down into the next turn as soon as possible. Generally, this means that you won't have time to completely finish your previous turn. That's why I call it the fast exit. If you repeatedly choose the fast exit from every bump, you will wind up skiing fairly fast, or at the very least you won't experience much braking action.

The long, or slow, exit from a bump turn is quite different. Here the skier keeps on turning, rounding out the bottom of the turn, passing that first gully exit and often finishing the turn by steering both skis up

Figure 6.8c *The short exit.*

the flank of the next bump to the side. This turn can stretch out to be more than twice as long as the short exit turn I described above. It's a question of using every available inch of space—to slow down. What I call the long, or slow, exit from a bump turn means stretching the turn out, as far as possible, really finishing that turn, while the fast exit implies that you have decided not to finish your turn.

Take a look at Fig. 6.8 to see a graphic representation of these two lines: the long line and the short line; the long, slow exit and the short, fast exit from bump turns. The amazing thing is that, generally, both these options are available to the savvy bump skier. And by choosing one or the other of these two options at the end of each turn, you can build an amazing variety into almost any bump run. Mixing and matching these two options pretty well defines how fast or how slowly you drop down through a mogul field.

If the bumps aren't too steep or oppressive, if you feel comfortable and quick, skiing the fast line (taking the fast exit below each bump) is a wonderful feeling. Such a run is smooth and fluid. Small guiding movements of the feet usually suffice to steer the skis directly from one gully to the next. But if the pitch steepens, if your speed rises past your comfort line, go for plan B. Start looking for the long line, and use it.

Skiing the long line—taking the long exit from your bump turns—is a lot less direct. It requires more patience, sometimes a little more technique, and much less daring. But life in the bumps isn't all black or white. Most of the time skilled skiers let their skis go, flowing like water down the fast line, only opting for the long exit from time to time, to slow down as needed. You can mix it up as the spirit moves you, and as your confidence level dictates.

But mastering these two different lines, these two different ways of ending (and thus linking) bump turns is the final piece of the speed control puzzle in moguls. Take your time and become comfortable with both options. Ski a whole run through big and rhythmic bumps, choosing the long exit for every turn. You will be amazed at how slowly you can ski through pretty serious bumps. In fact, the long line often allows you to make lazy, effortless runs through pretty mean-looking moguls. And then do the exact opposite on a bump slope that doesn't seem very scary; just let your skis go, guiding them with a light touch. Instead of finishing each turn, turn back down the hill at the first opportunity. Why slow down if you don't feel the need? This fast line is really a series of unfinished or only partially completed bump turns. The short fast exit is usually there waiting for you as soon as your ski tips have gotten past the vertical, the fall line.

By the way, I should tell you that this fast line, a series of short exits from moguls, is often called the "zipper line," an obvious and pretty accurate image. It is very impressive to see bold and athletic skiers take the zipper line through big, steep, mean moguls—but this simply isn't an option for most skiers. It's too fast, too scary. There's no rule that says you have to dash down through the moguls at top speed. Skiing bumps gracefully, fluidly, and comfortably is already quite an achievement for most skiers. It is for me. Mastering and then mixing the two lines, fast and slow, is the final key to relaxed, easy bump skiing. The possibility of setting your own pace brings you much closer to playing with bumps instead of struggling with them.

Once again we've seen that the tail end of our turns can be more important than the start. When you really feel that, you'll know you've taken a giant step forward in bump skiing. The start of your bump turns should feel pretty effortless, a given, like falling off a log (or actually, falling off a mogul). And instead of overdoing that start, you simply let it happen while concentrating on how each turn will end—where to end it, how to end it, already reaching down the hill for the following turn with the tip of your pole.

I don't want to say much more about hand-and-pole action in the bumps. But a small reminder is in order. I've already made a big deal about how important it is to quickly advance the tip of your outside pole every time you turn, reaching straight down the hill for your next rendezvous with destiny, for the next bump. But I should tell you that this hand/wrist action, flicking the tip of your pole down the hill, is really the move that stitches individual bump turns into long fluid bump runs. If my pole is advanced and ready, I'll make the next turn. If I leave my pole behind, I'll miss that next turn. It's that simple.

I should add that the harder the bumps become, the more vital this rapid pole-racing action becomes. This gesture is my speed limit in tight or difficult bumps. As soon as I advance my new pole I'm ready to turn again. And it's important to keep turning, even if every turn isn't perfect. Each new turn acts as a sort of dynamic recovery from any possible mistake, any loss of balance in the last turn. Your motto in the bumps might well be: One good turn deserves another. And even a crummy turn deserves another good one—as quickly as possible.

Have we achieved our initial goal of making friends with bumps? I hope so. You'll know it's happened when you start to look forward to bump runs, when you can't wait to jump back on the lift to ski those same moguls again. But there's still more. Because I confess, bump skiing is a totally open-ended endeavor. You never dominate the bumps completely. No matter how skilled a bump skier you become, you can always ski bumps better or ski still harder bumps. Bump skiing is a work in progress, even for mogul masters. So let's keep going.

Really Tough Bumps: Absorption and Other Tricks

If you've ever taken a bump lesson, you have probably heard about absorption, about using your legs like shock absorbers in the bumps. In ski school lessons, skiers usually get a good dose of absorption whether they need to or not—and usually they don't. Magazine articles and books about skiing also make a big deal out of absorption. But I've put this subject off till the end of our bump apprenticeship for a simple reason. Shock absorbers are used to absorb shocks. Only skiing very fast through bumps or skiing through very big and dramatically shaped bumps will create serious shocks or sudden pressure underfoot. Most bump skiing, at comfortable recreational speeds, over moderate-sized bumps, just doesn't create the sort of shocks that demand a shock-absorbing

Figure 6.9 *Absorption in bumps.* Or more exactly, absorbing the shock of hitting sharp bumps at higher speeds. Allow the bump to compress your legs, folding them up beneath you; and then as you pass the crest, extend your feet, toes, and skis down into the trough on the other side of the bump, filling up the available space and stretching your legs out again so they can absorb the shock of the next big one.

technique. I confess I use relatively little absorption in moguls, and I suspect you won't need much either—at least not at first. But eventually, growing confidence may push you to ski bumps faster, or you'll find yourself in the middle of really abrupt bumps, and all of a sudden, you'll feel like someone is punching you from below. Absorption is the ticket to smoothing out your ride.

I hate to dwell on misconceptions, but let me debunk one more before sharing the secrets of easy absorption with you. Rumor has it that bump skiers absorb the shock of hitting bumps by folding or retracting their legs beneath them. This folding of the legs even has a French name, *avalement*, but neither the fancy name nor the leg-folding action are really needed. Yes, your legs will definitely fold up beneath you if you hit a big bump with extra speed, but they will simply fold up on their own, especially if you're following my advice about skiing bumps in as loose and relaxed a manner as you can. The sudden pressure of the bump will collapse your legs, your shock absorbers; and your job is to stretch back tall again to fill in the hollow space on the other side of the bump. Reextending rather than flexing is the secret of effective absorption in the bumps.

You can get the hang of this absorption pattern by just traversing straight across some big bumps fairly fast:. Feel the bumps push your legs up, and then press your feet down on the far side of the bump as you straighten back up. That's the anticipation story. Don't overdo it because you think that this deep leg-flexing action looks cool. Relax your legs just enough to let the bump push them up beneath you, and then actively reextend to come back to your normal stance. You don't want to let successive bumps squash you lower, and lower, and lower.

And furthermore, we know exactly why it isn't desirable to ski in a low flexed position. If your knees are overly bent, and your thighs more horizontal than vertical, you will be supporting yourself with your quads and it won't be long before even those big thigh muscles begin to burn. But in a taller, looser stance, your leg bones not your leg muscles will be holding your body up. A good deal, all around. And I should add that maintaining your balance in a deeply flexed position is a bit of a trick because as a bump compresses your legs (either from extra speed or an abrupt terrain change), you will feel your knees coming up in front of your hips. Or to put it another way, your hips will fall back when you flex deeply, so you need to really extend your arms forward to maintain a centered balance. Absorbing sudden extra shocks in the bumps by letting your legs fold up beneath you (and in front of you) is a great strategy—just don't overdo it. And don't get stuck in that low flexed position.

To ensure the maximum flexibility and "give" in your legs during hard bump skiing, I also want to encourage you not to bend forward at the waist. The more you break at the waist, the tighter your legs will become. A tall vertical back guarantees the maximum flexing/shock-absorbing potential in your legs. A relaxed but vertical back is a real hallmark of skilled bump skiing, just as quick hands and poles are.

Finally here's one last tip for mega-bumps—not a serious ski technique

Figure 6.10 *A bumper's trick for difficult terrain. Keep your back upright, almost vertical. Sure, a big bump may flex you forward momentarily, but if you keep your upper body more or less vertical, you will find you have more flexibility in your legs for absorbing the sudden shocks of the meanest bumps.*

idea but simply an interesting image that you can focus on as you expand your comfort zone into ever bigger and ever more challenging bumps. Think about your toes, about guiding and pressing your toes down over each bump. That's right, focus on the toes of your ski boots, and try to push your toes down into the hollow of the trough on the far side of big bumps. The effort you make to press your toes down on the other side of the bump will help your skis hug the snow, especially if you extend your legs downward into that trough after absorbing the shock of the bump's crest. In continuous big bumps, your turns will exhibit an alternating pattern of flexing and reextending: flexing as you cross the crest of the bump; flexing (easily and naturally, allowing the bump to push your legs up) and then reextending as you complete the arc on the other side. This flexing-extending pattern has a big role in skillful deep powder skiing too, as we'll see in the next chapter.

But for now, just keep doing it. Skiing bumps with a smile on your face. The most important advice I've offered you in this chapter is to choose friendly bump terrain. And that means upping the ante slowly and progressively. By all means try harder moguls, but do it cleverly. Don't dive in over your head, but instead increase the challenge a little at a time and give yourself lots of successful bump runs along the way, at each level of difficulty, to build confidence, to build good habits. Bump action can be so fast and furious that there just isn't any time to think through your technique, your every move. Skiers respond to bumps, to the next bump in front of them. And your only chance of building strong, efficient bump skiing habits is to take it easy and avoid super-hard moguls until you are really ready. Making friends with bumps is just a beginning. You can pursue the challenge of bumps for years to come, and I'm sure you will.

IN SUMMARY

- Shaped, or super-sidecut, skis have several advantages in bumps. Shorter than classic skis, they fit more easily through the restricted space between bumps. Because they turn on a dime, they offer more options for changing your line and controlling your speed.

- For most skiers, the biggest problem in bumps is speed control. Many skiers find that their skis "rail in" and once caught on the edges shoot out from under them. The culprit is excess muscular tension.

- The answer is not merely to relax but to sideslip in bumps. Avoid edging. Your skis already have more than enough natural edging. Relax your feet and let your skis slip gracefully through the bumps.

- It is critical that bump turns start with both feet, both skis, turning at the same time. The one-two, step-step action of a stem christie is a disaster.

Focus either on early weight shift or on soft weight shift by relaxing/folding the downhill leg to trigger your bump turn. Or perhaps easiest of all, simply pivot both feet slightly but simultaneously to start your bump turn.

- Anticipation is essential too. Linking short turns with dynamic anticipation (the subject of Chapter 5) is a prerequisite for successful bump skiing. In moguls, there's no time to turn one's body back and forth. It's enough to guide one's feet and skis.

- Start your turns on the high spot, or crest, of the bump and use the side and gully of the bump to round out the turn (don't cut it short). Use the small smooth shelf between bumps to complete your turn, and slow down. The basic pattern for easy bump skiing boils down to this: a patient anticipated start on top of the bump leading to a delayed finish beneath the bump. Stretch your bump turns out to use all the available space.

- Good pole action rebalances you forward into each new turn, speeds up your reactions, gives you more time to respond to the next bump, and generally pulls things together. Efficient rapid pole work—flicking the new outside pole ahead with quick wrist action, and continually reaching down the hill for the next turn—is the glue that links good bump turns into great bump runs.

- Mix and match the long and short exits from each bump turn to adjust the speed and intensity of your mogul runs: sometimes dropping straight down toward the next bump below you, sometimes rounding out the turn to climb up over the next bump to the side—an efficient way to scrub off excess speed.

- Don't overdo trying to absorb the shock of hitting bumps; your legs will fold up on their own to absorb extra pressure when needed. Your job is to reextend them to be ready for the next bump.

CHAPTER 7

Powder Perfect

As Close As We'll Come to Flying

Powder is a dream come true. A child's dream of flying: weightless, free from the nagging tug of gravity, floating through space. Skiing powder snow is a fantasy barely becoming a reality, a slow-motion fantasy of effortless, graceful movement through an equally fantastic setting—mountains never look more magical than they do under a foot of new snow. This chapter is your passport to powder. As you become more and more comfortable in deep powder snow, I hope you will discover your own images, your own metaphors to describe this sublime experience. Powder and passion go together; for skiers they are virtual synonyms. You're about to discover why.

The mystique of skiing new powder snow runs deep. It's been a central part of skiing for as long as people have skied. But many skiers just don't get it. The powder mystique is definitely an insider's kind of thing. I suspect that many of my readers have heard all the usual tales of great mornings spent making fresh tracks through fresh powder snow, but haven't ever experienced this insider's delight—for a couple of good reasons. First, there just aren't enough powder days. A deep-snow enthusiast might well say there's never enough powder, but what I mean is that unless you live at a ski resort, it's very easy to ski all winter long without ever connecting with the aftermath of a big storm, a virgin mountain covered in new snow. Maybe you ski every weekend, but this season the storms all arrived midweek. You see what I mean. It's difficult to get enough practice time in powder to really get comfortable with the special balance and the special moves that deep snow demand. Which brings us right to the second reason that so few skiers are really comfortable in new snow: Powder snow requires that we adapt and modify our way of standing and reacting. It feels different and it is different. And to be honest, fresh snow, deep snow, powder snow is quite disconcerting at first. You can't see your feet and skis; they are lost somewhere down there under the snow; and you no longer have a solid firm surface of packed snow to stand on. You are floating in an uncertain medium. The neophyte in powder feels unbalanced, tippy, insecure. And the deeper the new snow, the more off-putting it seems—until you've made your peace with it, that is. Then everything changes and powder snow becomes very easy, really easy, technically easier, less demanding, and more effortless than anything you have experienced till now on packed slopes. Deep-snow aficionados—and I'm one—will all tell you that skiing powder snow is much easier than skiing on the pack. Hard to believe but true. I've always called this the powder paradox: Deep-snow skiing is easy to do but hard to learn. Well, not that hard. So let's get started.

Skis for Powder Snow

Many of the problems that used to ambush would-be powder skiers have now been solved by better equipment: either specialized powder skis, which are extra-wide, or "fat," skis, or by our new generation of all-mountain super-sidecut, or shaped, skis. These amazing deep-sidecut skis, which have become the standard in recent years, and that have given us a whole new range of carving possibilities on hard snow, also simplify our life in the deep stuff. Why? Not because of their deep sidecut per se, but rather because of their extra wide tips and tails. Overall, many of the new skis are wider than classical skis used to be, and this extra width translates into more surface area, which in turn provides more flotation in deep snow than classical skis

Figure 7.1 *Skis for powder snow. A specialized fat powder ski (left) and an all-snow shaped ski (right). The relatively wider tip and tail of many all-mountain, or all-snow deep-sidecut, skis make them very forgiving in deep snow. But even so, they don't offer anything like the flotation, ease, and security of an extra-wide powder ski.*

ever did. Of course, the pure powder ski, significantly shorter and much wider, provides even more flotation. But the modern shaped ski is sort of a halfway step toward the specialized powder ski. And the increased ease it offers in deep snow is very significant.

Let's look closer at this issue of flotation in deep snow, and ask why it's so important. Most of the time we ski *on* the snow, on the surface of the snow. But in powder we ski *in* the snow, skiing in three dimensions. Of course I'm talking about a real powder day, at least a foot of new snow. Not just a decorative dusting of two or three inches of light fluff. If we are looking at only a couple of inches of new snow, nothing really changes except the aesthetics. It's always a treat to leave your own tracks, your own signature in fresh snow, or to kick up a plume of light white dust behind you. But you will still be skiing on the solid packed layer beneath. Think of such conditions as "decorative powder snow." But as the inches add up, as your feet and skis disappear beneath the surface of the new snow, some interesting changes take place.

In real deep powder there is no longer a solid floor to stand on, so to speak; you find yourself floating not exactly on top of the snow, but a little way within it. And how well and how easily you float in the deep stuff depends on whether you are standing equally on both feet, on both skis. That's right, deep powder is the exception to the important rule of one-footed skiing that we have been pursuing like a holy grail through this whole book. Not to worry, special circumstances require special techniques. And nothing is quite as special as deep powder.

If you get all your weight, or even most of it, on one ski in deep snow, what happens? That ski dives down through the snow, the light ski floats up to the surface, and you, the skier in the middle, are seriously out of balance or worse. Conversely, if you can maintain roughly equal weight on both skis in deep snow, they will tend to float and to float you at the same level in the snow. The two skis really behave as one ski, like one big platform to support you in this fluid medium, and your balance isn't threatened. This is why specialized extra-fat powder skis work so well. They are so wide that each ski has about as much flotation as a pair of classical skis used to have. So if you do get off center and wind up with your weight all on one ski, that fat ski will still support you in the deep snow; it won't dive, and you won't crash. These fat powder skis are truly marvels. They protect you from the consequences of your own mistakes. And they do more. The amazing flotation of special fat powder skis actually turns difficult deep and wild snow into light powder—or so it feels. Whether in heavy, wet "Sierra cement" or breakable crust, fat powder skis seem to float you right over the toughest snow. You'll wind up riding closer to the surface on these seven-league boards, and I promise you won't even notice that the snow is awkward or difficult. But why, you may be wondering, if fat powder skis are so great, why shouldn't I just rush out and buy a pair and use them all the time? If you lived at a ski area you probably would—buy a pair, that is. But real powder is an infrequent treat, and most savvy skiers simply rent fat boards when a major storm starts to promise that tomorrow morning will be a powder day. Ski resort rental shops usually have a good selection of extra-fat powder skis for just such days. Yet you won't enjoy these skis very much on the packed slope. Many of them don't have much sidecut, and even those that do don't carve well on packed snow because it is quite hard to hold an extra-wide ski on edge.

But as I hinted above, many and maybe most of today's super-sidecut shaped skis are a perfect compromise: pretty easy to handle in deep snow because their wider tips and tails do provide extra flotation (although not as much as fat skis), and yet, of course, they give you all the performance you could desire on packed slopes. So unless you are facing a major dump of new snow—well over a foot of the white stuff—I'd recommend that you go out and dive into the new snow on your regular modern shaped skis. Rent fat skis when you get into trouble or when the powder gets really deep.

Powder Basics: Balance and Smoothness

As usual, stance and balance are at the heart of the matter. As we've just learned, deep snow does require a special stance, a two-footed stance, and a special kind of balance. I'm going to suggest that you develop both by postponing your first powder turns and instead just going for a long straight slide or two to get used to this new environment. No one feels at home in powder at first. But you will soon. Build up your confidence, your powder balance, and stability in several long, fast straight runs—either traverses or schusses straight down the slope, depending on the angle of the slope. Just cruise straight through that new snow, bouncing a little on both feet to get used to the fact that you are no longer standing solidly on a solid surface, but floating. Feels good, and it will feel even better after a few straight runs.

When you push off through deep snow, I want you to spread your hands laterally, a bit wider than normal, for better lateral balance. It's always trouble to spread your skis in powder, so spread your hands. And it's important not only to stand equally on both skis but to develop a kind of recovery mechanism to reequalize your weight when you get unbalanced onto one ski. The easiest way to do this is by sinking, collapsing both legs a bit, which will put you back firmly on both skis. Finding and maintaining two-footed balance in deep new snow isn't hard; it's just different. Or at least it feels different. But getting used to balancing on floating skis is half the fun.

But we're not really out on the mountain on a powder morning; you're probably reading this book on a sofa at home, maybe even in midsummer. And I bet you're already wondering if this is really the best approach. Why would you want to just go straight through the new snow when all around you confirmed powderhounds are tracing graceful curved arcs down the mountain? Trust me on this. It will make an incredible difference if you can

Figure 7.2 The powder skier's stance. The skier is centered, not leaning back, but definitely balanced equally on both skis for maximum and equal flotation. Hands are spread wide for extra balance.

get comfortable, feel stable and unshakeable, and grow accustomed to sliding fairly fast through powder snow before you start turning. Speed is the key. In deep snow, speed is your friend. The faster you go, the more your skis will float up toward the surface of the powder, and the easier it will be to turn, as long as you feel comfortable and stable. It's analogous to waterskiing—the boat has to pull the skier forward at a good speed before the skis rise to the surface of the water. Indeed, a very common problem in powder is trying to turn without enough forward speed. Such turns quickly become wrestling matches with the snow, and the snow usually wins. And straight running in powder isn't only a good balance exercise. It's the way experienced powder skiers start most every run. They push off down the hill at a steeper angle than they would choose on a packed slope, and then they wait, and wait, until they have picked up enough speed to make the first turn easy. Have I convinced you? I hope so.

But after a couple of good straight runs, I know you'll be itching to simply ski. Great. And here's the first trick I want to share about turning in deep snow. Do everything slowly and smoothly; avoid any sudden jerky movements. Powder skiing more than anything else is a slow-motion sport! Remember, there is new snow all around your skis, so if you make a sudden movement, if you twist your skis violently, they will run into a veritable wall of resistance … and trip you. Progressive smooth movements are a must in deep snow. The parallel between deep powder skiing and pure carved turns on the pack is striking—and curious. Although the snow is so different, both situations demand a slow, patient entry into the turn. If your ski tips lead you, if your skis are moving more ahead than sideways, you'll be in great shape in powder. In powder, try to make all your movements slow and long, smooth and steady. And it goes without saying that I want you to make all your turns round, not sharp.

What else? I should steer you away from one dreadful myth about skiing in deep snow. Don't sit back. This old bit of bad advice just won't die. And indeed a long time ago, when all skiers had were very stiff wooden skis, it made sense to lean back in deep powder to lever the tips of one's skis up in the deep

Terrible Snow:
Breakable Crust and Beyond

There is snow and there is snow; there's challenge and then there is challenge. I confess to a certain fondness for difficult and challenging snow. Perhaps my interest, even enthusiasm, for skiing in very difficult, unpacked, or wild snow conditions is due to the fact that I began my life in the mountains as a climber long before I ever put on skis. So I've always looked at skis as my own seven-league boots that could carry me safely and comfortably into every conceivable snow-covered mountainscape—if I could learn to do my part, that is. I've always assumed that no matter how frustrating the snow conditions were, there had to be a way of skiing them. And that's almost true.

So without spending too much time on it, I'd like to share a few tips for coping with snow that is beyond difficult—dreadful, lousy, terrible snow. But, first, a warning about breakable crust. Breakable crust is seldom found inbounds at ski areas. The grooming crews are too good to let it happen. But the backcountry is full of it. The name is self-explanatory. The surface crust that gives breakable crust its name is formed either by wind action or by repeated melting and freezing in spring. And, of course, this crust is not solid enough to support a skier's weight. Or else it will support your weight in some spots and collapse in others. Beyond being devilishly difficult to ski, breakable crust is quite dangerous because in a fall your skis can become trapped and held beneath the crust. So unless you are very fit and feeling both strong and strong minded, the best thing to do when you encounter breakable crust is to turn around and ski away. But if you're ready for a little excitement, ski it decisively. Lift your skis right up off the snow with a more or less sudden retraction of your legs and then smash them down onto the crust, forcing them to break through to the snow beneath. This ends the suspense of waiting for the crust to shatter without warning under your weight. You'll want to finish your turn with a vigorous twist beneath the crust, then pull your skis up out of the crust to do it all over again.

But that's only a rough strategy. Handling breakable crust is not a matter of elegant and efficient skiing. It is an athletic improvisation. It's also a bigger problem for heavier skiers. Sometimes a light skier can ride on top of the crust with delicate movements while her heavier companions break through and flounder. And, of course, fat powder skis help—immensely.

Skiing really dreadful snow like breakable crust often comes down to what I call "leap-and-land" skiing. Somehow, against all odds, you get your skis completely out of the bad snow. You pivot them in the new direction in the air. And you come down to earth again, ready to hang on. Hesitate, even for a second, and the crust will topple you.

The leap-and-land approach is not a bad way to go in other varieties of terrible snow, snow that's so difficult that your only motivation is to get down in one piece, to survive the run. Believe me, sooner or later this happens to everyone who enjoys skiing far from the beaten piste. There are other varieties of devilishly diffi-cult deep snow. Bottomless, wet, rotten, late-afternoon spring snow is one. Handle it with strong up motion, larger turns than normal, a strong forward push of both feet and a lot of inward banking of your whole body. Skiing wet deep slush reminds me of water skiing, and it reminds me that I should have quit a couple of hours earlier. Spring snow is best when skied neither too early in

(continued on page 220)

(continued from page 219)
the day (when it can be ice) nor too late (when it can be mush).

Turning mostly in the air—the leap-and-land approach—also works pretty well when you encounter "sastrugi," or wind waves, on high, exposed above-timberline slopes. Or when you are picking your way through a lumpy field of "death cookies"—skiers' slang for frozen ice lumps—either frozen morning-after spring slush or the debris from a sloppy grooming job. There is simply no way to cope with really terrible snow and feel graceful about it. Congratulate yourself on turning at all, and save your dreams of perfection until you are safely back on friendly snow.

snow. But that's almost skiing prehistory now. Don't do it. Stand neutral, even, flat-footed, right in the center of your foot, right in the center of your ski. Modern skis are soft enough that they tend to bend up at the tips anyway when you are cruising through deep powder. Leaning back doesn't accomplish anything except fatiguing your thighs. Enough said. Now let's take a look at the mechanics of good turns in powder.

A Powder Primer: Free Your Turns with Up-Motion

Deep snow, even if it's light powder, means extra friction, extra resistance, all around our skis, and this extra resistance tends to hinder the turning action of our skis. It sometimes feels as though our skis are stuck, trapped in the powder. And inexperienced skiers start to fight back, to use a lot of force to twist their skis through all this extra white stuff. We can do better.

To facilitate turning in deep snow, we'll use a threefold strategy. We'll make sure we're moving fast enough, fast enough for our skis to float up in the snow, and fast enough to push through this extra resistance easily. Second, we simply won't turn as much as we usually do. Certainly, we won't complete our

Figure 7.3 *Gentle up-motion to start an easy powder turn. A slight bounce, an easy lift off both feet is sufficient to lighten both skis and facilitate the start of an easy turn.*

turns very far across the hill. Instead we'll ski at a steeper angle than normal, and we'll guide our skis through only part of a completed turn, a gentle, sinuous partial arc, relying on the resistance of the new snow rather than our completed turn shape to keep our speed under control. It will. And finally, we will use a special move to start our turns. A smooth, strong rising, or up-motion, of the whole body to make our skis light right at the start of the turn.

This up-motion has a fancy ski name: unweighting. Time was, when skis were a lot stiffer and skiers needed to unweight their skis for every single turn. In those days, skiers had a mantra: down-hup-and-around. They would sink down to prepare their turns, rise up smartly to take their body weight off the skis, to free their skis (that was the "hup"), and then they would twist their skis more or less vigorously in the new direction. Well, such unweighting, or up-unweighting, to give it its full name, has all but disappeared from modern skiing. It just isn't necessary. In fact, the early weight shift that we practiced so

Figure 7.4 *Extra up-motion.* In deeper, heavier, or more challenging powder, you may need stronger, more ample up-motion to launch your turns. Here a powerful lifting and rising action starts a big turn in deep powder.

patiently and successfully in Chapter 4 is really the opposite of unweighting. We've learned to stand on our new outside ski even before it starts to turn. But powder, you already know, is different, very different. We are going to reach back into the history of ski technique and rescue unweighting from oblivion. Unweighting with up-motion lightens our skis right at the start of a powder turn.

You have already been practicing this up-motion if you followed my advice to cruise straight through the powder, bouncing a little on both feet, getting used to the new floating balance of powder skiing. A small bounce is a great form of up-unweighting. Try it now. In a big open slope of not too terribly steep powder, push off and when your speed is comfortable, flex your knees lightly and bounce back up. As you do so, turn your feet just a little. And voilà, your skis turn pretty easily. Once you've started a turn in powder, it's up to you to keep it going. Use a gentle, steady, continuous guiding action of both feet. Bounce to turn, and keep turning. Bounce to turn, and keep turning. Your turns will be patient, slow changes in direction, not sudden corners, right?

A little bounce provides a little unweighting, all you need for a gentle turn. In deeper or heavier powder, you may need more unweighting to do the job. It isn't difficult: Just flex a little deeper to prepare your turn, and then as you trigger the action with your downhill pole, lift your body strongly up (really, you are just standing up again from your flexed position) and start your turn with a gentle turning steering action of both feet at the same time. The notion of moving, or as I suggested, turning and steering, both feet is crucial. Equal action with both feet should result in equal weight distribution over both skis. That's it. Flex to get ready as you plant your pole, rise, and turn.

Let me add, parenthetically, that if you have taken my advice about renting extra-fat powder skis, this whole business about up-motion at the start of the turn is much less important. It's okay; indeed it will help. But fat boards float you so high in the new powder snow that you don't have as much snow resistance to deal with. And, probably, even if you forget this smooth, strong up-motion at the start of your turns, they are going to work anyway. Especially if you remember to turn both feet at the same time.

And while we are talking about feet, let me offer the first of several powder skier's tricks—pushing your feet ahead of you into the turn. Wherever you are reading this chapter, look down, right now, at your feet. Imagine for a moment that you are skimming through a foot of new snow about to turn. Focus on the toes of both feet, and push them straight ahead a few inches

Figure 7.5 *Subtle foot action in deep snow. Equal action means equal weight, which in turn means equal flotation. And one of the ways to achieve this optimum balance is with a subtle forward push of both feet at the start of a powder turn. Here we see this move (of only a few inches) from the side as well as head on. Such foot thrusting is not a basic powder technique but a nice extra that can help launch turns smoothly in a variety of deep snow conditions.*

while steering them to the right. That's it. Do this a few times, shoving your toes sometimes to the right, sometimes to the left, but always a few inches forward. This is a particularly effective powder skier's trick. And believe it or not, this slight action of pushing both feet forward and into the coming turn does not set you back on your heels. That's because the extra resistance of the snow slows your skis as you turn, and so your body always catches up, always stays centered, even when you push both boots ahead and into the turn. The reason this move is effective is that the equal push of both feet guarantees equal weight on both skis, equal flotation as you enter the arc of your turn. And momentarily, just for a split second, this foot-thrusting move takes some weight off the tip of your skis—a kind of stealth unweighting. Try it. It works. But it works better for some skiers than for others. If this funny move doesn't seem to help, just put it aside and keep skiing powder. The beauty of beginning your powder experience on wider skis, either fat powder skis or all-mountain shaped skis with extra-wide tips, is that even if you make every mistake in the book, you will still succeed, still turn. And then you will face a simpler problem. Not how to turn in powder, but how to make your powder turns better.

Your main strategy, as ever, is mileage and repetition. You become a powder skier progressively by skiing powder, not by thinking about how to ski powder. I'd like to suggest that you ski a smoother, straighter, more sinuous line. That you are careful not to guide your skis too far out of the fall line before turning back down the hill. From the chairlift on a powder morning, you can see what I am talking about by observing the tracks of the best powder skiers. These tracks never seem to cut back across the hill; in fact they almost never turn more than about 45 degrees from the fall line. The turns that these beautiful tracks draw in the snow are long ones. Think about the skiers who made such tracks. Were they in a hurry? I think not. And, of course, from that same chairlift observation platform you can probably watch not just tracks but the skilled powder skiers making them. Notice how fluid and slow all their movements are. As I said earlier, powder skiing really is a slow-motion sport.

But there's another important factor that will influence, even shape, your apprenticeship as a powder skier—and that is, where this introduction takes place: whether in the Rockies or closer to a coast, either coast. I'm referring to the difference between the cold, light, dry snow of a so-called continental climate, the very light powder snow of the Rockies, of Colorado, Utah, and their neighbor states, and the much denser, heavier snow that is more typical of the so-called maritime climates of California and the Pacific Northwest or even of New England. Learning to ski in untracked new snow is a very different experience in the Rockies than in the High Sierra, for example. Let me spell out this difference and how to deal with it.

A foot or so of light high-altitude snow in the Rockies won't slow you down that much. Even on a gentle blue slope you'll have no problem sliding, keeping your speed up enough to turn. But farther out west, the same depth of snow will seem denser, stickier, because of its greater moisture content, and immediately you will discover just how much new snow can slow you down. In West Coast mountains, whether California's High Sierra or the Cascades, you will need to seek out much steeper slopes for your powder apprenticeship. On a typical powder morning at Squaw Valley, for example, skilled skiers weave their multiple curving tracks down the steepest slopes, like KT-22 and Red Dog, and then, at the bottom of the steeps, all these tracks converge into one track leading out across the flats where the first skier has walked out. In short, on gentle slopes you just won't slide. And as a result, your first efforts in powder snow will feel quite different in these heavier maritime snow conditions.

In such heavy powder, I want you to find slopes that are perhaps a little too steep for you in regular packed conditions. You will quickly discover that the drag of this heavy, deep snow converts them into very friendly practice slopes—if you simply can't slide very fast, what is there to worry about? But make your first straight runs in the form of traverses. Pick an angle steep enough to slide, not steep enough to bother you. And after getting used to the deep snow stance I've described above (even, centered weight on both skis,

Figure 7.6 *Sinuous tracks in deep snow. These tracks tell a tale of efficient powder skiing: There's no evidence of sudden, last-minute moves; there are no jerky corners. These tracks record a slow-motion experience.*

arms spread more than normal), practice some uphill turns—just to get a feeling for how you will end your turns in this deep snow. In thick, heavy powder I suggest a special kind of uphill turn from your initial traverses, an uphill hook that you will create by pushing your skis sideways, out from under you. Technically, we could call this turning by extension, and it works like this. In a comfortable though moderately steep traverse, sink down to get ready; then from this low flexed position I want you to push the heels of both boots down the hill. To do so you are in essence stretching your legs back out; only instead of standing back up, you are extending your legs down the hill, pushing your feet away from you at the same time as turning them up the hill. And, of course, you come to a stop, but do so slowly, smoothly, progressively. Remember our first powder principle: no sudden jerky movements. And that means no sudden jerky turns.

Figure 7.7 *A very special kind of uphill turn in powder—turning with a twisting extension of both feet and legs.* From a very low position, the skier extends his feet sideways, out and down into the snow, moving three-dimensionally within the snow as he completes this turn to a stop. Great practice for steep fall-line powder skiing.

So let's say you have successfully made a few of these uphill turns to a stop by extending, pushing your feet out through the deep snow. Do a few more, but now do each one from a steeper and steeper traverse. And finally, from a straight run, or schuss, vertically down the hill. This pushing, turning extension into the snow that we have been practicing is really the tail end of a turn in deep and heavy powder. And with that move under your belt it's time to just dive in and ski, making complete turns with up-motion as I described earlier. Heavy, deep western snow calls for bigger, more ample, and powerful movements, so you'll need more than a small bounce to start your turns. And I want you to start your full powder turns from a steeper angle than normal with a little more speed than normal. Up-motion accompanied by steering both feet down the hill starts the turn. A smooth sideways extension of the feet finishes it. And repeat ...

Perhaps you are already discovering that powder skiing, whether in light Rocky Mountain powder or heavier West Coast powder, is largely a confidence game. Believe in it and it works. More or less well. If the novelty and strangeness of deep snow psych you out—the fact that you can no longer see your boots and skis, that you are no longer standing on a solid surface—then you'll tumble for sure. Powder is a comfortable medium to fall in but I'd rather you stayed on your feet. Which is why my first suggestion was to get used to the snow, to cruise straight through it before trying to turn.

But now that you are turning, I have one more powder skier's trick to share—especially for skiers dealing with heavier, wetter, denser powder. Lift your outside hand at the start of each turn. This move is a real no-no on the packed slope, as it will tilt you to the inside of the turn and rob your outside ski of weight and pressure. But in powder it is a veritable power move. Say you are about to start a left turn down the hill in deep powder. Your left hand is getting your left pole ready to plant—the signal that triggers your turn. As you do so, and begin to rise and turn your feet, I want you to smartly raise your right hand from around waist level to around shoulder level all at once. What happens?

Powder skiers form a kind of club, an in-group of sorts; they exchange knowing glances, secret handshakes (just kidding), and they have their own vocabulary. "It was face shots, all morning long!" Face shots? Of course, powder snow deep enough to rise in slow motion waves and wash over your face. I've been there. Never often enough. Maybe you have too. But there was a morning, one special morning, at northern California's Bear Valley, where face shots were the least of it.

It had been snowing for days, an old-fashioned Sierra blizzard, the stuff of tall tales. And gusty winds and low visibility had kept most skiers off the mountain for days; the snow was piling up deeper and deeper in vast pillows and long drifts; gullies were filling in; tree wells were deep enough to swallow you whole. For days, we instructors would look at each other and nod and say: Just wait, when this storm blows over … when these clouds lift … we'll have the biggest powder day of the year.

And we did. Suddenly it was morning, mother of pearl mist, slowly clearing. More snow than we could remember. Lift by lift, the patrol did its avalanche work; lift by lift, the patrol turned us loose; by 10:30 I was up on the topmost ridge with a couple of fellow ski pros, looking down between two big rock towers into a favorite couloir a usually hollow gully now filled in with whipped cream snow. Hard to see, hard to know. But, hey, I'd skied this slot a dozen times before. The snow was stable—a few great runs had already proved that. And deep— every turn proved that. So stop looking and dive in. All right, all ready. I'm going.

Really deep powder is an invitation to go straight until you find the speed to turn. I went straight, dropped over an edge from waist-deep powder to shoulder-deep powder in the narrow gully, kept on dropping. The whole world turned white. The snow was over my head. I was still dropping ... and turning. Instinct, I guess. My skier's reflexes kept firing; my skier's legs and feet kept turning. Under the snow. Miraculously, my skis didn't cross. Three turns later I came back out to the surface and breathed, gulped, kept going. I couldn't believe it. Neither could anyone else. Hey, Lito, you just disappeared, disappeared under the snow, and then reappeared way down the hill, When they caught up to me, my buddies were babbling. I was too. I was already wondering if it had really happened. It happened. Who needs face shots?

Just as linked short turns with dynamic anticipation represented a final step after we had learned to carve clean, round arcs on packed slopes, linked short turns in powder, especially in very steep and very deep powder, represent the final step in our evolution as powder skiers: fall-line powder skiing. The secret is the way our skis work within the deep snow. And in a curious way, fall-line powder skiing resembles mogul skiing, but let's not get ahead of ourselves.

You already know how to link turns with dynamic anticipation. On a packed slope you're an ace. You can move easily from turn to turn to turn, guiding your skis only with foot and leg action, while your quiet upper body keeps on keeping on, moving straight down the slope without turning from side to side. All we have to do is adapt this pattern to powder and, in particular, to steep and deep snow. I make this distinction because already I'm sure you have found it easy to link minimal turns straight down the fall line, provided the new snow was light enough and friendly enough, and the slope wasn't too steep. As with bumps, continuous, rhythmic pole action is the mechanism that links one turn to the next. Like bump skiers, powder skiers too are continually reaching down the slope with their new pole. Reach and turn. Reach and turn. And of course, it's the pole that is reaching and moving, not the skier's arms and shoulders. The same efficient wrist action—tilting the pole forward without disturbing our basic balanced position—is all we need. So I am going to assume the continuous rhythmic aspects of fall-line skiing are a given, that they are now a basic part of your skiing habits. And that if you are playing in six inches of fluffy new snow at Aspen or Steamboat or Vail, you naturally string your powder curves together in long sinuous lines, that your body floats along above your turning skis. But I know that when you get to a really steep pitch of deep, the picture is no longer as pretty. For one thing, on seriously steep powder slopes speed control is once again an issue. And we have a new way of dealing with it.

In steep and deep snow, expert skiers finish their turns not by guiding their skis farther across the fall line, but instead by sinking their skis deeper into the snow. This is such a wonderful and subtle notion that I want to say it again in a different way: Experts are able to finish their deep powder turns in three dimensions instead of two by pressing their skis deeper into the snow at the end of their turns. This has some interesting advantages. Of course, this move slows you down, always a reasonable thing to do on a very steep slope. But at the same time because you haven't twisted your skis very far across the hill, you don't have very far to turn back into the fall line to launch your next turn. And best of all, the action of pushing your skis downward into the snow, sinking the tails of your skis at the end of a turn, produces resistance and pressure underfoot as the deep snow compresses under your skis. All you have to do then is relax your legs and voilà, this pressure will push your skis back up through the snow—unweighting them for the next turn. In essence, you are creating a sort of invisible "pressure bump" under the snow that will push your skis, your legs, and thighs up, just as a big bump does.

As was the case when we practiced linking short turns with dynamic anticipation, the end of each turn seems more important than the start of the next one. And so it is. If we end our turns well, we'll enjoy a kind of free start

Figure 7.9 *The final step: steep fall-line powder skiing with retraction and extension. You begin this turn by relaxing your legs. The pressure of the snow beneath you will lift your skis to the surface. You turn them toward the new direction and finish this turn with a strong downward extension of both legs—pressing the tails of both skis deeper into the snow, building resistance that will push your skis upward for the next turn. A steady alternation of relaxing and retracting, and extending and pressing. Smooth, efficient, exhilarating.*

to the next one: action/reaction, turn/return. So we need to practice that three-dimensional ending, sinking our skis deeper into the snow rather than turning them farther out of the fall line. Attentive readers will remember that I proposed a series of exercises to do just that in the previous section on getting used to heavier new snow, when I talked about making a series of uphill turns by extension.

Remember? From a traverse, sinking down and then extending our bent legs to push our feet (and skis) away from us, down the hill. There's no better way to get the hang of finishing powder turns with extension, or twisting extension, to use the full technical term. Just remember to do a series of these uphill turns, each one from a steeper and steeper traverse. Ski pros sometimes call such an ever-steepening sequence a fan pattern: steeper and steeper until eventually you're heading straight down the hill before you make your move: sinking down; then pushing your feet out laterally into the snow. This stretching out, or extension, is really a combination of two movements: You are pushing your feet, especially your heels down and out into the snow, and at the same time you are turning your feet a little. Twisting extension. The deeper the snow, the deeper you can sink your skis with this extension move, which slows you down and ends a good deep-snow turn.

Now, let's use this very interesting move. On a fairly steep powder slope, a little steeper than you usually ski, push off, start a turn, and as you come out of the fall line, press down and extend your feet down into the snow. Can you feel the snow press back? You will. Immediately relax and let this pressure push your legs and skis upward. As your skis float up in the snow, turn them back down the hill, and do it all again. You simply have to play with this sensation. You won't get it all at once—partly because there are so few opportunities to ski in really deep snow. But you will certainly get it.

Try to get a sense of this rhythmic alternation: pressure underfoot, then relaxing to release that pressure. Pressure and release of pressure. Press and release. With each release of pressure, a new turn begins, and it ends with increasing pressure. Once again your feet are where it's at. Creating and releasing pressure in the soles of your feet is much of what advanced powder technique is all about.

And this holds true even if you are skiing on specialized extra-wide powder skis. Of course they will float higher in the snow. And even extending your legs strongly downward you won't be able to "sink" fat skis as deep in the fluff as a pair of all-mountain shaped skis. But the same pattern still works and works well. It is just more subtle on fat skis. Pressure to finish one partial arc, relaxation and release of pressure to start the next one.

Figure 7.10 *Continuous fall-line powder skiing with retraction and extension.* The real thing. Your legs folding and unfolding, floating up, then pressing down. A nearly effortless rhythm that feels as if it can go on forever.

In essence, this more advanced fall-line pattern that I have been proposing simply replaces the up-motion of the whole body with an alternate up and down motion of the legs beneath the upper body. That same old dynamic anticipation story in a new context: active legs and feet beneath a quiet almost motionless upper body. Your new pole always reaching ahead for the next turn. Our anticipated style of fall-line skiing turns out to be almost infinitely adaptable to a variety of exciting and challenging and deliciously satisfying expert ski conditions. For me, personally, nothing is quite as satisfying, quite as delicious as powder skiing. The deeper the better. Fresh powder snow is one ski condition that I will never ever get tired of, never get enough of. It probably won't take many days in powder snow for you to feel the same way.

But I'd say that if you get bitten by the powder bug, then there are really only two choices if you want to log enough practice turns, enough practice hours to begin to feel completely at home in deep snow. Either go snowcat skiing. Or go to the Alps. You will find snowcat tour operators at or near most of the large western ski resorts, and a day in the backcountry with a snowcat guide is remarkably affordable and usually chock full of powder. Far more powder than you can find in-bounds at a ski resort where most runs will be tracked up in a few hours. Likewise, because timberline is so low in the Alps, and because European ski resorts are so vast, there is simply a lot more untracked snow at the large Alpine ski areas than you are likely to find at any American resort. But that's another tale, worthy of another book. What I really mean to suggest is that in order to complete your powder skiing apprenticeship, nothing is as important as mileage in the deep. Turn after turn, run after run. You know what to do. Now it's time to do it.

Enjoy.

IN SUMMARY

• Skis can help: extra-wide powder skis are ideal. Wide tips (and wide skis) provide extra flotation in deep snow.

• Develop a special powder skier's stance and balance: Weight both your skis evenly, spread your hands for lateral balance, and don't lean back. Your first task: Get comfortable in this new environment.

• Speed is your friend—with enough speed your skis overcome the resistance of deep snow and begin to float. Nonetheless, deep-snow skiing feels like a slow-motion sport; move slowly, smoothly, and continuously.

• At first, use smooth up-motion to help start your turns. Start with medium to long turns. Take your time.

• As powder gets steeper and deeper, control your speed not by turning farther across the hill but by sinking the tails of your skis deeper into the snow. This downward extension at the end of one turn can be followed by a relaxation/retraction of the legs to start the next turn—a great way to handle steep fall-line powder skiing.

Part III

The Rest of the Story

CHAPTER 8

Even More Challenges

Multiple Subworlds of Expert Skiing

You walk out to the lift, toss your skis down on the snow, scrape the snow off the soles of your boots, two healthy clicks, and you have become another person, a skier. But what skier? What skier today? They say no two snowflakes are the same. Why should any two days on skis be the same? Is this an adventure day, a relaxing day, a day to share your favorite runs with friends, a day to push your skis and your technique toward new limits? Your choice. Your choice every time you step into your bindings. All you know for sure is it won't be the same mountain it was yesterday: Life—or is it only winter?—is always conspiring to create a new mountain. Melting, freezing, thawing, the unpredictable action of wind, and the too predictable action of high-tech grooming machines. New snow in new patterns or simply old snow getting older, moguls getting deeper, spring ice getting crunchier every day or light winter crystals even lighter, even drier after a bitter January night. It's a new mountain. You're a new skier. You know you are about to ski something new today. You skate off toward the lift line. You can't wait.

Is this the whole story? Are we there yet? The answer is a resoundingly ambiguous *yes* and *no* and *sort of*. When exactly does one become an expert skier? A real expert? If, by expert skier, we mean someone capable of carving beautiful modern turns down most slopes on most mountains, then

I'm pretty sure you can already congratulate yourself on a terrific break-through into a new world of expert skiing. But if, by expert skier, we mean a vir-tually perfect skier, capable of brilliant turns and brilliant runs on every slope, on every mountain, well, then, you probably still have a way to go. And for that matter, so do I. The truth is—and for me this is good news—that it never ends: the beauty, or the challenge, of expert skiing. No matter how skilled you become, you can always get better. You can always push your limits a little fur-ther, ski harder slopes, ski tougher snow, ski faster or more gracefully, set your-self nearly impossible new challenges and meet them.

That's what this chapter is all about. I hope to look beyond the normal definition of expert ski performance and visit a few of the unusual subworlds and specialized domains of high-level skiing far from the beaten piste. To explore some of the different ways we can use and adapt our solid basic expert technique and our phenomenal shaped skis. I'm thinking especially about ski-ing ice. I'm also thinking about an intriguing form of carving (which I call "supercarving," very nearly a sport in itself), about racing (at least about what is usually called recreational racing—ski racing for the rest of us), and about skiing extremely steep slopes. Let's start with a frustrating condition that chal-lenges the very notion that skiing is fun—ice.

Too Slick for Comfort: Skiing Ice

Ice is a condition that skiers put up with, not one they look forward to. But ice happens. Indeed merely to cope with ice demands well-tuned skis, a finely honed technique, and Zen-like calm and concentration. I can't guarantee we'll make friends with ice the way we did with bumps, but I can arm you with some very effective strategies for skiing the slick.

Start with this easy idea: An icy ski slope is a place where there just isn't enough friction, enough gripping between your skis and the mountain. This in turn means that any sudden strong action, any sudden movement, and, above all, any sudden pivoting of your skis, will be too much. On packed powder this just isn't a big deal; if you twist your skis suddenly on packed powder, you'll simply wind up skidding a bit instead of carving a pure turn. But if you over-twist your skis on an icy slope, they will spin right around and wash out side-ways in a hopeless skid. The number one motto, then, for skiing ice is, above all, be gentle.

My friend and skiing guru Dick Dorworth, a former U.S. men's ski team coach and world speed-skiing record holder, gave me my first real insights into skiing the slick. That was years ago, but his suggestions still work and I've never forgotten those striking images. Dick put it this way: Imagine that the icy slope in front of you is covered with eggs, those large cardboard flats of eggs you see in bulk grocery departments. And now imagine that your mission is to ski down over all those eggs without breaking a single one. A nice way of say-ing: Be gentle. Be soft and smooth and almost delicate with your skis; no sud-den, harsh movements whatever—and you stand a chance of guiding your skis in a very positive clean arc.

But maybe we ought to pause a moment to distinguish between two dif-ferent kinds of conditions: In the first, there are only patches of ice here and there—scraped sections below big bumps, for example— and in the second, much more challenging, condition, the entire mountain seems to be one sin-gle sheet of ice. If you are dealing with icy patches, my best advice is just to grin and bear it, to avoid trying to ski them with something resembling solid tech-nique and to simply slide across the icy spot, knowing full well that all that snow that has been scraped away is probably waiting for you on the far side of the icy patch. Then once you arrive at that pillow of scraped-away snow, it's no problem to guide your feet and your skis into a real turn. So the answer to icy patches is don't try to ski them. Turn instead on the real snow that is always waiting a little farther down the slope. Delay the turn or, at the very least, the finish of your turn until you are back on respectable snow.

But a solid icy mountain is another story. A less amusing story altogether. Ski mountains get icy for a number of reasons, the most common being an

Figure 8.1 *Slice the ice.* Your skis will grip best on slick and icy surfaces if they are moving forward, not sideways. So a slow and patient entry into the turn is your best bet in very slick conditions.

alternation of melting and freezing weather: warm temperatures followed by freezing temperatures. But ice can also be formed by high winds scouring the slopes. And early season artificial snow has a way of packing down into something that really resembles pure ice, especially with the passage of crowds of holiday skiers, all over-turning and sliding and scraping sideways.

Here in the United States, the iciest slopes can probably be found in New England. New England ice is legendary, and I can attest that there is a solid basis in fact for this legend. A relatively wet maritime climate, bitter cold, and occasional high winds are a recipe for, well, for very challenging icy conditions. Eastern skiers are a tough breed; they grin and bear it. In my adopted home state of Colorado, we are completely spoiled by a wealth of soft dry snow, powder, and packed powder. Ice is incredibly rare in the Rockies, but still some skiers complain about ice when conditions are merely firm and a long, long way from real ice. But let's say that wherever you ski, fate has caught up with you and you are looking at least at a few days of very icy slopes at your favorite resort. What to do?

The first step is to sharpen your skis' edges—or have someone do it for you if you aren't very handy with a file. When a mountain is extremely icy, I carry a small (8-inch) mill bastard file with me and touch up the edges of my skis at noon! But once your skis' edges are sharp, paradoxically, you have to resist the temptation to overedge your skis. By this, I mean that for any given speed and hardness of snow or ice, there seems to be an optimum edge angle that gives you the greatest holding power. Edge your skis more than that and—presto—they slide away. Skilled skiers often speak of "feathering their edges" on ice: rolling their skis up onto an edge, for sure, but just enough to feel those skis begin to bite and arc around. And no more. And by the way, once your skis have begun to skid, no amount of further edging will stop that skid. Your first goal, in terms of having your edges hold on ice, will be to slice forward into the turn rather than twist into it. In just the same way that a somewhat dull kitchen knife will still often be able to cut a tomato if you slice it forward across the tomato's skin, so your skis will hold better, even on the slickest ice, if they are slicing forward rather than simply pressing down or moving sideways.

So what do we have so far? To hold and more or less carve turns on ice, you want to make a slow, patient entry into each turn, allowing your skis to slice forward rather than pivoting them quickly into a new direction. And this in turn commits you to a medium- to long-radius turn. Short turns on icy slopes are a recipe for skidding out. But we can do still more.

Try the following. On an icy mountain, turn as much as possible in the hollow places on the slope. Why? Normally, skiers tend to start their turns on top of high spots in the snow, whether those are actual bumps and moguls or simply larger rolls and humps in the terrain. As we pass over the top of these

Figure 8.2 *Balance on slick slopes. One of the keys is quiet hands. Wave your arms and hands around and your skis are sure to skid. Quiet hands, quiet movements, quiet technique—a discreet and winning combination on ice.*

crests and feel the snow drop away on the other side, our skis get lighter and we experience a delicious, light floating sensation as we turn. But not on ice, where this lightening, or "unweighting," of the skis caused by the terrain dropping away actually tends to make our skis skid out. On the contrary, if we turn in the hollow spots, the concave areas on the slope, our skis will be slightly compressed by the ground coming up under our feet, not dropping away. And this extra pressure, or compression, will tend to make our skis grip the surface just a little bit better. Try it. It works. Turn in the gullies and just before the top of a mogul, and see if your skis don't hold better.

And one last trick or tip for ice: Don't wave your hands around. Years ago, my ice skiing mentor, Dick Dorworth, told me I had to calm my hands and arms down if I hoped to carve or guide my skis in a smooth round arc on icy snow. This was the most important ice skiing lesson I ever learned. The logic of this advice runs somewhat like this: Because one's skis have such a tenuous grip on an icy slope, it is critically important that your turning ski's edges grip equally along the entire length of the ski. For this to happen, the skier's weight needs to be equally distributed all along the edge of the ski. And that in turn requires that the skier's weight be equally distributed along the edge of the boot, equally from the toe and ball of the foot, along the arch, all the way to the heel. And it so happens that where you hold your hands affects and even controls this weight distribution. Dick told me to find the perfect spot for my hands, the usual hand position to be sure, about waist high and spread in front of my hips—but even more precise. "Find a sort of magic circle, about six inches in diameter," Dick told me, "and don't move your hands from that special spot. If you reach your outside hand forward," he continued, "it will pull too much weight onto the tip of your ski and the lightened tails will slip away and skid out. Conversely, if you drop your outside hand back, even six inches or so, it tends to pull your hips back, which overloads the tails and, again, makes them skid out." And sure enough, Dick was absolutely right. On packed powder one can get away with all sorts of hand movements without provoking a skid. But on ice, even a small hand gesture will unbalance the pressure along the edge of your ski and will cause you to skid. Naturally, Dick wasn't recommending a stiff or frozen arm position. But calming down my hands, finding that perfect spot and balancing there with my hands, really did the trick. I still don't like ice, but I can ski it. And so can you.

Supercarving: The Next Game on Skis?

We've already spent a lot of time talking about carving turns. And I know that most likely you've already paid your dues, learned to balance easily and strongly on your outside ski, learned to enter your turns slowly and patiently, slicing forward into a pretty pure arc. I know that you can already carve a helluva turn. But there are carved turns and carved turns … all carved turns are not created equal. At a certain level, carved turns can become so pure and so perfect that they almost seem to belong to a separate sport. They do, and I call that sport within a sport supercarving.

Supercarving, or hypercarving, is carving carried to an extreme. And it's really neat. The extreme I am talking about has nothing to do with extreme steepness or speed, much less extremely challenging snow. Supercarving is something you can only achieve on a well-groomed slope. It is all about leaving lines on the snow, pure narrow lines, the line that a bent ski edge makes as it tracks forward in an arc: thin, pure, and perfect. A very exciting challenge—as amazing to do as it is to look at. But before trying supercarving, let's watch some.

A supercarving skier tends to ski in a moderately wide stance. And for good reason. Here comes my friend Bill Thistle, probably Aspen's best pure carving skier, arcing down the immaculately groomed slopes of Buttermilk Mountain, an international meeting spot for fanatic carvers on snowboards

Figure 8.3 *Supercarving—a close-up view. Here we can see some of the most important aspects of carving tight turns at moderate speeds. High edge angles, of course. Feet wider than normal and hips well to the inside. And it's clear that the skier is carrying some of her weight on the inside ski, even though the outside ski is doing most of the carving. An intriguing exception to the rule of 100 percent weight shift.*

or, as in Bill's case, on specialized carving skis. Bill is leaving two parallel lines in the snow, like very sinuous railroad tracks. He is riding a pair of 165-cm carving skis with a very deep and radical sidecut. And between Bill's boots and bindings and the skis themselves are two "risers," or carving plates, stacked one on top of the other to raise his boots farther off the snow. Risers have become a part of the modern expert skier's kit, as they give you more leverage to hold your skis on edge and allow you to tilt your boot farther over to the side without it hitting the snow. But double risers are a phenomenon unique to supercarving. Bill seems to dive into his turns, his body moving rapidly sideways down the hill each time he rolls from one arc to the next. And like almost all skilled skiers, pure carvers or not, Bill is always turning, always arcing. He moves his body so far and so quickly to the inside of each new turn that his outside ski and foot are way out there, off to the side as he enters the turn. Bill's outside leg is extended sideways at a strong angle to the snow, not at all vertical above his boot and ski. And as we watch Bill, it seems for all the world as though he is really skiing on both skis equally. Huh? Whatever happened to our all-important notion of skiing on the outside foot and ski? Not to worry. Bill is indeed carving on his outside ski. His outside ski, which is rolled over to a very high, or steep edge, angle, is indeed making the turn happen. Bill is not really breaking our golden rule. But he is modifying it to keep about one third of his weight on the inside ski and leg. Why? To achieve the extra-high edge angles needed to carve a moderately tight arc at more or less normal speeds, Bill has tilted his body much farther to the inside of his turn than most skiers do, and yet because he isn't traveling at the very high speeds of a GS, or super G racer, Bill's turn doesn't generate enough centrifugal force to support his body at this extreme inward lean. And so he needs to carry some extra weight on the inside ski simply to keep from falling over to the inside. Watching a gifted carving skier like Bill Thistle come down a slope is like watching a ballet. Bill's movements and, for that matter, those of his skis are smooth and continuous—continuously graceful. The two skis, parallel but fairly wide apart, are rolling from one set of edges to the other as they take a longer circular line around each turn than Bill himself does. He is always somewhat to the inside of the circle his skis are carving. His center of gravity follows an arc in space right above his inside ski while his outside ski, foot, and leg all work a little like an outrigger, out there, to the outside, biting into the snow and slicing around. Looks great. Sounds great. Now how can we learn to carve like Bill?

First things first. You need a pair of carving skis set up for supercarving, i.e., with plates under the bindings. A few specialty ski shops at big resorts actually rent carving demo skis. Look for them before you rush out and buy a pair of these amazing little machines. And, in fact, the relatively new super-short skis, modeled after World Cup slalom skis, only a little softer, will do the trick as well. Start on a very easy, freshly groomed slope, facing diagonally down and across the slope. Now spread your skis two feet or so apart and flex your uphill leg so that your hips move laterally over that ski. (That ski, by the way, is virtually flat on the snow.) Your other leg, your downhill leg, meanwhile, feels stretched out, almost straight (a skier's leg is never completely straight). And you'll notice that the other ski, out to the side of your body, is actually tilted way up on its edge. Now, in this strange position, push off and feel how that edged ski bites into the snow and guides you in a long smooth arc. A pure carve, for sure, but still a long way from the continuous pure carved turns we've been watching.

Do this a couple of times in both directions, tracing long carved arcs across the hill to a stop. And then it's time to try to link these long carved some-thing-or-others together. Start straight down the hill in a wide stance, flex one leg, and settle your hips to that side as you feel the opposite ski begin to carve; after a few meters of this, move your hips across to the opposite side and feel your stretched-out leg and ski start to carve back the other way. And so on.

So far, nothing hard. This is only a sort of experiment to feel the edge of your outside ski bite and carve. Now, how do we get from this patient, slow, and—admit it—rather awkward carve into a dynamic exciting carve, some-thing that feels a little more like skiing? The answer is: gradually. And our

Figure 8.4 *Supercarving again.* *In this image it's clear how much the skier's hips, or center of gravity, have to move inside the turn. This strong movement of the hips from one side to the other helps roll the skis over to an unusually high edge angle.*

method is simple: Go faster. With feet still apart, build up more speed and then speed up this whole process, moving your hips rapidly from one side cleanly across to the other side to change directions. (But beware: You are **not,** and I repeat **not,** turning your hips, merely moving them laterally to set one ski, the outside ski of these proto-carved turns, strongly on edge.) Does this remind you of something? Of course, it does. Crossover, the commitment of your body, and especially your hips, into the new turn, which we played with in Chapter 4. Supercarving demands extreme crossover, extreme commitment of the skier's hips and upper body down the hill, to the inside of the coming turn. This is what more or less guarantees the extreme edge angle needed to carve a fairly tight curve at a moderate speed.

You'll have to feel your way into this extreme crossover turn by turn. But I can describe how it feels, how it works. You're racing across the slope, with most of your weight on your bottom ski, ready to start a new carved turn. Now you are going to do two things at the same time. Move your hips down the hill so far and so fast that if nothing else happened, you would fall right over into the snow. But at the same time, you relax your legs, folding them slightly, and let your feet move forward ahead of your hips. So it seems as though your crossover move is no longer a move forward and down the hill, but almost backward and down the hill. You aren't really moving backward; it's just that your feet are getting ahead of you. You are diving into the center of a short turn that is about to happen. And what happens is this: Your top ski rolls way over onto its new edge. Its radical sidecut makes the ski bite the snow in a curved arc (we remember that the higher the edge angle, the more a ski can be pushed and bent into reverse camber, into a deeper bend). And the turn starts and keeps on going, fairly fast.

Supercarving is like that. These turns aren't necessarily patient long radius carved turns; most of the time, they are amazingly tight carved arcs. And this is possible only because the skis are very, very short, because they have a very, very deep sidecut, and because the skier's body is way, way to the inside (the result of such a radical crossover move). By the way, does it sound as though I have just described a skier losing his or her balance backward? That's not really true—although for an instant you are behind your feet—because the carving skis catch up with you and you leave the turn not only balanced but even pressing forward a bit in your boots.

And that's the path—increasing your speed and exaggerating your crossover—that I suggest will take you into the fascinating subworld of super-carving. My friend Bill Thistle has done a good job of initiating me into the mysteries of leaving lines—and nothing but lines—on the snow. But I confess I am a long way from being a master of this esoteric side discipline in skiing. Big mountain skiing through all kinds of unpacked, fast-changing, gnarly snow conditions is more my passion.

But I can say that supercarving is a delight. And that you can carry the sensations you master and the elegant lines you pursue down virgin corduroy snow with you when you trade your supercarving skis for all-mountain skis. Two brilliant Austrian coaches who teach in Australia in the Southern Hemisphere's winter season have baptized this style of skiing "fun carving." And that's a very good note on which to end this section. Supercarving is simply fun. Keep it fun. Don't take it too seriously. Carving is hardly a moral virtue and the inability to leave two perfect lines in the snow is hardly a moral failing. Skiing is a joyful game, and pure carving only a game within the game. Enjoy.

Recreational Racing and Higher Speed Skiing

"Racers ready … go!" Almost every American skier I know has skied in a NASTAR race (NASTAR is an acronym for national standard race) invented by the folks at *Ski Magazine* years ago, and held at most serious ski resorts. And yet only a tiny minority of skiers have ever been involved in intense amateur racing, junior racing, collegiate racing, regional- or national-level racing. Serious racing demands almost year-round commitment as well as talent and quickly takes over a young skier's life. Understanding, supportive parents and dedicated coaches can guide young competitors along that road. What I want to discuss, briefly, in this section, is racing for the hell of it: club racing, NASTAR racing, fun racing, or (as it's often called) recreational racing. I've often claimed that life is too short not to become an expert skier. And once you enter those ranks, it's a shame not to qualify for a NASTAR gold pin, which is more of a reward for not screwing up than for really skiing fast. Let's take a closer look.

Most fun races, nowadays, are of the giant slalom variety, sort of. In traditional Alpine racing, there are four events: slalom, giant slalom, super G, and downhill. Downhill races, of course, are the straightest and fastest of the lot, and slalom races involve the tightest turns. So a giant slalom course, for example, is set for longer rounder turns. In traditional Alpine racing, skiers pass between sets of flags and/or poles—nowadays, these are spring-loaded "breakaway poles," which flop down to the snow when racers hit them. By contrast, most recreational race courses are quite short and are so-called one-pole courses where only the inside of each turn is marked, usually by a giant slalom–type flag tied between two poles. NASTAR races are a perfect example: set on a fenced-off hill (which is not too long), a NASTAR race course consists of a series of smooth, not at all tight turns with, however, a modern electronic timing system. As most skiers know, NASTAR participants race against a pace-setter's adjusted time, and depending on how far away you are from this fast time, you are awarded a bronze, silver, or gold pin.

Let's quickly share the secrets of getting a gold. First, remember that it's easier to lose time by making mistakes, by overturning and skidding, than it is to gain time by poling and skating and pushing for speed. A smooth poised run, a series of nearly perfect carved turns with no sideways skidding, is your recipe for a fast time and a gold medal. At first, you might think that the straightest line between poles is going to be the fastest. And, indeed, it would be except for one thing. If you connect all the poles on the racecourse with straight lines, the corners will be too sharp, and you will tend to skid, and lose time, by turning too hard. So keeping that idea of skiing as straight a line as possible from pole to pole, make an effort to round out the corners, the turns, in the smoothest possible way without skiing very far from those theoretical straight lines.

This isn't hard to do if you focus on one idea—the golden rule of recreational racing: Turn early. Ideally, in a NASTAR race you should start each turn well before the pole that marks the inside of that turn. And when you pass that pole, you should be heading straight for the next pole. What happens if you don't turn early, before the pole? If you turn too late—say, when you are very close to the pole or passing the pole—then you will tend to drop too low and you'll have to cut back across the slope at a less steep angle to reach the next pole and the next turn. Your line between the two turns will be slower, and, worse yet, late turns tend to multiply, each turn getting progressively later,

Figure 8.5 *The secret of a NASTAR gold medal. A clean carving turn that doesn't waste precious tenths of a second by skidding. Dynamic step turns like this one are just the ticket for a fast NASTAR race time. Skier and skis are continually moving forward, never sideways.*

forcing you to turn back farther to reach the next pole. It's a simple rule of thumb: Turn early, turn early, turn early.

What else? Unless you are very good at skating I don't recommend taking a few skating steps out of the starting gate to build up speed. One awkward step will cost you more time than you are gaining. And although it often isn't necessary, I recommend you experiment with a smooth decisive step to your outside ski. In a typical NASTAR course, with wide flowing turns, a small lateral step at the start of your turn will allow you to take a steeper, straighter line toward the upcoming pole (remember, steeper and straighter means faster), and then as you step laterally, you gain just enough clearance to pass the pole smoothly in an efficient minimal arc. Play with this idea to see where it is most helpful.

But my main advice is simplicity itself. Ski smoothly and efficiently, and avoid skidding. In a racecourse, any sideways skidding, even for a few feet, will probably put an end to your hopes for a gold.

Racing is clearly about speed. But in larger context, so is skiing, period. Without the wind in your face, skiing just wouldn't be skiing. Yet speed on skis is a very subjective thing. A beginner might feel that schussing straight down that green practice slope at the bottom of the mountain is altogether too frightening to contemplate. Experienced skiers, heading back down to the lodge, flying straight down that same hill might wonder why their skis weren't moving faster and might make a mental note to get their skis waxed before tomorrow morning. Speed, in short, is relative.

But because speed and racing go naturally together, I thought this would be the perfect spot to share a few tips with you about skiing fast, really fast. For now, let's define fast skiing as skiing significantly faster than your normal speed, whatever that is. And let's talk about the best way to deal with such unaccustomed speeds. But I can already hear some skiers saying: Hey, that's not me. I'm just not interested in skiing fast, period. And that's okay. There is no speed threshold one has to cross to enter the company of expert skiers. But I would say that even the most prudent or speed-averse skiers will sometimes find themselves skiing faster than they had in mind. Someone falls in front of you, and you have to straighten out your turn to avoid a crash, and suddenly you are really hauling. These things happen. What then?

The most important strategy for skiing fast or extra fast is that you, the skier, must move slowly, extra slowly. Think about driving a car. At slow speeds, say in a parking lot, you can spin the steering wheel or stomp on the brakes, and you will be okay. But if you spin the wheel or hit the brakes while you are moving at 65 miles per hour on the freeway, you will probably spin out and crash. Behind the wheel of our cars we have learned to look ahead when we are traveling at high speeds and to act and react slowly, patiently, progressively. Same on skis. The faster you go, the slower and more patient your turns must be if you don't want to lose it. Another way of saying the same thing is that if you find yourself moving too fast on snow, the solution is to slow down slowly—with long, progressive turns. That at least is the recipe for getting things back together if you realize suddenly that you are going too fast. Take it easy; no sudden moves or quick turns. Slow down slowly.

But the quest for speed is something else. If you find yourself jazzed by a little extra speed, I can only encourage you to pursue these delicious sensations. There's no reason that high-speed skiing should be a racers-only pleasure. But racers train and race on fenced-off and, generally, empty slopes—never on crowded runs. As a recreational skier, your best bet for finding a safe and sensible situation to ski fast is to be among the first skiers on the lift. At Aspen and Snowmass, where I have been organizing intensive ski weeks for quite a few years, the first hour of the skiing day is close to ideal for fast skiing. The mountain is still relatively empty; the overnight grooming crews have provided immaculate fresh corduroy surfaces for high-speed, top-to-bottom nonstop runs—runs that would be ridiculously dangerous later in the day. Be sensible. It doesn't matter how good you are; skiing at high speed close to other skiers is both foolish and downright rude. You can ruin other skiers' experience by giving them the impression that they barely escaped a collision even if you were skiing well within your limits. And skiing fast on an empty run, early in the morning, is simply more fun.

What else? At higher-than-normal speeds, spread your hands a bit wider than normal for better lateral balance. And really focus your attention on balancing over that outside ski. Use more patience than normal in starting and entering your turns. And avoid twisting your feet. Skids are much less enjoyable at high speeds. In fact they can be downright unnerving. Long, patient carved turns are the ticket. Take your time. And don't forget to smile with all that wind in your face.

Steeps and Extreme Steeps

Steep is hard. Steep is scary. Steep slopes are intensely challenging and intensely rewarding. Skiing a steep slope is, almost by definition, an adventure. And in my book, adventures are always good. But I certainly don't want to encourage you to go looking for steeps, steep black slopes, and double blacks, and slopes steeper still that have resisted naming and trail signs until and unless you are ready. You guessed it. There's a sort of prerequisite to feeling at home on very steep slopes. Naturally, I'm talking about short linked turns, turns linked with a pattern that I've called dynamic anticipation, and that we covered together in Chapter 5.

The logic of skiing very steep slopes goes like this. On the steeps, you can't afford to linger in the fall line—you would quickly accelerate out of your com-

How's it look, Edgar? Will it go? My friend Edgar Boyles is out of sight, around the corner, down below. The snow drops away, out of sight too. I pay out the rope that connects me to Edgar and wonder what I'm doing here with skis on my feet. We're just above the narrowest part of the Tram Chute, the steep, snow-choked gully in the rocky face of Granite Chief, just beneath Squaw Valley's big aerial tram. Edgar and I have been looking at this thin wedge of snow all season. We can ski that, I know we can. And one morning we looked at each other and thought: Why not today? Problem was if you lost it and fell

during this descent, you would be smashed on rocks, tumble over cliffs, the full catastrophe. The solution: a climbing rope. We would belay each other down, skiing one at a time, with one skier anchored to the side of the gully, then the other. We thought then, and I still think today, that no ski run, no matter how exciting, is worth risking your life for.

So here we are, trying not to trip on our rope, making quick hopped, or "pedaled," pivots from side to side, sliding like madmen till we can get our edges in again and bounce off the snow again. And it's working. The chute is more scary than hard. One rope length. Two.

fort zone, and who knows where it would all end. So steep slope adepts opt for very short turns, bringing their skis around—past the fall line or gravity line and back across the slope—as fast as possible. Clearly, turning your body from one side to the other isn't going to help. There just isn't enough time to turn your trunk first right, then left, then right again, then left again, and so forth. So anticipation, total anticipation, feet and skis pivoting beneath a quite stable upper body, is an absolute necessity on very steep slopes. But as you can imagine, steep slopes are hardly the place to master this pattern. When your

Three. We're through the narrows, almost down. I ski out of the bottom of the long narrow gully onto an open face of snow, still steep but no longer confined between sandy-colored walls of weathered Sierra granite. We're home free. I ski over to a notch above a pine tree growing out of the slope and take in the slope while Edgar comes down with his patented loose-limbed leap-and-land turns. Looking good ... And then he trips, falls, slides in a disorganized tangle right by my tree. I pull in as much rope as I can, hang on, and jump off the other side of the tree.

It's over. We hang on the slope, *laughing and giggling, held by a red 9-mm climbing rope passing behind that single tree. Guess I relaxed, Edgar allows; guess I lost my concentration. Yes, but not his cool. There's an unpleasant cliff just 50 feet below us, Whew ... We untangle ourselves, say goodbye to our thank-god tree, and traverse around the cliff band. Still smiling and laughing. It all seems like Squaw Valley prehistory now. Other much better and much braver skiers have skied the Tram Chute fairly often since then. Without ropes. But the first time was a grand adventure on skis. Any adventure that becomes a memory is a successful adventure.*

linked short turns, straight down the fall line, are working well, then you're ready to tackle seriously steep slopes.

On extreme steeps, the game is to get your skis from one horizontal position to another, aimed the opposite way, of course, as fast as possible: sometimes leaping and pivoting, and then virtually falling down the mountain, between turns. But let's leave the drama of extreme skiing and extreme steepness to one side for a moment, and concentrate first on some tricks and tools for handling those merely breathtakingly steep slopes that usually merit a double-black-diamond designation on trail maps.

Even when your short linked turns are rather good, a sudden increase in steepness can make things fall apart. The psychological problem of a very steep slope is obvious, especially if it's a long one. You can't help thinking, if only for a second: Wow, I might fall all the way down there. In addition, although it's actually an optical illusion, all slopes look steeper when viewed from above than from across or below. And that doesn't make steep slopes any friendlier either. But, technically, there's another problem, one that I've already mentioned in connection with bumps. On a steep slope, our skis automatically and naturally have a big edge angle in relation to the snow, and that gets us in trouble. By that I mean that even without any edging effort on our part, with our skis simply horizontal, they are already biting into the slope at a considerable angle. And if we tense up, which is all too easy to do on a really steep slope, the edges of our skis can lock in, or rail in, and shoot us forward across the hill, adding to the general impression that things are getting out of control. Overedged skis are harder to steer on a steep slope and can easily accelerate out from under the skier. The answer, of course, is to relax and let go of this steep slope with the edges of our skis. In a word, to sideslip.

It isn't that easy. In fact, it is quite counterintuitive. But letting go of the slope is a big part of taming the steeps. It can get you going when you start to feel: Uh, oh, I don't belong here. And when you know that first turn is going to be a big challenge. My suggestion: When you find yourself at the top of a very steep slope, simply sideslip down into the slope forty or fifty feet or more, before turning, just to get used to the pitch. You will feel and adjust to the extra natural edging I mentioned above. You will adapt your stance and balance to the new angle of the steep slope, and you will start to relax. And your first turn is more likely to be a good one after this short sideslip than if you started by diving down the hill or traversing into this intense situation on locked edges.

Your strategy for handling steep slopes will be just as important as your technique. For instance, you can find yourself a short but steep pitch to practice on before you venture out onto long, exposed steep runs. And in this calmer context, you can work on a couple of aspects of linking short turns that will pay off on very steep slopes. Your goal: Start these turns quickly; finish them quickly.

Up to a certain steepness, I prefer to use the kind of soft weight shift that I described at the end of Chapter 4, flexing and folding and, so to speak, collapsing my downhill leg into each turn. With this kind of a start, your skis will hug the snow as they pivot rapidly back around underneath you. And you will be able to steer them quickly back across the hill. Obviously, you will not be carving. Throw out any notion of carving on extremely steep slopes.

But beyond a certain steepness, even this rapid pivoting on the snow seems to take too long and threatens to build up too much speed for comfort. Then it's time to pivot your skis clear around in the air, launching your turns with a bounce or a hop or a quick retraction of boots, legs, and skis beneath you. In essence, you pick 'em up and turn 'em. To facilitate such rapid action, whether folding your legs beneath you or lifting your skis clear off the snow, pole action is critical. The steeper the slope, the more you want to support yourself on your downhill pole as you make your move. With solid support on that downhill pole planted straight down the slope beneath you, you'll find it much easier not only to lift your skis quickly off the snow but to pull your heels up beneath you as you do so, thus tilting your skis down the slope and making sure the tails of your skis don't catch on the snow as you flip them around. This

Figure 8.6 *A trick for very steep slopes. Beyond a certain angle, it just doesn't pay to keep your skis on the snow. Rebound or even jump into the air and pivot your skis around rapidly beneath you. But on a steep slope like this, you'll need to pull your heels up underneath you to keep them from hanging up on the snow.*

move is very similar to what you have perhaps already learned to do in bumps when you press your toes (and ski tips) down into the hollow space of a trough as you pass the crest of the bump. Pressing the toes down the hill involves pulling your heels up beneath with a kind of retraction/folding movement of your legs: vital on very steep slopes. You can even feel what I'm talking about right now, sitting in a chair, if you just pull your feet up and back under you— notice how your toes point downward as you do so. This move is a winner on steep bumps and steep slopes generally as it makes your skis stay more parallel with the angle of the slope as they are turning rapidly.

So we've looked at a rapid start to our turns on very steep slopes, leading, we hope, to an equally rapid finish to keep the lid on our speed. This truncated follow-through phase should be pretty easy if you start relaxed and manage to keep your weight centered fore and aft. Balance too far forward and your skis will run away from you as you come out of the fall line. Balance too far back and the same thing will happen, although in a different way, as your tails catch and edge and rail in. Stay centered, stay loose, and let your skis slip through the tail end of an abbreviated arc before stopping this inevitable slide with a quick edge set.

"Edge set"? I think this is the first time I've used this expression in this entire book. The term means exactly what you think, quickly edging into the hill, especially with the edge of your downhill ski. Edge sets used to be a big part of expert-level skiing; no longer. But like strong unweighting, we keep these older moves in reserve for special circumstances, and a very steep slope is about as special as it gets. At the end of a quick short turn, if you stop the slipping of your skis with sudden sharp edging (an edge set), you will get a reaction off the snow, a kind of bounce or rebound that helps to spring you back off the snow into the air, so that you can once again pivot your skis rapidly around to the other side. Feeling this edge set and rebound effect, practicing it, and ultimately using it to launch rapid turns on steep slopes will take a bit of time. But I'm assuming that you have decided you really want to master steep slopes, that you have taken the trouble to find a short steep practice pitch, and that you are willing to put some time into the effort. Start by sideslipping straight down the pitch in a very anticipated position, then slam your downhill edge into the slope with a quick movement of your foot and ankle. (Pressing your knees into the slope to "set your edge" is much less efficient—always start with the feet.) The amount of reaction, or rebound, you get from this move depends more on how fast you set your edges than on how strongly you edge. This move has more or less disappeared from normal everyday skiing for several reasons: Our skis turn so easily that we just don't need to unweight them through rebound or any other form of up-motion, and nowadays skilled skiers seek to avoid any sudden moves that will break the steady forward flow of their skis' motion. But extreme situations still demand extreme movements. And very, very steep slopes certainly qualify as an extreme situation.

So now we have a pattern, a plot, for mastering the steeps. Let me list the elements. Short turns with lots of anticipation. Staying as loose and relaxed as possible, no matter how excited we feel inside. Triggering our turns either with a rapid folding/collapsing action of the downhill leg or with a quick lifting move, a bounce of rebound. And then finishing our short turns, without locking our edges and shooting off across the hill, by means of a snappy edge set that can provide the bounce or lift to start the next turn.

Let me add that this edge-set-and-rebound pattern is dynamite on smooth steep slopes, for example, wind-blasted walls of snow above timberline. But when there are bumps, even the beginnings of bumps, on steep double-black slopes, it makes more sense to use these shapes to launch and guide our turns.

And here's a safety tip. Falling, cartwheeling, and tumbling down a long steep slope is more than merely frustrating. It can be very dangerous indeed. So if and when you lose it on the steep—and I'm sure you will, we all have— act fast. Dig in to stop your slide before you build momentum, before things get out of hand. This advice applies equally to steep mogul runs and to steep smooth slopes. Get your feet below you and scrape to a quick stop if you can. You can also use your elbows to dig in to the snow, which not only will slow and stop you but will tend to keep your head uphill (whereas digging in with feet and skis can flip you over). On very steep slopes where I know that a long tumble is the last thing I want, I will often take my pole straps off my wrist, so that in case of a fall, I can grab one pole, slide both my hands down to the point of that pole, and slowly grind it into the snow around shoulder level in a version of the mountaineer's self-arrest. This self-arrest has saved me more than once after I made a mistake on a potentially dangerous steep slope. But a good rule of thumb is that if you think you can't stop a fall, you just don't belong on that slope. If you can hear a little voice inside you whispering: *Don't do it!* then you had better listen.

I can promise you, though, that if you pay your dues, first mastering short linked turns and then practicing them on some short, safe but steep pitches, you will find that steep slopes become less steep, less daunting, less forbidding. Yes, you can even enjoy runs on radical double-black slopes. I do. And when you're ready, you will too.

Open-Ended Challenges

No, that's still not the whole story. Because no matter how good you get, just when you think you have it wired, you run headlong—or should I say, ski headlong—into a new challenge. I haven't tackled the scary mysteries of skiing breakable crust or the obvious athletic challenges of jumping (and landing). And there's more.

No, you won't run out of challenges, you won't get bored, and, for that matter, you don't really need to pursue perfection on skis like a holy grail. Perfection, my ski pro friend John Philips likes to say, isn't really in the cards, but simple excellence will do just fine. Expert skiing is a sort of practical coming to terms with excellence on skis. Expert skiers are at home on the mountain, any mountain.

Figure 8.7 *Still more challenges.* Here we have both extreme steepness and deep spring snow—two challenges combined and multiplied. It's time to improvise. And there will always be new challenges whenever you want to look for them.

You don't have to pursue and master each and every new challenge to know that you have discovered a new relation with mountains and snow and winter. To know that you belong out here, up here, on a windswept snowy slope, the world spread out below you, a white world full of choices, full of challenges, full of possibilities, full of pleasure. Most of this book has been about ski technique, modern expert ski technique. And just by reading this far, you have proved yourself a good student. But there are one or two more aspects of expert skiing that have more to do with strategy and style, with vision and attitude than with pure technique—a few more patterns to explore in our quest to feel completely at home on every slope. And that's what we're about to investigate in the next chapter.

IN SUMMARY

- Ice: The slicker the ice, the smoother and more subtle the skier's movements have to be. Sharp edges will help, but excess edging won't. Quiet hands help keep your weight balanced along the whole edge of your ski. Sudden pressures and sudden edging lead to sudden skids on ice.

- Supercarving: Extreme carving requires special extra-short super-sidecut skis, lifted bindings, and very high edge angles. To create sufficient edging, you need to move your hips far to the inside of each turn. And this, at anything less than racing speeds, requires the supercarving skier to support some body weight on the inside ski of each turn—even though the outside ski is doing almost all the work of carving.

- Recreational racing and higher speed skiing: The recipe for a fast time in a NASTAR race is simple: Don't lose precious seconds by skidding your turns. Turn early; turn cleanly; carve a smooth progressive arc around each pole. In general, the faster you ski, the slower and more patient all your movements must become.

- Very steep slopes: Practice turning on steep but short and safe pitches before you find yourself on a big, scary steep slope. Serious steeps demand total anticipation, a rapid start, and a rapid finish to each turn. Use rebound and a rapid pivoting of your skis from one horizontal position to the next. Don't try to carve; accept sideslipping as an inevitable part of skiing extremely steep slopes.

CHAPTER 9

Soft Skiing Down Hard Slopes

Subtle Secrets of High-Performance Skiing

They're having so much fun, you've just got to stop and watch: a group of instructors skiing together early in the morning before their first lesson. Fresh snow, ice crystals suspended in midair, and what skiers! what turns! Outrageous arcs, slippery S-curves, backlit plumes of snow like a scene from a Warren Miller film. What a sight. And you know enough to know just how good these off-duty ski pros really are. You watch them with educated eyes; after all, you have become an expert-level skier yourself, although these skiers have years more experience than you do. And then it dawns on you, there are experts and then there are experts. All these skiers are impressive but two or three are really dazzling; their skiing is a cut above. And you start to wonder: Why? And how?

You've just become aware of the difference between good and very good skiers, between the skilled and the superskilled. The difference is real; you can see it easily, but it's hard to put into words. And now that you think about it, it's not just a question of reaching instructor-level skiing. There are many levels of expert skiing. Some very skilled advanced skiers seem to do everything right, but ... They make great carved turns, they ski the steepest, meanest slopes with great control but even so, their skiing doesn't appear effortless and playful. It's almost as though they are still working at skiing well. It hasn't become 100 percent natural or inevitable. I'm going to try to explain this difference and see if I can't help you make that transition into this higher level of subtle, stunning, and seemingly effortless ski performance.

First, let me quickly add that I applaud each and every skier who moves from the ranks of plateaued and frustrated intermediates into the polished parallel world of carved turns and fall-line skiing, into the new world of expert ski technique. Totally brilliant peak performance on skis is not such an important life goal that you need to feel disappointed because there are still skiers who are more comfortable, more dashing on their skis than you are. There always will be. There are skiers I've admired for years, knowing full well that I'll never be able even to come close to their consummate ease of performance. No big deal. But I still find it fascinating to study differences in skiing performance at high technical levels and to try to understand, communicate, and share what it is that makes certain skiers so special.

This phenomenon, the remarkable and seemingly effortless skiing of a small minority of professional skiers, is very noticeable in ski schools across the country. By the time they have passed all their exams and qualified for all the possible certifications available, ski pros are more than merely competent, more than just marginally skillful. Nonetheless, some of them merely ski well while others ski beautifully. It's like the difference between a talented student who has learned to speak French in school and a native French speaker. Where does this extra dimension of ease, fluency, and fluid motion come from? I've wrestled with this problem for years, and I confess I haven't yet succeeded in distilling and bottling this extra dimension of ease on skis into a magic potion that I can hand my students and say: Here, drink. But I do think I'm zeroing in on some of the reasons for this performance gap and what to do about it.

The answer has a lot to do with relaxation—in situations where relaxation is not the obvious response. And I'm also convinced that this next level of refined expert performance is a real possibility for almost anyone, although differences in sheer talent will always be there to haunt us. Let's start our quest for this kind of peak performance in a roundabout way by first getting rid of one of the most persistent myths about skiing performance.

The Myth of Aggressive Skiing

As long as I have been teaching skiing, I've listened to other instructors telling their students that if they wanted to ski better, especially on harder slopes, they had to ski more aggressively. Don't hesitate; just be more aggressive. Attack the slope. Ski aggressively. Such advice absolutely floors me. I'm not buying it. And it never really works. Indeed, I hope to convince you that trying to be more aggressive on skis is generally counterproductive. It will probably make you ski worse. Yes, of course, I know that's an overgeneralization. I'm the first to confess there are a few skiing situations, notably during the intense short struggles of high-level Alpine racing, where an aggressive attitude pays off. But not for most skiers most of the time. And certainly not in a learning situation.

I suppose these well-meaning instructors who talk about skiing aggressively are trying to exhort their students not to be timid, not to shrink back from the hill but to move forward to meet the mountain. A worthy goal. (Although I also believe that simply cheering skiers on is never enough. It's clearly more important to train our feet to ski well than to hype ourselves up into a state of false bravado.) Let's look more closely at this confusion about skiing aggressively, starting with words and ending with action on snow.

In my lexicon, the opposite of timid is not exactly aggressive; it's confident. There's a big difference. The word *aggressive* implies struggle and tension, forcing something to happen, pushing harder. And in many situations—for example, in challenging bumps and steeps—we have already seen that powerful, sudden, aggressive movements on skis tend to create too much muscular tension, which in turn can make the edges of our skis catch and "rail in" so that we actually lose control over our skis rather than increasing it.

In fact, for many ambitious and athletic skiers, an aggressive attitude toward skiing, toward one's skis, toward the mountain, seems almost natural. Yet I have to tell you, it almost never works. Because an aggressive attitude leads to a sort of overacting—movements that are too violent, too sudden, too strong, and tend to interfere with the smooth sliding of our skis over the snow. So I want to suggest a different ideal, a different image of what an expert skier's attitude and posture and style of movement should be—one of relaxed confidence. A state in which you can work *with* the mountain rather than attacking it.

Working with the mountain means adapting your movements to fit the terrain. And it also means making every move, every turn, every run as efficiently as possible—skiing with the least amount of energy. Letting your skis go. Letting turns happen and forces build progressively rather than forcing them all at once. Skiing, as I noted in Chapter 1, is a sport of borrowed forces. Gravity is the engine propelling us down white mountainsides. We are not strong enough to move this fast. Gravity pulling us and the friction of skis against snow, snow against skis, pushing back, is what produces these exciting carved turns, these heart-pounding runs. We couldn't do it on our own. And we don't need to contribute much muscular force. The role of the expert skier is to coordinate and direct these amazing external forces. Calm and collected, smiling wildly, but not moving wildly, we can observe the action down at the snow level. And enjoy it. And control it. But the more in sync you are with your skis, with the snow, with winter, the less there is to feel aggressive about. Or toward. "Ski more aggressively" is about the most pointless advice one can give an aspiring skier. Let's move beyond this foolish myth once and for all.

Try Softer: Relaxation in Expert Skiing

I often tell my students that skiing is a basically un-American sport. That's because most of our sports stories and our sports metaphors revolve around the idea of trying harder. It's as American as apple pie. The football team is down twelve points at halftime; the coach gives his boys the traditional pep talk before they return to the field: Okay, guys, go out and really hit 'em! I want you to drive harder, tackle harder, run harder, play harder. Try harder, in short. Well, in skiing it's just the opposite; the trick is to try softer.

Try softer is a nice phrase. I use it in several different senses. One aspect of *trying softer* on skis is to develop a soft touch on the snow. French skiers have

a perfect word for this, *la glisse*, literally, sliding. But actually *la glisse* implies unimpeded, unhindered sliding, a delicate state with the minimum of shocks, with no sudden friction catching at one's skis.

Try softer also refers to the fact that often the best way to make something happen in expert skiing is by the selective relaxation of certain muscle groups rather than by contracting other muscles. This is true when it comes to shifting weight and changing the edges of our skis, to launching turns, to absorbing excess pressure, whether in bumps or in deep powder. Or even getting out of trouble, making emergency stops, avoiding rocks in the bottom of a bump's gully, and more. And an intriguing corollary of this notion is that if you can maintain a background state of relaxed readiness, when quick muscular response is required, you don't wind up fighting your own tensed muscles.

Figure 9.1 *Trying softer.* *I often tell my students, tongue in cheek, of course, that they should try to "ski like a girl," and then, in all seriousness, I explain that watching skilled women skiers will provide them with the best possible images of soft skiing on hard slopes. Expert women skiers tend to solve skiing problems with finesse and relaxation rather than power and strength. There's an important lesson here that we can all learn.*

And a last sense of *try softer* is equally important—the psychological sense. Backing off, letting things happen, giving your skis room and time to do what they do best. Learning to diffuse the anxiety often triggered by tough snow and steep slopes.

Let's look at each aspect of trying softer in some detail. A soft touch or a light touch on the snow is the sure sign of a consummate expert. You can develop this subtle feel for sliding on snow by focusing on a couple of key points. Ski tall. You want your skis to flow and glide over this snow as smoothly as possible. To maintain this supple sliding over constantly changing terrain requires that whenever your skis hit some obstacle in the terrain, tiny or large, you'll need to absorb the extra pressure, or compression, that this encounter generates. And you do this, first, by relaxing your foot and ankle and, second, by relaxing your whole leg and letting it flex loosely like a very elastic shock absorber. A tense leg will resist the small shocks transmitted from the snow up through your boots and feet, and you will experience a bouncier and jerkier ride. And when you ski in a low position, with ankles, knees, and hips deeply flexed, your legs will automatically be tense. This is because in such a low position, the strong quad muscles in your thighs have to contract to keep you upright. You pay for this extra leg tension with more fatigue and a jerky ride.

In a tall stance, however, most of your body weight is supported by your skeleton. The bones in your legs, in particular, are stacked up on top of each other, almost vertical (but not quite), and you only need a small amount of muscle tension to stabilize this mostly skeletal structure. Result: looser muscles, an increased ability to flex with the terrain to absorb all the sudden little excesses in pressure between skis and snow. You can go one step further and make a habit of standing even more on one ski. Not just in turns, which I know you are already doing, but as you cruise across the mountain in traverses too. If you are traversing on two feet, the combined strength of those two legs is too great, and they tend to resist or push back when you experience small shocks from uneven terrain. But if you are really traversing on one ski (in a traverse this will naturally be your downhill ski), then that leg, which is already doing the job of supporting your body, doesn't have much extra strength available. When your skis ride across bumps or high spots in the terrain that would normally produce solid shocks, this downhill leg will simply give and flex, equalizing the pressure, absorbing shocks big or tiny. So a tall stance, and dominant balance

The Hidden Bonus of Foot-to-Foot Skiing

Now that we are getting close to the end of this book, it might seem that I have said just about all I have to say on the subject of foot-to-foot skiing—moving to the new ski, the outside ski, and staying balanced there while that ski flexes under your weight and carves a beautiful arc. Almost, but not quite. In the context of this chapter devoted largely to ease, efficiency, and relaxation on skis, I want to underscore one last, vital advantage of this style of riding and working one ski at a time. It's a helluva way to avoid tired legs, to rest and recover in the thick of the action.

I mean, of course, that while one leg is supporting all your weight, the other one is taking a break, more or less relaxed, not really working. This alternation of tension and repose, first one leg then the other, is a large part of what I sometimes call aerobic skiing. Try an easy experiment. By now I trust that you can ski down a slope either in the way I have been proposing—shifting totally onto the outside ski of each turn—or the exact opposite way, standing solidly on both feet. Maybe the turns won't be quite as good, but what the heck. Pick a very long slope and ski it both ways: foot to foot, and then, right afterward, with your weight as equally distributed as possible on both skis. I'm confident that you'll feel the difference. Carrying weight on both legs, both feet, all the time—although necessary, for example, in deep snow—is a good recipe for increased muscle fatigue. Imagine hopping down the street on both feet compared to walking. The reason we can hike 20 miles in a long day and not be cramped up at the end is that in walking, one leg works while one leg relaxes, every other step. The same principle applies in efficient skiing.

on one ski even when going straight, and a more or less relaxed foot in your boot are all a part of developing a light touch on the snow.

Another big part is your ability to feel all the changing pressures on the sole of your foot and to respond to them in a subtle, quick, almost instinctive way. This takes time. But you can do it. One of my favorite ski stories involves Guy Périllat, a great French ski champion of the Jean-Claude Killy era. When a journalist asked him to explain the difference between good skiers and great skiers, Périllat responded (or so I've been told) that to be a great skier one needed to have an educated foot. He was right, and he was ahead of his time because back then, in the 1960s, official ski technique was very involved with all sorts of upper body actions, rotation, counterrotation, and instructors and coaches weren't paying that much attention to skiers' feet. But we've been focusing on the feet from the very first chapter of this book. And I hope you are beginning to develop that educated foot that Guy Périllat talked about: feeling your feet and responding with gentle muscle adjustments inside your boots. Foot awareness is a big part of developing a light touch on the snow. And so is a kind of backward and forward sliding of your foot beneath your body that we might call foot adjustment. The implicit goal is to maintain even pressure all along the length of our ski. To do so, the skier must sometimes push the foot ahead a bit or pull the foot back a bit to compensate for changing terrain (and remember there is a change of terrain throughout every turn). There is no pat formula for such foot awareness and foot adjustment. But by paying more attention to sensory input from the feet, you'll develop the ability to sense and maintain even uniform sliding pressure as your skis glide over the snow. The basic mechanism is always the same, back off, relax the foot and leg whenever sudden pressures would interfere with the smooth sliding of the skis. In a word, try softer.

And then there is the whole range of actions, especially ski-on-snow actions that we can trigger by the selective relaxation of certain muscle groups. Chief among these is what I call soft weight shift, a way of moving the skier's stance from one foot to the other by the simple expedient of releasing all the muscle tension in one foot. I described this in some detail at the end of Chapter 4. And I think this might be the single most important technique I've proposed in this book. So if you skipped over that section, go back and review it now. Softening and loosening and hence lightening one foot is a powerful move that doesn't require any power and one that doesn't interfere with the smooth forward motion of our skis over the snow. The application of this letting-go/folding/relaxing action of the downhill foot and leg to very short turns also facilitates the important pattern of dynamic anticipation. Why? Because this relaxation of muscle tension in your legs also affects the muscular connections linking your legs to your hips and waist, the area that has to stay relaxed, soft, and loose to create upper-lower body separation. This is another example of skiing better by trying softer.

Relaxing/collapsing one side, the downhill side, of the skier's lower body does more than just shift weight smoothly. It creates crossover, tilting the skier down the mountain toward the center of the new turn. Because your downhill leg no longer supports you, you begin to topple gently over down the hill—just what you want, to a greater or lesser degree, at the start of each turn. And as your body moves inexorably to the inside of the coming turn, your edges change, smoothly, progressively, inevitably. That's a lot of action, a lot of results, from just relaxing one foot and leg. Keep playing with this pattern until you have integrated it into your skiing at a deep and habitual level. It's hard to see from the outside just how much relaxation the most impressive expert skiers build into each turn, each run. But you can trust me when I tell you, it's a lot.

And lest you think that I am becoming a one-dimensional proponent of laid-back, lazy skiing, I want to add that even the quickest and most powerful skiing movements are more effective against a background of relaxation. There are lots of moments in skiing when you will want to make a quick and dynamic movement: twisting your skis suddenly through a bottleneck gap in mean bumps, lifting them out of a mess of cut-up crud and turning them in the air—last-minute moves to avoid rocks. The question: How do you make such sudden moves most effectively?

The answer is found in a principle that we discussed back in Chapter 5: ballistic motion versus co-contracted muscles. Remember? Every joint in the body has at least two pairs of opposing muscles associated with it—flexors and extensors, or, as physiologists call them, agonists and antagonists. Your quadriceps, for example, are extensors and your hamstrings are flexors. When both these opposing sets of muscles are contracting at the same time, fighting each other, movement is inefficient and fatiguing. We see this effect often when inexperienced skiers get nervous; they stiffen up all over, their limbs almost trembling from co-contracted muscles. At the opposite extreme is so-called ballistic motion, during which the set of muscles that contracts is

We've been skiing all day. And haven't taken the same run or the same lift twice. This is big country, even though it's also the old country, in skiing terms—the Austrian Vorarlberg, where it all began: ski schools and resort hotels and legendary local champions. In early morning shadow, we took the first lift up out of Zürs, shivering past a frozen lake. Then down toward Oberlech, turn after turn, kilometer after kilometer of rolling wavelike terrain, a lot of untracked snow still

left from the big storm last weekend. Exploring the lifts and runs of Lech. Riding the Rüfikopf cable car up the opposite side of the valley to a wide rooflike plateau of snow on the far side of Zürs. And now the sun has set.

We've scarcely stopped all day: just once on a sunlit terrace above Oberlech for a tall glass of Weissbier and now at this little hut on the flank of the Trittkopf, still thousands of feet above Zürs, where we sip glasses of country schnapps while waiting for the completely unopposed by the opposite set that remains relaxed. Obviously, such movement is very efficient: more and faster movement for less effort. Of course, this is precisely the way that extremely skilled—but basically very relaxed—skiers make sudden, powerful moves. Their skis respond in a flash because such skiers aren't fighting their own bodies. Action against the backdrop of a very relaxed stance is always more effective. Another interesting example of our notion of trying softer.

Finally, there is the psychological application of this mantra of ours: Try softer. Here I will be even less specific in terms of easy-to-follow one-two-three instructions. But I guess that's inevitable because this part of the top-level performance package takes days and months and years to develop. It is largely a question of defusing the crisis atmosphere of very challenging ski situations,

moon to rise so that we can finish our skiing circuit under its milky glow. One of the longest, best days of skiing I can remember. And the damnedest thing: I'm not even tired. I reach down and rub my thighs as though they ought to feel sore. They don't. I realize there might even be a name for what we've been doing: aerobic skiing— resting and recovering in the thick of the action. I realize too that there's a physical, technical side to this—skiing with as little tension, as much relaxation as possible—

and a psychological side to it— trusting my skis and my skill, trusting the snow, knowing that I don't have to fight for these runs, that I can just accept them. And, finally, as the moon rises and we walk outside to step into our skis, I can't help thinking maybe there's another, indefinable side to this experience too, something close to luck—choosing the right friends, the right romantic mountain range to ski, the right star-filled night to finish this longest day on skis—as fresh as when we started.

of slowly accepting at some deep inner level that everything is okay, of realizing that you really belong on this scary double-black slope—that it's not the end of the world. Building your expert-level movement patterns takes time. But coming to believe in them, and in yourself, takes even more time.

I can recall an experience at Squaw Valley during my early days as a ski instructor that illustrates this point perfectly. It was a very snowy winter, powder day after powder day, and I was pursuing the elusive goal of becoming a good deep-snow skier with something like single-minded devotion. Finally, after a big dump of snow, I found myself on the West Face of KT-22, steep and smooth and deep. I pushed off and was enjoying a great run, turn after turn, all face shots, snow flying over my head. And then, after at least a dozen wonderful turns, I crashed—because a little voice inside piped up: Lito, this is absurd, you can't ski this well! I crashed because, suddenly, I stopped believing that it was possible for me to ski like that. I can remember that wild five-foot Sierra storm like yesterday, and I remember how that single crash made me wake up and say: This is silly. It's time to admit that you're a good powder skier. The doubts will get you, not any flaws in your technique. Just let it happen. And I did. From that season on, I've known I was a powder skier. And I discovered that with that acceptance, I stopped trying so hard and began to ski powder much better. Letting it happen in a more free-form way, letting the deep drifts of Sierra powder and sometimes Sierra cement, push my skis where they would, riding my skis instead of trying to overturn and overcontrol them. Letting go. Letting it happen. Just another version of trying softer.

I can't predict just how or when you will experience a similar epiphany—but you will, I'm sure of it. It's all about realizing and accepting how good you have become. How everything will work out fine, even on runs where your skis are bouncing from crisis to crisis. You suddenly realize that you belong here—that you have crossed some invisible abstract boundary into the inner world of expert skiing. Accept this revelation with enthusiasm and gratitude. Realize what a long and successful journey you've made from the frustrating doldrums of the intermediate rut to this new sense of freedom on skis. Grin. Relax. Try softer. And ski better.

Reacting to the Mountain: Skiing the Big Shapes

As skiers we have one helluva playing field. Ski mountains come in all shapes, all flavors. What kind of a skier do you feel like becoming today? What kind of skiing did you have in mind this run? And what do you feel like skiing after lunch? Decisions, decisions.

In at least one sense, moguls are easy—you don't have to make many decisions. There's a bump in front of you, you turn around it. And then around the next one, and the next. There is a lot of technique involved in bump skiing, but very few choices. Yet when you push off from the top of a big ski mountain, a tabletop winter fantasy of bowls and trees and trails spreading out below you, you are faced with an almost infinite number of choices. You can create a run from scratch, tailor it to your mood and your skill and to the particular pair of skis you picked up this morning. I used the word "create" on purpose. For this is the creative side of skiing. Choices and more choices. All of them intriguing.

Expert skiers respond to these choices differently than average skiers. I've hinted at this difference earlier, but now let me make it explicit. One of the biggest differences between average stuck-in-a-rut intermediate skiers and true experts is this: Intermediates tend to repeat themselves all the way down the mountain. They have usually zeroed in on a favorite turn, often a medium-short, pushy, overinitiated, overskidded turn, and this turn has become their security blanket. As long as they keep on making that same turn, wherever they find themselves, they're going to be okay. And that's just what they do—ski the same turn over and over and over again, no matter where on the mountain they find themselves. Experts, by contrast, are constantly varying their skiing patterns to respond creatively to the mountain in front of them. Long turns and short, carved screamers and quick little wiggles. A morning in the mountains in midwinter is too precious to let yourself fall into a skiing rut.

I want to encourage you to constantly vary the way you ski different slopes.

Of course, along the way you will certainly discover that you have favorite ways of handling certain kinds of terrain. You may have already developed your own signature style of skiing, your own way of relating to the mountain. But you should still make a conscious effort to vary the way you ski different slopes. It will pay off handsomely by increasing your versatility as a skier.

Let's start with a few basic situations that seem to call for different approaches. Consider transitions, especially the transition from steeper to flatter slopes and from narrow to wider trails. When the pressure eases up, I recommend you take a deep breath or two, stand a little taller on your skis, and let your turns stretch out into long easy arcs. The tendency of too many skiers is to tighten up their turns for the steeps and then forget to stretch out again when that particular challenge is over. Big turns are a quintessential expression of confidence and relaxation. A few times each skiing day, make a point of exploring the limits of really big long-radius turns. Surprise yourself. Make some turns that are much larger, much longer, and much more patient than usual.

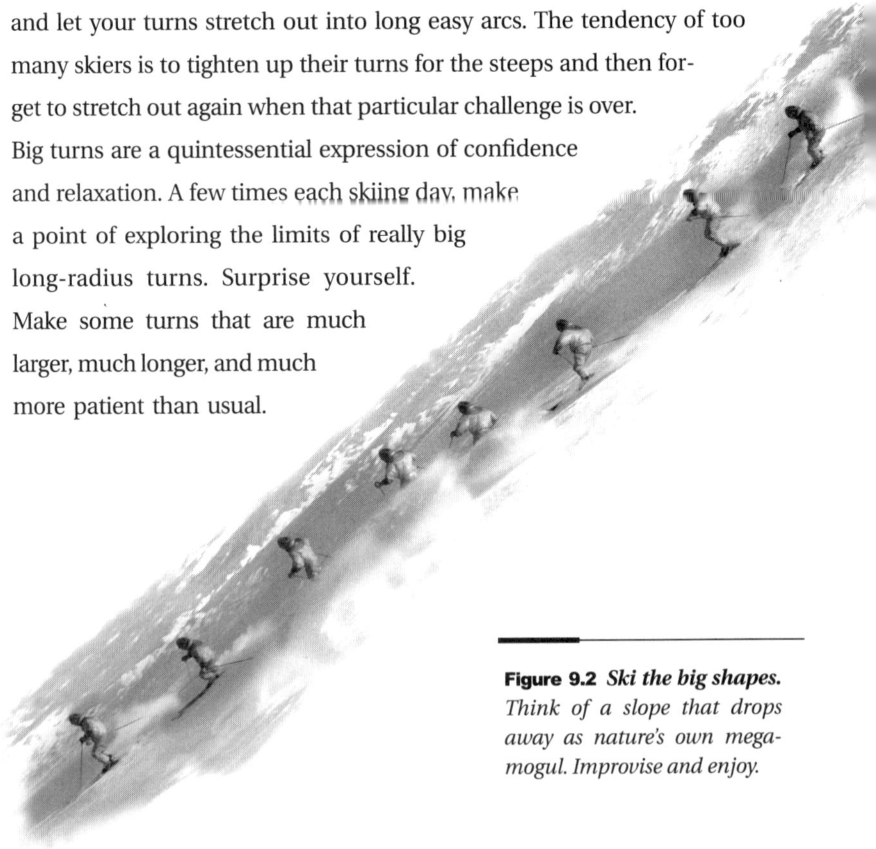

Figure 9.2 *Ski the big shapes. Think of a slope that drops away as nature's own mega-mogul. Improvise and enjoy.*

It's a great feeling in itself and also in contrast with the short turns you need to handle steeper slopes.

Transitions in the opposite sense are exciting too: skiing from a wide-open slope into a far more challenging situation without stopping to think things over, maintaining your rhythm and then adjusting it on the go. What does it feel like to shift from big cruisers to short tight turns? You'll find yourself flexing more deeply to facilitate the increased leg action that characterizes short turns, folding your legs, especially your downhill leg deeper into each shorter turn. You'll also begin to feel more upper and lower body separation as your legs start to turn faster while your torso seems only to move straight down the hill, our now familiar pattern of dynamic anticipation. But make this transition (from turn A to turn B, so to speak) smoothly over the space of a few turns; if you shorten your turns all at once, you are more likely to over-turn and skid out.

Play with transitions and challenge yourself to keep going. The ability to make transitions in your style while you ski across transitions in the terrain without stopping to think things over or to psych yourself up for the new pitch is a definite hallmark of your emerging expert skill. And keep mixing it up.

The logical move is to make short turns on the steep and long-radius turns on gentler slopes. But often it's fun to do the exact opposite. Throw in a few very big turns on a steep wall or see how many tiny turns you can make across a flat section—just to avoid the feeling of skiing in a rut. And perhaps I was guilty, once again, of oversimplifying when I said that in bumps there were few choices to make. How about ignoring the shapes of individual bumps and making, or trying to make, long-radius turns through a mogul field, letting the arc of each turn carry you up and down the flanks of whatever bumps you find in your way.

Not always advisable, to be sure, and not always possible, but a challenging game when you feel up to it and, in a kind of contrarian mood, decide to make a run that is the exact opposite of what the terrain is telling you to do.

Still, skiing with the mountain rather than against it is always a good strategy for starters. How about the big shapes: fall-away rolls and dips, large, rounded ridgelike shapes, larger humps and dimples on ski runs, undulations in the terrain made by nature and not by skiers? Every high point, the crest of every roll or ridge in the terrain, is an invitation to turn. These are God's own moguls. And the reason it is so much fun to turn on the high spots and let your skis follow the long, rounded contour of big shapes is that such rolling shapes provide the skier with a terrific sensation of lightness, of floating. When the ground drops away on the far side of such rolls, you will feel less pressure pushing your skis down into the snow. They skim and fly through such turns.

In the old days, skiers always sought out such high spots, the tops of these rolls and hummocks, because this natural "unweighting" from the shape of the terrain actually helped them to start their turns. We no longer need to unweight our skis, making them light in order to get them to turn. (In fact if you think about it, nowadays we do the exact opposite because early weight shift is really a way of preweighting the new outside ski, not unweighting it.) But the sensation of lightness, of floating, of skimming lightly over the surface of the snow is still a delicious one. Explore it by shifting to your new ski just as your skis cross the crest of these larger rolls in the terrain. In this way you can fashion a kind of megamogul run, skiing the big shapes of the mountain.

And as usual, the opposite approach can yield some intriguing new sensations. Try banking your skis off the walls of a gully or off the uphill side of a catwalklike trail cut across the mountain. In this case, rather than feel your skis get light, you will feel how they are momentarily compressed as they run into the side of the gully—the snow pressing up underneath them instead of dropping away on the far side of a roll. I sometimes refer to such turns as turns on a counterslope, a term I picked up in the French Alps. I've already mentioned turning in the hollow spots on the slope in Chapter 8 as a possible strategy for icy mountains, where the added pressure from the counterslope will press the edge of your ski against the icy snow, helping it to grip and hold. But, additionally, flying up the side of a big gully and then turning back down is a wonderful roller-coasterlike sensation. Many ski mountains have long, wide natural gullies where you can play with this pattern, nature's own half-pipes. The trick, of course, is not to run out of speed as you ski up the wall of the gully, and when you are ready to turn, it helps to stretch out tall (extend) and simply lean your whole body downhill away from the slope to counteract the way the gully's counterslope is compressing your skis.

But behind all these specific suggestions, I hope you have zeroed in on my main theme. Although there is no right or wrong way to ski any given mountain or any given slope, it would be a shame just to repeat yourself, run after run, weekend after weekend, season after season. Ski it new. Once you've mastered the basics of modern expert technique—carved turns, anticipation, all the rest—playing with different approaches to different slopes will turn skiing from exercise into something more like exploration and discovery. Not that it was ever merely exercise.

Getting in Shape: Developing Kinesthetic Awareness

In this chapter we've put our concern with modern expert ski technique aside to enter a world of increasing subtlety, looking for the differences that separate pretty good expert turns and runs from dazzling, breathtaking ones. My recipes for getting there have been general, not specific. I think that's normal. Because we're talking about how you can become the very best skier you are capable of becoming. And we know that every skier, like every snowflake, is different. There are so many factors that can either enhance or limit an individual's athletic potential and performance, that even with the best will in the world, even working on all the same moves and exercises, even skiing the same slopes, we're not all going to wind up skiing with the same finesse, the same polish.

Some performance factors in skiing, and in sports in general, are innate—strengths and weaknesses we are born with—and such factors constitute natural limits to our performance. Reaction speed seems to be one of these. But that's no big deal. Skiing is not skeet shooting. Strength and stamina, on the other hand, can be developed by the right exercise program. And indeed, ski magazines, all ski magazines in all countries, have a long tradition of publishing how-to-get-in-shape-for-skiing articles at the beginning of every season. You know the kind of story I'm talking about: lots of photos of attractive young ski racers in bright-colored workout togs, smiling as they lift weights and jump and stretch. And easy-to-follow instructions on how we can do these exercises; although common sense tells us, we're never going to be as fit as these fierce members of the U.S. Ski Team. I do want to encourage you to pay more than just lip service to this sort of advice and to get in shape for skiing. For a couple of reasons, the most interesting of which is this: Paradoxically, you can't ski in a relaxed, efficient soft way if you don't have quite a bit of strength in reserve. Even though I've put a lot of stress on trying softer, on avoiding big, sudden, powerful movements, you won't be able to ski from that relaxed place if you are right at the end of your reserves of strength and endurance. As we get tired, our bodies tense up—that muscular co-contraction I talked about earlier. It's counterproductive but perfectly natural. We seem to be hard-wired that way. So I'm all for a preseason program that builds leg strength and aerobic endurance or general fitness. You can't lose. And, indeed, a balanced program of leg exercises that strengthens both the flexors and the extensors equally—for example, both the quads and the hamstrings—can greatly reduce the likelihood of knee injuries on the slope.

But that's only part of the story. And not the most important part. For me, kinesthetic awareness is the ultimate factor that determines how far you can go in skiing, how subtle and skillful and playful an expert skier you can become. Kinesthetic awareness is a fancy term for how sensitive you are to the movement of your body through space. Skilled gymnasts, dancers, skaters, and, of course, really skilled skiers are blessed with great kinesthetic awareness. All these activities involve precise, efficient, graceful, rhythmic, and relaxed movement through space. So the big question is whether we are born with a certain amount of kinesthetic awareness or whether we can develop more than we seem to possess naturally? I've never found a definitive answer to this question. Perhaps because different authorities and researchers have defined this gift differently. But I am convinced that we can all improve our sense of balanced, fluid, rhythmic movement—whether to some predestined limit, I don't know. And perhaps it doesn't matter. As long as we can cultivate more kinesthetic awareness than we've got now, we'll come out ahead. We'll ski much better.

How can you do this? My suggestion is simple. Find an off-season activity that embodies a lot of balance and continuous rhythmic movement—something you think you'll enjoy—and dive right in. Number one on my list is ice skating, but any kind of skating—in-line skating or conventional roller-skating—is fantastic. There is no better way to improve your skier's coordination in the off-season than skating. And it's really fun. And wonderfully graceful.

Next, I'd suggest dancing, any kind of dancing: ballroom dancing, Latin dancing, folk dancing, square dancing, tango, modern dance, jazz, or even ballet. Well and good if you are already a dancer. Some folks are. Some haven't gone dancing since high school, if then. You can always take a class. Community colleges everywhere offer dance classes. Take one of these classes, and next season you won't believe what it's done for your skiing.

My final suggestion for developing or increasing your kinesthetic sense has an Oriental flavor. Consider Aikido or Tai Chi. Aikido is a relatively gentle sort of martial arts practice, primarily defensive and not aggressive, in which participants use their opponents' force to their own advantage—much as we use the mountain and its shapes and the pull of gravity to our advantage when skiing. Tai Chi is a wonderful slow-motion exercise routine, widely practiced in Chinese communities around the world and also widely taught in the United States. It develops balance, slow, continuous, patient movement, and a great sense of one's center, and how it moves through space—the real foundation of kinesthetic awareness. Both these practices, Aikido and Tai Chi, really require a good teacher. You can't get there on your own or with a book or video lesson. Either one will do wonders for your skiing balance and awareness. Either one will give you a significant push in the direction of that subtle higher level of performance we've been talking about.

And that's about it. My vision of soft skiing down hard slopes. A vision of ease and poise and excitement on skis. A grab bag of tips and thoughts and suggestions on how you can continue to refine your new expert skiing skills, on how you can grow into your new expert skier's persona and relax into it. How you can take all this expert technique we've shared and practiced and mastered. And live it. And make it your own.

IN SUMMARY

- The difference between good and great skiing is often a matter of relaxation. The most gifted skiers never let their bodies tense up. Excess muscle tension disturbs the smooth sliding of your skis across the snow.

  .

- Don't fall for the notion that to ski better you have to ski more aggressively: Expert skiing is more of a collaboration with the mountain than a pitched battle with it.

- Trying softer, not harder, is the way to go. The most effective techniques I teach—especially soft weight shift—are those in which a skier creates movement by releasing rather than increasing muscle tension.

- In the off-season, in addition to basic exercise, pursue physical activities that will develop and increase your sense of balance and rhythm, your kinesthetic awareness.

All Snow, All Terrain

The Dream and the Reality of Expert Skiing

Skiing is sliding, and mountains, and winter. And skiing is more than sliding, and mountains, and winter. Skiing is a summer-long dream and a winter-long reality that never seems 100 percent real. Skiing is freedom. Expert skiing is still more freedom. And skiing on the latest generation of super-sidecut, shaped skis is freedom squared.

Skiing is a shared passion and a uniquely individual experience. Your mountain is not the same as mine; your perfect day on skis is probably quite different from mine. And your vision of expert skiing, I know, is different too. As skilled skiers, though, we have a lot in common. We can ski for hour after hour without really getting tired. When we see a new slope, the question is no longer: Can I ski that? but: How do I want to ski that? When we wake up to find a foot of new snow has reshaped the mountain, our reaction is one of pure unalloyed delight. Soon we'll be flying. We can't wait, but do anyway, and eventually the lifts start, and we enter a white planet where all the rules have been suspended, where we feel as light as the snow, where we move in a state of grace. Putting on skis is like coming home.

This is where we belong—on a tilted mountainside covered with snow.

Expert skiing—our shared goal throughout this book—resists easy definition. But surely that's a big part of it: the sense of feeling at home on the

mountain, anywhere on the mountain, of belonging here, no matter what the snow is like, no matter how steep the hill.

I got serious about skiing years ago in the small resort village of Leysin, in French-speaking western Switzerland. And there, during my first exciting season on skis I picked up a French definition of expert skiing, one that has stuck with me for a long time, one that still works. *Toute neige, tout terrain.* All snow, all terrain. By this yardstick, expert skiers are generalists, not specialists. We aren't mogul skiers, at least not just mogul skiers. We aren't racers, at least not just racers. We ski powder as easily as pack. At the top of any slope, every slope, our pulse speeds up. We can accept what the mountain offers us today and work with it, play with it. It doesn't matter if it's snowed all night or if it hasn't snowed for two weeks. It doesn't matter if the temperature has dropped 50 degrees or climbed above freezing. Packed powder is great. Unpacked non-powder is great too. All snow, all terrain.

Expert skiing is not, at least in my view, just about difficulty. An expert skier isn't someone who only skis double-black slopes. On any slope—easy, moderate, challenging, or scary—a real expert can always do something creative with nothing more than skis and snow. Expert skiing is an adventure, an adventure in spontaneity and creativity—and great memories are one part of what we are creating. Days well lived, runs so exciting, so intense, so perfect that they stay with us for years and years and years to come.

Toute neige, tout terrain. All snow, all terrain.

This doesn't mean that to the expert skier all snow is perfect. In a funny sense, all snow is less than perfect, but we transform it, make it virtually perfect by skiing it well. The experience approaches perfection turn by turn by turn.

And I should add that expert skiing is a never-ending project. One day, after a particularly challenging and pleasing run that you skied without any hesitation, without a lot of tension, either inner or outer, you have a kind of epiphany: Damn! I really am a good skier, I really am an expert—amazing!

And of course, it feels wonderful. Has this happened to you yet? If not, I'm sure it will before long. But that isn't the end of the story. If anything, it's only the beginning. Because once you've crossed that hard-to-define border into expert skiing, those epiphanies just keep coming. Every season, you discover new moves, new horizons; you push past old limits and find yourself making turns that you never even imagined were a possibility. I know this is true for me, for my skiing friends. I know it will be true for you. There's simply no reason not to keep getting better and better and better.

Together we've made some giant strides, or should I say, together we've carved some amazing turns. Let's not stop now.

It's all yours. *Toute neige, tout terrain.* All snow, all terrain.

For Newcomers to Skiing

Getting Started and Avoiding the Pitfalls of Intermediate Skiing

What happened? Did you see a Warren Miller film and find yourself dreaming about skiing powder in slow motion, even though you'd never been on skis? Was it the influence of friends and co-workers who spend the first half of the week telling excited stories about their adventures on the slopes and the second half of the week planning their next trip? Was it simple curiosity that led you to the rental shop to get these strange heavy boots and cumbersome skis? Or a half-price coupon in the paper? Whatever it was, you took the plunge and here you are on the slopes—not those big slopes stretching up out of sight, just a practice slope not far from the parking lot and the day lodge. You are a stranger in a strange land. A beautiful land to be sure, you can already tell that. You just wish that skiing was a little more intuitive, a little more obvious, the equipment a little less weird. And looking around you can also tell that the magic of skiing probably isn't down here on the practice slope. It's up there, where all those confident, brightly dressed skiers are heading, up there closer to that heartbreakingly blue sky. That's where you really want to go—as soon as possible.

To a new skier, it's a brave new white world, cold and bright and different: The slopes look steep, skis seem slippery and not entirely trustworthy, and you feel excited and uncertain at the same time. If it didn't look like such fun, if your best friend wasn't so crazy about skiing, you might be somewhere else, trying something else. But here you are, ready to ski.

Skiing isn't hard. You'll do well provided you don't let a friend talk you into taking a chairlift straight to the top to the mountain ("Oh, don't worry, you'll get the hang of it on the way down …"). In fact, if you start skiing by taking lessons, you will discover what thousands, probably millions, of other skiers have discovered: It's dead simple to become an average intermediate skier. Curiously, that's a problem.

American ski instructors are so enthusiastic, so eager to see you succeed, that they have more or less perfected a series of learning shortcuts that will allow you to slow down and stop, to turn and steer your skis down easy slopes, to avoid crashing and falling in a very short time. But these same shortcuts, if mastered too well, will also peg you for all time on the intermediate plateau. In most ski schools you won't acquire the deeper foundation skills that you'll need if you ever hope to advance to the more exciting realms of expert skiing. So I'm going to propose a slightly different early learning pattern that will keep your options open, that will get you through the novice and low-intermediate stages of skiing quickly without getting you stuck there. Let's go.

Beginner's Balance Versus Expert Balance

Skiing is sliding downhill over snow, and your very first concern is not to fall, to stay upright during this delicious slide. The simplest way of maintaining your balance is to spread your feet and skis. The proverbial wide stance. Skiing in a wide stance has become something of a religion in ski-teaching circles for a very simple reason: It more or less guarantees that you aren't going to fall over. That saves ski students a lot of hard knocks, bruised hips, and bruised egos, and it saves instructors the time and effort of helping their students back up onto their feet. Altogether a good thing. The reason that spreading your feet and skis into a wider stance works so well is that it gives you a broad base of support. Exactly the way that a tricycle is much easier for a young child to ride than a narrow bicycle. When skiers spread their skis in a wide stance, they are, in essence, turning themselves into tricycles. There's nothing wrong with this; just don't let it become too comfortable a habit. For many skiers, a wide stance becomes a sort of security blanket merely because this kind of balance over a wide base is the only kind of balance they have ever developed.

We'll do better. In a minute I'm going to describe some very simple moves for slowing down, stopping, and turning. Moves you will want to practice on your very first runs, your very first hour on snow. Braking, stopping, and turning add up to a sensational concept: control. But, in addition, from your first moments on skis I want you to play with a different notion—sliding, sliding freely. Ski teachers sometimes call this straight running and it includes everything other than turning and braking and stopping. Just letting yourself slide straight, straight down the slope or straight across the slope at an angle, comes very close to the essence of what makes skiing so special. Gravity pulls you down; you relax, smile, and enjoy the ride. Even as a first-time beginner, going straight gives you an opportunity to play with your balance, to develop a new kind of balance, a balance that will work for you when you eventually reach the level of expert skiing. And, of course, I'm talking about narrow-stance balance, balance without spreading your skis wide apart. Moving from that tricycle back to a narrow bicycle. Or, to stretch our image a little, you can think of a wide stance on skis as being similar to those training wheels that parents attach to the rear wheel of a bicycle when a young child hasn't yet learned to balance on a narrow two-wheeler. What you are going to do as soon as possible is to remove those training wheels by learning to stand with your feet closer together. Not all at once, but whenever you feel comfortable and especially when you are sliding straight down the hill. Enjoying the ride *and,* at the same time, experimenting with balance on a narrower base of support.

Developing a more sophisticated stance is absolutely critical. If you begin to depend on spreading your skis as your basic mechanism to avoid falling, everything will be harder in the future. You will have sacrificed mobility for

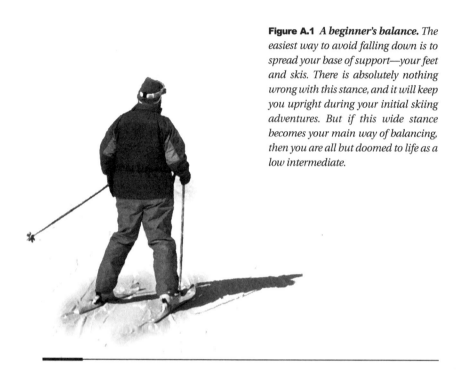

Figure A.1 *A beginner's balance. The easiest way to avoid falling down is to spread your base of support—your feet and skis. There is absolutely nothing wrong with this stance, and it will keep you upright during your initial skiing adventures. But if this wide stance becomes your main way of balancing, then you are all but doomed to life as a low intermediate.*

stability, and it just isn't necessary. Balance has been a key theme in this book; balance is basic. And we all have a lifetime of balance practice behind us, practice staying upright. What makes skiing balance so tricky is the fact that you don't have a solid motionless surface to balance on. Everything is moving. Balancing on a sliding ski is naturally harder than, for example, closing your eyes and balancing in place on the sidewalk in front of your home. But it isn't that bad. Here are a couple of tricks that will help you develop a real skier's sense of balance.

Spread something—just don't spread your skis. Pushing your skis outward into a wide stance improves your lateral balance. It keeps you from wobbling side-to-side. So, instead, with your feet comfortably close together (not jammed together, please), spread your arms and hands out in front of you. Exactly like a tightrope walker or a kid balancing on a fence. With your hands

Figure A.2 *An expert's balance. The same underlying principle applies: We need to spread something for lateral balance. But expert skiers spread their arms, not their feet. By keeping feet and skis directly beneath your body, not spread wide, you will find that your two skis encounter the same snow and don't get in so much trouble. An expert's narrower base of support and poised, balanced stance should be your goal from your very first day on skis. It's easier than it looks.*

spread wide in front of you, you can make small, almost automatic adjustments to preserve your balance. Try this whenever you feel comfortable enough to let yourself slide straight down a gentle hill without putting on the brakes.

Eventually, I want you to develop good balance, dynamic sliding balance, not just on two skis held more or less close together, but also on one ski or the other, on one foot at a time. Obviously, balancing on one foot at a time is trickier still. Standing on only one ski, you will have an even narrower base of support. But fortunately, balance is something you can develop, with patience, on fairly easy terrain. Balance is not like perfect pitch, something you are born with. I believe all skiers can develop an expert's narrow stance, an expert's narrow-track balance, provided they don't become too dependent on the security of a wide platform in the early days of their skiing career. So be forewarned.

And don't worry about falling. If you're not falling from time to time, you're not really learning, not testing your limits, or discovering new abilities to cope and to recover your balance in moments of crisis. Skiers' balance, the ability to stay over your skis, poised and ready, in a fast-changing white world, is something to play with, to develop through experimentation, not by gritting your teeth, hunkering down in a low wide-track stance, and defying the gods to push you over.

Now, with this all-important subject of balance out of the way for the moment (although we'll return to it often in different contexts), let's quickly look at how a newcomer to skiing can learn to slow down, stop, and turn.

Coping with the Hill: Slowing, Stopping, Turning

The French have a saying: *Plus ça change, plus c'est la même chose*—the more things change the more they stay the same. So it is with skiing. For generations, novice skiers have learned to slow down, stop, and turn by placing their skis in a V-position, variously referred to as a snowplow or a wedge, and using the extra friction and the angled shape of this V-position to slow down and turn. And for just as long, creative ski teachers have been looking for a way to get the job done without resorting to this effective but totally inelegant position, the snowplow. But this V-, or wedge, position is still with us today, and that's okay. Wedging, or snowplowing, won't hurt you as a skier, even though it's definitely not the way experts slow down and turn—provided you don't come to depend on it. It works quite well at the slow speeds that skiing newcomers tend to favor, and you can even learn some priceless skiing lessons while you practice wedging during your very first morning on skis. The key lesson is this: *Ski with your feet.* That's right, with your feet. Not with your legs. Not with your hips, much less your torso. The feet are really where all the action in skiing starts and finishes. And that's where we'll start right now.

You've just walked up a little hill, placing your feet sideways (like walking up a staircase sideways) to avoid slipping back down. And maybe you've already pushed off for an exciting slide or two down to the flat snow below you.

Maybe several such straight slides. (By the way, sliding straight down a hill is called a schuss, a borrowed German word.) But now it's time to learn how to stop and how to turn.

Get ready in place before you start sliding down the hill. As you steady yourself with your ski poles, I'd like you to lift one foot and its ski a little off the ground. Focus on your foot. Turn it in the air: toe in, toe out, heel in, heel out. Move your foot around a bit in space just to prove that you really can move it, encased as it is in a heavy armorlike plastic boot and weighed down with an unfamiliar ski. Now, turn that same foot slightly so that the toe points in and the heel twists out. Voilà, you've made half of the V-position I mentioned, and more importantly, you've learned that the front of your foot (your toes) controls the tip of the ski while your heel controls the tail of the ski. Now pick up your other foot and move it around in the air in the same way. Finally, standing once again on both skis, give a little bounce and push the heels of both feet outward. That's it. A wedge, or snowplow.

What can you do with your skis in this funny V-position? Try sliding in this position. That is to say, push off, down your gentle beginner's hill and as you slide along, push your heels outward—just a bit—which will push the tails of your skis outward. You're still sliding, but slower now. The edges of your skis are scraping the snow—brushing across the snow might be a better way of putting it—and slowing you down. It's simple: The wider you spread the tails of your skis, the slower you go. Push out strongly enough with both heels and you'll come to a stop. This wedge, or snowplow, stop is hardly graceful, but it does work. You can figure all this out and practice it easily during your first half hour or so on skis. This is important progress because knowing that you can stop when and where you need to liberates you to try other, newer, and better moves on skis. Imagine learning to drive a car without knowing where the brake pedal was. This wedging action, making a V and then pushing outward until you stop, is your first crude brake pedal on skis. Trust it and go on to better things.

Figure A.3 *Turn with a narrow wedge. If you can avoid pushing your skis out into a wedge that is too wide, you will find that your smaller wedge quickly tends to disappear. In a wedge, one ski is always pointing the way you want to turn. Make that ski dominant, stand on it, and steer it. And pretty soon—as in this illustration, which only begins with a wedge—you will find that the other ski is turning too, which often produces a spontaneous parallel finish to the turn.*

Going on means sliding. You surely didn't rent skis and hike over to the beginner practice slope in order to perfect slowing down and stopping. Your goal is to move, to move swiftly and gracefully, across the snow. That's what skiing is all about. So use your new wedge sparingly. When you want to slow down a bit, wedge, but only wedge a little. A thin or narrow V-wedge is far more effective (and far less tiring) than a fat wedge. Ski teachers have often called such a narrow wedge a "gliding wedge," and that's a pretty good description.

Now let's quickly use this narrow wedge to make turns to the right and left. First, stand on some flat snow, make a small wedge, and look down at your feet. "Curiouser and curiouser," as the Mad Hatter said. Your right foot and ski are aimed to the left while your left foot and ski are pointing right. This is a clue that one foot is going to be responsible for turning or steering you in one direction and the other foot will do the same job in the opposite direction. Now push off and slide down a comfortable, more or less gentle hill in a rather narrow wedge. As you slide, look down at your right foot; look where it's pointing. Now guide that foot a bit more in that direction by pushing down on it and steering it a bit to make that foot and ski dominant. Your right foot takes over and seems to guide the whole package, you and your skis, to the left. Bravo! Your first turn on skis. Now another one. This time make the other foot, your left foot, dominant, and steer it in the direction it is already pointing—to the right. Already you are tuning in to the connection between foot and ski. Wherever the foot points, that ski will point. Whatever the foot does, that ski will do.

It isn't hard to make one foot and ski more important than the other—to make one foot dominate to guide you around. Just stand on that foot a little harder, a little more solidly than on the other foot. (This is the beginning of a very important move that skiers call weight shift.) And if you need to, guide that ski into a curved path with your foot. That's about all there is to it. There are a host of tricks that ski pros have come up with over the years to make one foot turn more than the other. (One instructor friend of mine always told his students to press down on their right big toe in order to turn left; and vice versa. And it worked. But most such tricks are overkill. Just stand more on one foot than the other and that foot will take over and create a turn. Your job is to concentrate on guiding that foot where you want it to go. It takes almost no effort, especially if you are learning on a pair of modern skis—not modern high-performance skis but what we can call a modern learning ski.

Special Skis for Rapid Learning

A big theme of this entire book is the impact of a new type of ski on our snowy sport: skis with deeply curved sides, so-called shaped, or super-sidecut, skis. It took a while for this wonderful design innovation to find its way into the racks in rental shops and onto beginner slopes. But now, very short learning skis with deeply curved sides are common, almost ubiquitous. Did I say very short? Yes, learning skis should be even shorter than today's fairly short performance skis. Try to start your skiing apprenticeship with skis that are between 120 and 140 centimeters. They behave very well at slower speeds, and the movements you master on these skis will transfer easily to the somewhat longer skis you will be using soon.

Up to this point, I haven't put any particular emphasis on the kind of skis you were using as a newcomer to our sport. And, indeed, almost any ski will do—though some do better. But I need to stop right here to point out some advantages to these short, deep-sidecut skis and also to warn you against certain oversimplified teaching patterns that many ski schools have developed with these new learning skis. (When you read Chapter 1, you will find a full discussion of how shaped, or super-sidecut, skis work.)

The problem I've just alluded to is that many ski schools have become carried away by the amazing ability of these new skis to carve perfect arcs in the snow and have decided that if they can put their beginners on very shaped short skis, they can attempt to pursue an exclusively parallel, exclusively carved-turn approach. No more wedges, no more skidded or slipped turns, just pure carving, but in a fairly wide stance. Pure carved turns on these short learning skis are very easy for a skilled ski instructor, and, indeed, they are more or less possible for most students, who are encouraged to make such turns by simply rolling their skis from one set of edges to another in a wide stance.

But—and this is a very big but—students who learn this way have a very limited repertoire of movements and a very limited span of terrain that they can cope with. They are singularly ill equipped to handle steeper or narrower slopes, to make quick emergency stops, and although they manage to break into skiing, they find themselves comfortable only on gentle wide-open slopes. One-dimensional skiers, as it were. And then they discover, on their own, that they can twist both skis sideways and skid. A classic low-intermediate coping strategy, made even easier by the fact that very short skis are very easy to twist. And presto, what started as a would-be avant-garde teaching program, determined to eliminate wedges and skidded turns, has produced the same old intermediate skier.

Don't let this happen to you. There's more to modern skiing than a limited wide-track carving move on tiny shaped skis. We're in it for the long haul, and we're looking for freedom on skis, for movement patterns that will open up the whole mountain. For this, you'll need to feel your skis' edges both carve (or hold) and also slip (or skid)—the whole spectrum of skiing possibilities, plus sense of balance in motion, which can adjust to different styles of turning. The good news is that you can get there. The bad news is that there is really no shortcut, no single movement pattern that does it all. Not to worry, the journey is just as enjoyable as the goal.

Breaking into Christies: Two Skis Turning Parallel

Let's go back for a moment to our very small wedge position, that gliding wedge we learned earlier. Look down at your skis as you glide down a green (or novice) slope in this very slight wedge. Can you see how your right ski is brushing lightly on its left, or "inside," edge? How your left ski is really sliding along mostly on its right, or inside, edge? Now if a ski is even slightly on edge, and we stand solidly on it, our weight will bend that edge into a deeper curve, pushing it down a little into the snow. And voilà, the ski follows that curve in a more or less carved arc.

That's exactly what one ski has been doing in our early wedge turns, the ski on the outside of the circle, which we'll just call the "outside ski" of the turn. But of course, its companion, the other ski, has been resisting your turn. After all, in a wedge it is pointed in the opposite direction from the direction in which you are turning. So now it's time that our inside ski gets with the program and stops fighting the foot and ski that's doing all the work.

As soon as you can, start skiing faster. And keep making patient smooth turns, S-shapes down the slope, standing solidly first on one foot, then the other. It won't take long for this to become second nature. Now, let's vary the pattern a bit. As you stand on your right foot to guide it in an arc to the left, start to relax your left foot and move it smoothly and gently inward, parallel to your other foot and ski. Speed helps, so on every run, try to ski just a tad faster. And keep playing around with the inside foot of each turn. There's no best way to do this, but your goal is to relax that inside ski to reduce the pressure and muscle tension that is keeping it pushed out in a slight V and let it float in parallel to the ski that is really turning you. This is a job for your foot, only the foot, and nothing but the foot. Ride through each turn standing on the outside foot, and pull the other foot in parallel until it feels as though it's cooperating, not opposing, the turn.

Turns like this tend to start with your feet in a very slight V-, or wedge, position, but the skis soon become parallel. These turns are generally referred to as christies. A christie is any turn that ends with the two skis parallel. (And I should tell you that there's a lot of ski history in that term. Christie is short for Christiania, the old name for Oslo, Norway, where parallel skidded turns were first done, on wooden skis, hundreds of years ago.) I can also tell you that parallel or even parallelish turns like these first christies of ours come in two main flavors: turns in which we feel that the dominant outside ski is biting into the snow to create a continuous curved arc, and softer turns in which we feel that our skis are slipping loosely across the surface of the snow instead of biting into it, but turning nonetheless. These two styles of turns will develop into what we call carved turns and slipped turns—although the distinction isn't always black and white. What's the difference? I'd say that the cutting, arcing, more or less carved style of turn depends on strong and tight feet, whereas if you can relax your feet during a turn, your skis are more likely to float and brush and slip across the snow. Which is better? Neither. You will need both as you move on toward expert skiing.

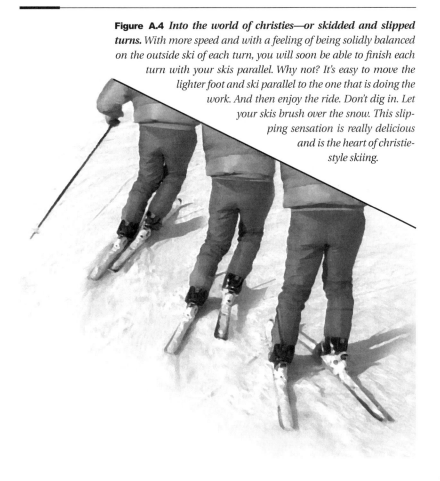

Figure A.4 *Into the world of christies—or skidded and slipped turns. With more speed and with a feeling of being solidly balanced on the outside ski of each turn, you will soon be able to finish each turn with your skis parallel. Why not? It's easy to move the lighter foot and ski parallel to the one that is doing the work. And then enjoy the ride. Don't dig in. Let your skis brush over the snow. This slipping sensation is really delicious and is the heart of christie-style skiing.*

So let's go skiing. I hope you are still patient enough to stay on green runs. It's probably still your first day on skis. Maybe the afternoon of that first day. And I'm proud of the fact that I haven't insulted your intelligence (as most ski books do) with instructions on how to ride lifts. I know you have easily figured that out by watching other skiers. So now I want you to make alternate runs: some with your feet relatively relaxed, loose inside your boots, and others with your feet feeling somewhat tight and strong, a bit tensed up inside your boots. And notice the different feelings each time. We are beginning the process of educating a skier's foot that will eventually give you a kind of sixth sense, an amazing sensitivity to what your skis are doing on the snow—just by paying attention to what your feet are doing in your boots.

What do your turns look like and feel like now? You cruise off down this gentle smoothly groomed slope. Your feet aren't touching, but I hope they aren't too far apart either. You have resisted the temptation to turn yourself into a tricycle. To start a turn, you begin to put more weight, more pressure, on one ski; you feel as though you are standing more solidly on that foot. It will become the outside foot of your turn. If you shift onto your right foot, you will wind up turning to the left, and vice versa. And you are probably helping that ski to turn by steering your ski in that direction with a patient guiding action of that foot. Well and good. The guiding action of that outside foot has pushed your skis into a slight V-shape. But we'd rather have them parallel, so as soon as this turn starts, as soon as you feel comfortable standing on that ski and guiding it, move the other foot to make your inside ski parallel. Do it now; don't just wait there while your skis turn in a V.

There's a kind of one-two effect to such turns. You start guiding one ski and then match the other one to it, parallel again. And then the turn proceeds with both skis lined up with each other, matching each other, parallel—one ski (the outside ski of the turn) solid and heavy; the other one (the inside ski) kind of light, floating along for the ride. But that one-two effect doesn't have to be very pronounced. As soon as these christie-style turns start to feel comfortable, you can play around with the idea of doing both things at once. Simultaneously, you can stand on one foot and guide it into a turn while at the same time relaxing the other foot and keeping it parallel. This is easier for some skiers than for others. But as soon as you can, this is the way to go. Instead of standing on one ski *and* pushing or twisting it out at an angle to start your turn, simply stand on it and guide both skis directly into the turn. One ski with pressure on it; one without. As your comfort grows, as your speed increases somewhat, you will probably find yourself making less of a one-two move and instead guiding both skis into the turn at the same time even though you are still shifting or pressing or standing on one ski more than the other. And that's another big step forward.

Perhaps you have already figured this out, but let me confirm your suspicion—skilled skiers control their descents by turning. A good turn will do it all: Turns determine your path down the mountain; turning up the hill slows you down; if you keep turning, you're going to stop. So I want you to hold that snowplow (or wedge) stop, our first crude brake pedal, in reserve. I'm sure this wedge stop gave you an initial feeling of security. But after your first day on skis, try not to use it. Instead, try to do everything with smooth, patient round turns. Turns are the ticket. (And for a thorough explanation of the importance of round turns in modern skiing, let me refer you again to Chapter 1.)

But since you will need a variety of turns to ski a variety of conditions, I've suggested experimenting with different feelings in your feet: letting go and relaxing your feet on one run; then holding them tight and strong on the next run. And so forth. You will discover that if you relax your feet, your turns become softer, more drifted. Your skis will tend to break loose off their edges and brush or drift or slip across the snow as they turn. Conversely, if the muscles in your feet are a little tighter, and if you can resist the temptation to twist or turn your foot very much, you will probably feel that your skis are drawing a cleaner curved line across the snow. Again there's no right or wrong here. Both feelings are important. See if you can tell the difference.

What Next? Balance, Balance, Balance ... on One Ski

Congratulations! You have survived your first day on snow on skis. As soon as you can ride a lift and slide back down with some semblance of control, then you are a skier—although still a very unpolished one. You've already done a lot.

But there's another task ahead of us that I hope you will tackle and master during your first few days on skis. I'm talking about developing what I think of as expert skiers' balance: balance on one ski at a time. In short, I'd like you to be able to pick one foot and ski up off the snow and stay balanced, so you keep on sliding on one ski. And then, of course, do the same thing on the other side. This isn't too hard if you pick a friendly, not very steep slope. But it's sure to feel very strange. At first those heavy boots, bindings, and skis on each foot feel like anchors weighing you down, gluing each foot to the snow. But, actually, we have a whole history, a whole lifetime behind us, of moving easily and smoothly, even gracefully, from one foot to the other. Everything we've done in life since we stopped crawling has been from foot to foot: walking, running, striding, going up and down stairs. We have an amazing store of reflexes and habits that involve balancing first on one foot, then on the other. I'd like to suggest that the real inner feeling of skiing is similar to walking—walking in slow motion to be sure, first on one foot, then on the other, riding first one ski, then the other. During your first few days on skis, it's your job to make sure that you get back in touch with those amazing foot-to-foot reflexes that you've built up over a lifetime.

To reinforce your balance reflexes, spread your hands out in front of you about waist high, always in front of your hips, and a foot or more to the side. Like a tightrope walker you can make small and subtle balance adjustments with tiny moves of your hands. But if you leave your hands at your side, in your pockets so to speak, it will be much harder to balance first on one foot, then on the other.

You don't need to pick one ski up very far off the snow. Just play with lifting it a wee bit while you balance on the other foot. Don't overdo this. Just play with it from time to time. As you get more and more comfortable balancing on one foot, you will find that your turns get better too. You will feel more stable, more solid on your outside ski, the one that's really doing the work, really making the turn. And this is a pattern that you will pursue right through the highest levels of expert skiing: the weighted outside ski creating the turn; the lighter inside ski smoothing things out by coming along for the ride, cooperating.

The basic exercise to practice this pattern is simply straight running, schussing, and alternately lifting one foot, balancing like that, and then repeating the move on the other side. But you can do more. Start walking, stepping from foot to foot as you move about on the slope. Especially on those boring roads that skiers call catwalks, it's a good thing to make simple stepping, walking movements from ski to ski, from foot to foot, as you glide along. Most skiers, novices or intermediates, simply freeze up, hunker down on both skis and wait. Passive. Motionless. Growing stiffer and more tired the longer they ride along in that position. Very skilled skiers, you will soon notice, are constantly moving, slowly, smoothly, gracefully, from foot to foot. Be one of those skiers!

Letting Go of the Slope: Balancing over a Slipping Ski

Before I congratulate you on breaking into skiing, becoming an new intermediate—but not a terminal intermediate—in only a couple of days on snow, I want to share one more skiing pattern with you: sideslipping. Well, actually you have already been sideslipping somewhat when you relaxed your feet in a faster turn and felt your skis brushing the snow beneath you. Sideslipping means just what it says: letting your skis slip sideways, a little or a lot, instead of tracking forward in a straight line. Sideslipping has a psychological as well as a technical message for emerging skiers. It is a way of letting go of the mountain instead of clinging to it. It is a way of lightening up and loosening up in challenging situations. And, of course, it will slow you down, and you can use it to sneak down slopes that are too hard for your current technique. But, above all, sideslipping is important because it is the single most relaxing maneuver in skiing, a welcome antidote to the excess tension all skiers feel when a slope gets a little too challenging. It turns out that just telling yourself to relax is a losing battle; it just doesn't work. But sideslipping is a ski technique that is also a way of relaxing. And it will help you find your balance over one ski, and, for that matter, it's sure to improve your turns. Wow, almost a panacea. So let's do it.

But, first, another fancy skiing word: "traverse." Like schussing, traversing is a borrowed ski word, this time from French. But in skiing to traverse means to point your two skis at an angle across the hill. By varying that angle, steeper or shallower, more down the hill or more across the hill, you can easily control your speed. You've probably already figured this out, but I mention it now because you are going to practice sideslipping from a traverse. A couple of small details, though. In a traverse, remember to keep your top ski ahead of the lower ski—that way your skis can't get crossed. And try to carry more of your weight on your bottom, or downhill, ski—because your downhill leg is straighter, it is also stronger and won't get tired as quickly.

Now, if you want to traverse across the hill from point A to point B, just tighten up your feet so that the edges of your skis grip the snow and push off in the position I've just described: most of your weight on your bottom ski, top ski advanced about half a boot length, hands ahead of your hips and spread laterally for balance. And away you go. But what if you relax your feet, especially your downhill foot—as you traverse across the slope? Well, your edges will grip less, and you will start to drift downhill. You wind up slipping sideways down the slope at the same time you are moving forward across it. Sideslipping. This isn't the time and place to go into all the refinements of sideslipping (which I cover in more detail at a slightly more advanced level in Chapter 2). I just wanted to call your attention to sideslipping and to let you know it was cool. Something to enjoy and embrace. Not resist.

Be sure you don't practice sideslipping on slopes that are too flat. When you relax your feet, your skis flatten out on the slope instead of edging into it, and on flatter slopes it's all too easy to catch your downhill edge, to trip and crash. But even green slopes have small rolls and short steeper pitches. So you can find a steeper but not scary pitch to play with sideslipping, starting, as I described above, in a traverse across the slope, and then letting go with your edges to start a sideslip.

Why bother? And just what can you do with sideslipping once you've figured out how to do it? There are some moments in skiing when you really want your edges to hold and grip; guiding a long, round turn on fairly hard-packed snow is a perfect example. But in many other situations you actually have more control over your skis if you can release the grip of their edges. It's a great way to stop quickly. Say you're traversing across a slope and someone falls in front of you. You need to stop fast, so you sideslip and quickly pivot both skis crosswise to your direction of travel. If your skis are brushing, slipping, then it's very easy to steer and guide and reorient them with relatively small movements of your feet in your boots. On the other hand, if your skis are stuck on their edges, it is almost impossible to quickly twist or guide them in a different direction. Letting go of the slope is actually a powerful and effective strategy.

Sideslipping vertically straight down a slope is rather tricky. Sideslipping forward across the hill, from a traverse, is a lot easier. And sideslipping a bit during your turns, feeling your skis slip or skid a bit as they come around, is easier still. All it requires is a little extra speed and relatively relaxed feet. Let it happen. As you gain confidence in your ability to guide your turning skis with your feet, you will inevitably begin to ski faster. Speed is a relative thing, relative first and foremost to your level of experience. What seemed quite fast your first day on skis will seem comfortable, almost slow a couple of days later. So onward and downward. As your confidence grows, try to minimize the V-opening of your skis. And play with the notion of always standing more on one foot than the other. I don't want you to ski around with one foot and ski in the air. Lifting one ski off the snow in a straight schuss was just a practice exercise to prove you could and to get used to balancing on one foot. Sideslipping too works best when you are balanced solidly on one foot, your downhill foot. But there's a kind of trick to it.

What makes sideslipping easy for skilled skiers is the fact that as their skis slide away down the slope, they lean or tilt down the slope too. This is a subtle, but real move. You have to go with your skis, leaning out and down the hill, and not in toward the mountain. This outward tilt is counterintuitive. Initially, no one wants to lean down the hill because in that direction there's a longer distance to fall. But do it anyway.

You'll quickly get comfortable with this new move. An important move, indeed, because what you are really doing is keeping up with your skis, rebalancing yourself down the hill as your skis move down the hill. Rebalancing over a ski (your downhill ski) that is slipping out from underneath you. This is a perfect introduction to the sort of dynamic balance that characterizes so much advanced skiing. Moving toward a position where, a split second from now, you will wind up in balance again. Not frozen balance, but a dynamic moving balance. A skier's balance. An expert's balance.

And now it's time for congratulations. You've become a skier, you're on your way.

IN SUMMARY

- A wide stance will help you cope with your first adventures and your first insecure emotions on skis. Spreading your feet and skis to create a wide base of support almost guarantees that you won't fall. But if you start to depend on this wide stance for stability, your future progress will be compromised.

- From your first day on skis, begin to develop a more sophisticated type of balance. Balance over a narrow base. Balance on one foot and one ski at a time, patiently balancing first on one foot for a while, then on the other.

- You don't need to avoid the V-shape of a wedge, or snowplow, in an attempt to learn so-called "parallel only" skiing. But don't let that wedge turn into a security blanket, like the wide stance I warned you about above. A small, or narrow, wedge can give you some instant control on your first runs down easy slopes.

- Focus on your feet: on guiding your feet; on turning your feet. Steer and control your skis with your feet. Every turn, every maneuver in skiing should be initiated and controlled with the feet. They are the only part of your body in contact with your skis.

- As you ski faster, learn to enjoy the sensation of both skis "breaking loose" and slipping, or sliding laterally across the snow. This sensation of parallel slipping is like letting go of the mountain and allowing your skis to do their own thing. Begin to finish your turns with this slipping action of both skis. Welcome to the world of christies.

- Letting go of the slope and slipping laterally is also called sideslipping. This important skill can improve your basic turns greatly. As you become more comfortable with this slipping sensation, try to stand more solidly on one ski, the outside ski of each turn.

About the Author

Lito Tejada-Flores was born at 13,000 feet in the Bolivian Andes, and he's spent much of his life in high places: rock climbing and mountaineering in Yosemite Valley, the Alps, Alaska, and Patagonia; pursuing his central mountain passion, skiing; and sharing his love of skiing through writing, teaching, and filmmaking.

As a long-time contributor to major national skiing publications, Lito has become one of the best known ski instructors and ski writers in America. Lito's earlier book, Breakthrough on Skis, *his companion* Breakthrough on Skis *videos, and his intensive week-long ski courses in Aspen, Colorado, have helped thousands of skiers to break out of their intermediate doldrums and realize true expert performance. And his Web site for alternative ski writing and instructional material, www.BreakthroughOnSkis.com, has become a popular destination for passionate and literate skiers.*

Lito is also a documentary filmmaker and graphic designer. He was one of the founders of Mountainfilm in Telluride, Colorado, America's first festival of mountain films. He has also collaborated with his wife, photographer Linde Waidhofer, on three books of Western landscape photography, the most recent being Stone & Silence.

Today Lito lives in southern Colorado, near the New Mexico border, directly under several 14,000-foot summits in the Sangre de Cristo Mountains, in a house he designed himself. Among his most memorable adventures, Lito counts first ascents on Mount Fitz Roy in Patagonia and Devil's Thumb in Alaska, glacier skiing in New Zealand and the Alps ... and falling in love with Linde Waidhofer.

For an ongoing exploration of the techniques and approaches presented in this book—and to keep an eye on the nonstop evolution of the sport—Lito hopes you will visit his Web site at www.BreakthroughOnSkis.com. He welcomes your feedback and suggestions for future editions. You can also write Lito at P.O. Box 2, Crestone, CO 81131, or e-mail him at feedback@BreakthroughOnSkis.com.